CW01432188

KILLING
MONARCHS

To my children, Rachel and David, and my grandchildren,
Sophia, Isabelle and Ambrose, with much love.

KILLING MONARCHS

REGICIDE IN THE TUDOR AND STUART AGE

RICHARD HEATH

PEN & SWORD HISTORY

AN IMPRINT OF PEN & SWORD BOOKS LTD.
YORKSHIRE – PHILADELPHIA

First published in Great Britain in 2025 by
PEN AND SWORD HISTORY
An imprint of
Pen & Sword Books Ltd
Yorkshire – Philadelphia

Copyright © Richard Heath, 2025

ISBN 978 1 03610 531 0

The right of Richard Heath to be identified as Author of
this work has been asserted by him in accordance with the Copyright,
Designs and Patents Act 1988.

A CIP catalogue record for this book is available from the British Library.

All rights reserved. No part of this book may be reproduced, transmitted,
downloaded, decompiled or reverse engineered in any form or by any means,
electronic or mechanical including photocopying, recording or by any information
storage and retrieval system, without permission from the Publisher in writing.
NO AI TRAINING: Without in any way limiting the Author's and Publisher's
exclusive rights under copyright, any use of this publication to "train" generative
artificial intelligence (AI) technologies to generate text is expressly prohibited.
The Author and Publisher reserve all rights to license uses of this work for
generative AI training and development of machine learning language models.

Typeset in Times New Roman 11/13.5 by
SJmagic DESIGN SERVICES, India.
Printed and bound in the UK by CPI Group (UK) Ltd.

The Publisher's authorised representative in the EU for product safety is
Authorised Rep Compliance Ltd., Ground Floor, 71 Lower Baggot Street,
Dublin D02 P593, Ireland.
www.arccompliance.com

For a complete list of Pen & Sword titles please contact
PEN & SWORD BOOKS LIMITED
George House, Units 12 & 13, Beevor Street, Off Pontefract Road,
Barnsley, South Yorkshire, S71 1HN, England
E-mail: enquiries@pen-and-sword.co.uk
Website: www.pen-and-sword.co.uk

or

PEN AND SWORD BOOKS
1950 Lawrence Rd, Havertown, PA 19083, USA
E-mail: uspen-and-sword@casematepublishers.com
Website: www.penandswordbooks.com

MIX
Paper | Supporting
responsible forestry
FSC® C013604

CONTENTS

PART 4

RUSSIA'S 'TIME OF TROUBLES': FROM RURIKIDS TO ROMANOVS

PART 5

UPHEAVAL IN THE OTTOMAN EMPIRE: THE KILLING OF OSMAN II AND IBRAHIM I

PART 6

CHARLES I AND THE REGICIDES: THE WORLD TURNED UPSIDE DOWN?

FAMILY TREES

Tudor Family Tree

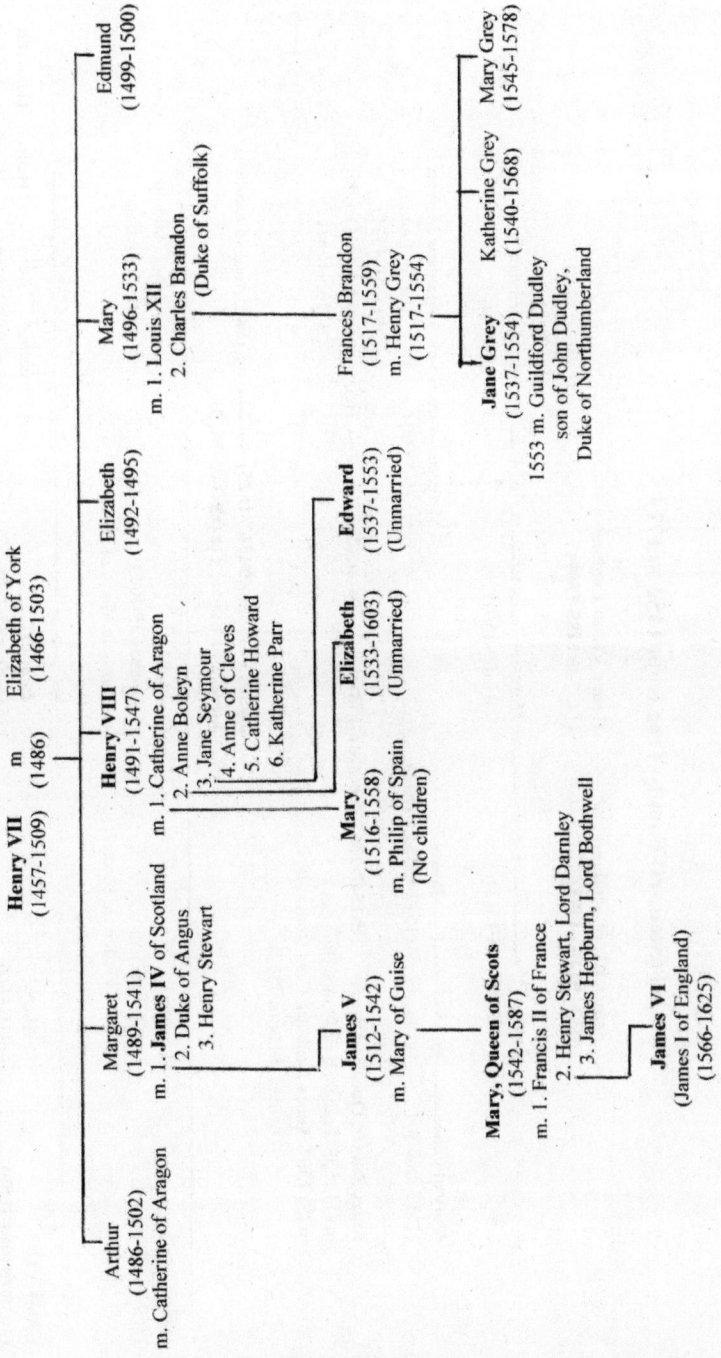

Henry VII (1457-1509) m (1486) Elizabeth of York (1466-1503)

Arthur (1486-1502)
m. Catherine of Aragon

Margaret (1489-1541)
m. 1. James IV of Scotland
2. Duke of Angus
3. Henry Stewart

Henry VIII (1491-1547)
m. 1. Catherine of Aragon
2. Anne Boleyn
3. Jane Seymour
4. Anne of Cleves
5. Catherine Howard
6. Katherine Parr

Elizabeth (1492-1495)

Mary (1496-1533)
m. 1. Louis XII
2. Charles Brandon (Duke of Suffolk)

Edmund (1499-1500)

James V (1512-1542)
m. Mary of Guise

Mary (1516-1558)
m. Philip of Spain
(No children)

Elizabeth (1533-1603)
(Unmarried)

Edward (1537-1553)
(Unmarried)

Frances Brandon (1517-1559)
m. Henry Grey (1517-1554)

Mary, Queen of Scots (1542-1587)
m. 1. Francis II of France
2. Henry Stewart, Lord Darnley
3. James Hepburn, Lord Bothwell

James VI (James I of England) (1566-1625)

Jane Grey (1537-1554)
1553 m. Guildford Dudley son of John Dudley, Duke of Northumberland

Katherine Grey (1540-1568)

Mary Grey (1545-1578)

Stuart (Stewart) Family Tree from 1452 to 1714

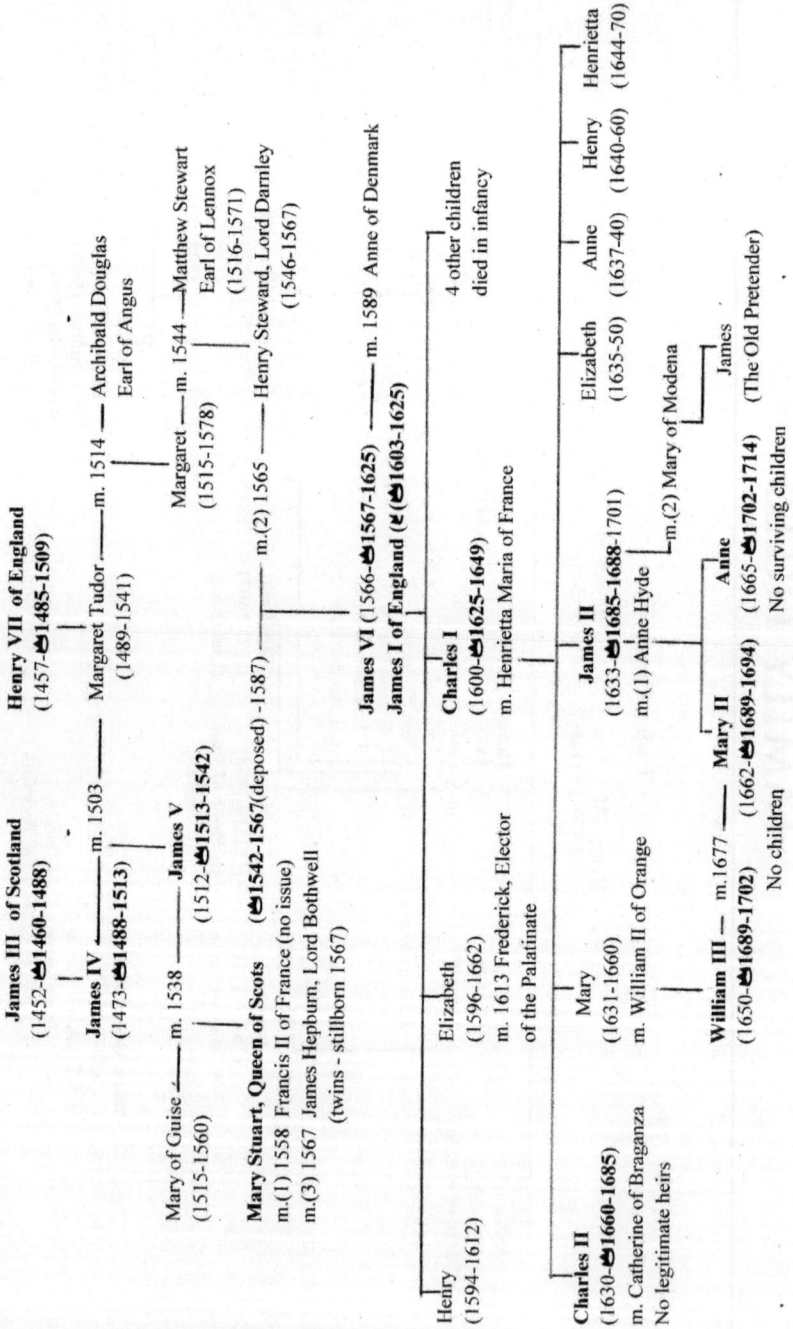

James III of Scotland (1452-♔1460-1488)

Henry VII of England (1457-♔1485-1509)

James IV (1473-♔1488-1513) — m. 1503 — Margaret Tudor (1489-1541) — m. 1514 — Archibald Douglas Earl of Angus

James V (1512-♔1513-1542)

Margaret (1515-1578) — m. 1544 — Matthew Stewart Earl of Lennox (1516-1571)

m.(2) 1565 — Henry Steward, Lord Darnley (1546-1567)

Mary of Guise (1515-1560) — m. 1538

Mary Stuart, Queen of Scots (♔1542-1567(deposed) -1587)
m.(1) 1558 Francis II of France (no issue)
m.(3) 1567 James Hepburn, Lord Bothwell (twins - stillborn 1567)

James VI (1566-♔1567-1625) James I of England (♔1603-1625) — m. 1589 Anne of Denmark

Elizabeth (1596-1662) m. 1613 Frederick, Elector of the Palatinate

Henry (1594-1612)

Charles I (1600-♔1625-1649) m. Henrietta Maria of France

4 other children died in infancy

Charles II (1630-♔1660-1685) m. Catherine of Braganza No legitimate heirs

Mary (1631-1660) m. William II of Orange

James II (1633-♔1685-1688-1701) m.(1) Anne Hyde m.(2) Mary of Modena

Elizabeth (1635-50)

Anne (1637-40)

Henry (1640-60)

Henrietta (1644-70)

William III (1650-♔1689-1702) — m.1677 — Mary II (1662-♔1689-1694) No children

Anne (1665-♔1702-1714) No surviving children

James (The Old Pretender)

The Houses of Valois and Bourbon from 1515 to 1715

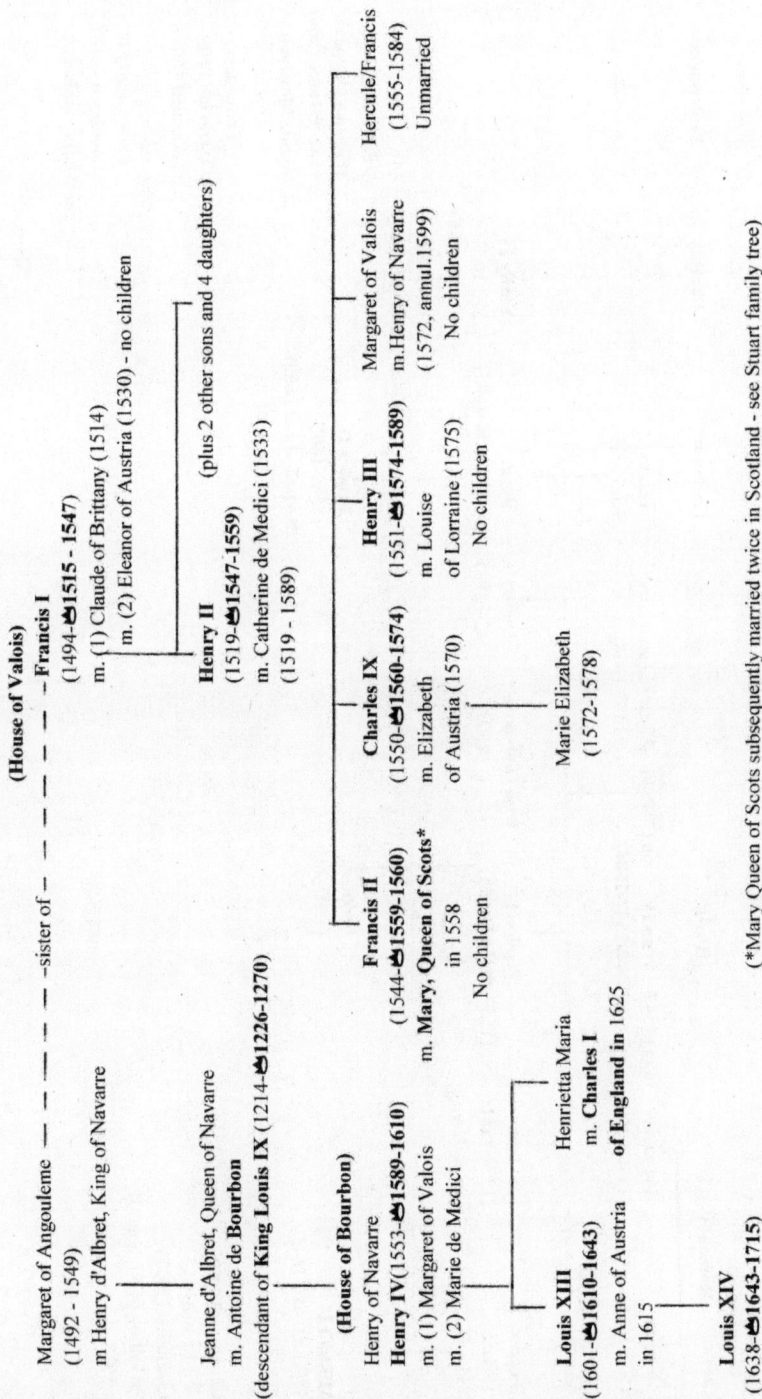

(House of Valois)

Margaret of Angouleme — — — — — — -sister of — — — — **Francis I**
(1492 - 1549)   (1494-⚔1515 - 1547)
m Henry d'Albret, King of Navarre   m. (1) Claude of Brittany (1514)
                                                                                            m. (2) Eleanor of Austria (1530) - no children

Jeanne d'Albret, Queen of Navarre   **Henry II**   (plus 2 other sons and 4 daughters)
m. **Antoine de Bourbon**   (1519-⚔1547-1559)
(descendant of **King Louis IX** (1214-⚔1226-1270)   m. Catherine de Medici (1533)
                                                                              (1519 - 1589)

(House of Bourbon)   **Francis II**   **Charles IX**   **Henry III**   Margaret of Valois   Hercule/Francis
Henry of Navarre   (1544-⚔1559-1560)   (1550-⚔1560-1574)   (1551-⚔1574-1589)   m.Henry of Navarre   (1555-1584)
Henry IV(1553-⚔1589-1610) m. **Mary, Queen of Scots*** m. Elizabeth   m. Louise   (1572, annul.1599)   Unmarried
m. (1) Margaret of Valois   in 1558   of Austria (1570)   of Lorraine (1575)   No children
m. (2) Marie de Medici   No children   No children

                          Henrietta Maria   Marie Elizabeth
                          m. **Charles I**   (1572-1578)
                          of England in 1625

Louis XIII
(1601-⚔1610-1643)
m. Anne of Austria
in 1615

Louis XIV
(1638-⚔1643-1715)

(*Mary Queen of Scots subsequently married twice in Scotland - see Stuart family tree)

Russian Tsars 1547 - 1645

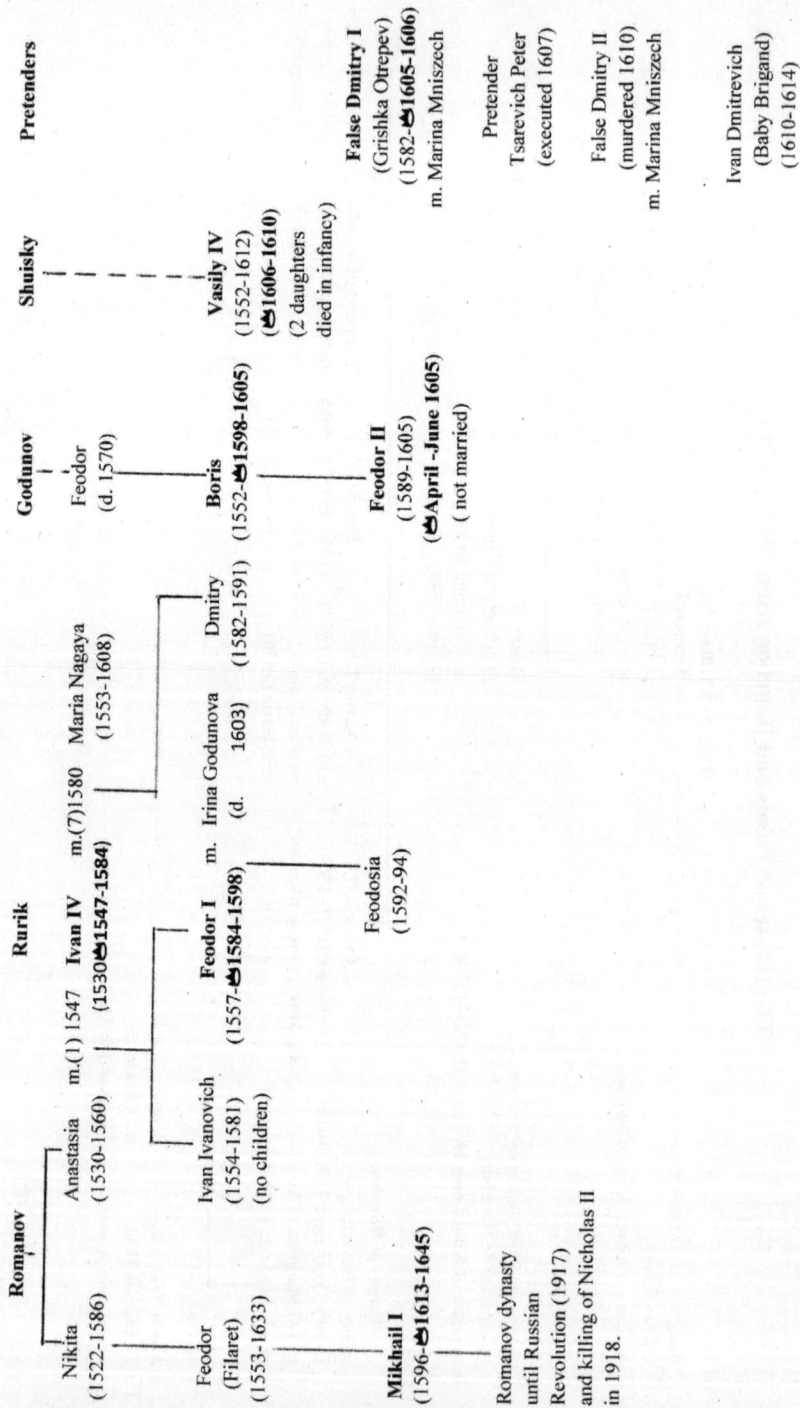

Romanov	Rurik	Godunov	Shuisky	Pretenders

Romanov

Nikita
(1522-1586)

Anastasia
(1530-1560)

Feodor
(Filaret)
(1553-1633)

Mikhail I
(1596-⚔1613-1645)

Romanov dynasty
until Russian
Revolution (1917)
and killing of Nicholas II
in 1918.

Rurik

m.(1) 1547   **Ivan IV**
(1530⚔1547-1584)

m.(7)1580   Maria Nagaya
(1553-1608)

Ivan Ivanovich
(1554-1581)
(no children)

Feodor I
(1557-⚔1584-1598)

m.   Irina Godunova
(d.   1603)

Dmitry
(1582-1591)

Feodosia
(1592-94)

Godunov

Feodor
(d. 1570)

Boris
(1552-⚔1598-1605)

Feodor II
(1589-1605)
(⚔April -June 1605)
(not married)

Shuisky

Vasily IV
(1552-1612)
(⚔1606-1610)
(2 daughters
died in infancy)

Pretenders

False Dmitry I
(Grishka Otrepev)
(1582-⚔1605-1606)
m. Marina Mniszech

Pretender
Tsarevich Peter
(executed 1607)

False Dmitry II
(murdered 1610)
m. Marina Mniszech

Ivan Dmitrevich
(Baby Brigand)
(1610-1614)

The Ottoman Dynasty from 1566 to 1695

Selim II (1524-⚓1566-1574)

4 known daughters

2 sons died in infancy and
5 sons executed by Murad III
on his accession in 1574

(mo. Nurbanu Sultan)

Murad III (1546-⚓1574-1595)

Over 30 daughters

19 sons executed by Mehmed
on his accession in 1595

(mo. Safiye Sultan)

Mehmed III (1566-⚓1595-1603)

10 daughters

Mustafa I (1600-1639) No children
(⚓1617-18 and 1622-23)

Mahmud (1587-1603)
(executed)

10 others sons

(mo. Halime Sultan)

11 daughters

(mo. Kosem Sultan)

Ibrahim I (1615-⚓1640-1648)

(mo. Handan Sultan)

Ahmed I (1590-⚓1603-1617)

At least 5 other sons

(mo. Mahfiruz Hatun)

Osman II (1604-⚓1618-1622)
(2 sons died in infancy)

Murad IV (1612-⚓1623-1640)
(All 15 sons predeceased him)

10 daughters

(mo. Turhan Sultan)

Mehmed IV (1642-1693)
(⚓1648-1687 - deposed)

(mo. Asub Sultan)

Suleiman II (1642-⚓1687-1691)

(mo. Muezzez Sultan)

Ahmed II (1643-⚓1691-1695)

(mo. = mother of the Sultan)

INTRODUCTION

The murder of rulers, or even their attempted murder – whether they be emperors, kings, sultans, princes, military dictators, elected presidents or prime ministers – can have profound consequences, not only for those directly involved but also for whole nations. Many rulers have been removed by force, and some of them killed by their own subjects. A few of these deaths have received a great deal of attention. The stabbing of Julius Caesar in the Roman Senate, the beheading of Charles I outside Whitehall Palace, the guillotining of Louis XVI in the Place de la Révolution (now the Place de la Concorde), the shooting of Abraham Lincoln, the murder of Tsar Nicholas II of Russia and his family, and the assassination of John F. Kennedy in Dallas, are familiar to many people around the world. However, the killings of most leaders, including monarchs, remain largely unknown outside their own country.

It has been estimated that in the 1200 years from the beginning of the seventh century to the end of the eighteenth century twenty-two per cent of European monarchs died a violent death. This includes death in battle, such as that of Richard III of England at Bosworth Field in 1485, and accidents, as when Henry II of France died after a jousting injury in 1559. But by far the greatest cause of these violent deaths was regicide,[1] the deliberate killing of the monarch. This is calculated to have accounted for fifteen per cent of all monarchs during that period.[2] Some monarchs were murdered by a lone individual, though these killers were often influenced by the prevailing mood of the time. Others were the victims of plots, often within their immediate entourage in palace coups, frequently from within their own family. Some were killed as a result of rebellion or widespread disorder that got out of hand, while others were executed at the culmination of some form of legal proceedings.

During the sixteenth and seventeenth centuries across Britain and Europe, the period of the Tudor and Stuart dynasties, numerous monarchs were put to death. In England three monarchs were beheaded after a trial – a failed claimant to the throne, Lady Jane Grey, a deposed queen regnant of Scotland, Mary, Queen of Scots, and Charles I after his defeat in the civil wars.

Two French monarchs, Henry III and Henry IV, were stabbed by lone killers, though the assassins had absorbed the strong feelings that were prevalent in sections of society at the time. In Russia's 'Time of Troubles' three crowned Tsars were put to death, as were other pretenders to the throne, in a ten year period of social and political turmoil, though only one of these Tsars had inherited the throne. In the Ottoman Empire two sultans of the ruling dynasty, Osman II and Ibrahim I, died in palace coups backed by the armed forces. These ten killings provide a fascinating variety in terms of the perpetrators and their motives, with a cast of religious zealots, self-interested nobles, hugely ambitious power-seekers, defenders of dynasties, palace plotters and those seeking to overturn the political structure. The deaths involved beheadings, stabbings, strangulation, shooting and being hacked to death.

The term 'regicide' is also used to refer to those who are responsible for such an action, the 'killers of monarchs'. In Britain the best-known example of regicide is the execution of King Charles I of England, Scotland and Ireland in 1649. Those who signed Charles's death warrant and a few others directly involved in his trial and execution are referred to as the regicides, as are those in France responsible for the execution of Louis XVI almost 150 years later. Both groups argued that the executions resulted from a legitimate trial carried out in the name of a parliament or assembly representing the people of the country, and that at the time of execution neither Charles nor Louis could be regarded as the king. The same claim might be made about the shooting of Tsar Nicholas II of Russia, though in that case there was no formal trial. Conversely, many people regarded the death of these kings as nothing less than murder. They would argue that any such trial had no legal standing. Charles himself wished to know from his judges 'by what authority, I mean lawful authority' he had been charged and brought to the court.

Such trials and executions make up only a small proportion of the violent deaths experienced by monarchs at the hands of their subjects. Although the absolute number of monarchs being killed had been in decline since the early Middle Ages,[3] and never matched the numbers of Roman emperors murdered, being a monarch was still a risky enterprise in the sixteenth and seventeenth century. One reason for this was that there was rarely a procedure for the removal of a hereditary monarch who had lost the confidence and support of large sections of society, especially the nobility. So what could be done if a king was clearly incompetent or, in the view of the political elite, leading the country to disaster in foreign wars or causing widespread domestic unrest? They would not wish to support the actions of a king that they knew to be harmful to either the country or to their own personal and family interests. They might be willing to put up with the situation in the hope that when that monarch died his successor, assuming a clear line of succession, was more capable. But how long would they have to wait and how much damage might be done in the meantime? Attempts could be made to restrict the power of such a king. Many might accept the situation if they could control a weak monarch. But that could result in dangerous rivalries between different groups of nobles. In any case most kings would not readily accept a reduction of their power. Even if some restrictions were forced upon them, as with King John when he was compelled to sign the Magna Carta in 1215, monarchs frequently reneged on any agreement if the opportunity arose to regain their full powers. King John did just that and if he had not died in 1216 a prolonged civil war could have ensued.

In such circumstances there might well be attempts to replace the king. Many 'over-mighty' subjects, frequently close relations, had their own ambitions. If they were not appointed to prestigious positions of influence from which they could dominate royal policy, the most powerful might seek the crown themselves, and this often resulted in rebellion and, if successful, the murder of the monarch. In England during the fourteenth and fifteenth centuries this was not uncommon. In 1327 King Edward II was forced to abdicate in favour of his son and soon afterwards he was murdered. Richard II was removed as king in 1399 and then starved to death by his cousin, Henry Bolingbroke, who became King Henry IV, the first of the Lancastrian monarchs. In 1461, during the Wars of the Roses or Cousin's War, the mentally unstable King Henry VI was deposed by Edward of York (Edward IV). After a brief restoration ten years later, Henry was placed in the Tower of London and within weeks was reported to be dead, killed on the orders of Edward IV. The sons of Edward IV, the 'Princes in the Tower', the elder of whom, Edward, was the rightful king of England, also met their death in the Tower just over a decade later, almost certainly on the orders of their uncle, Richard III. Richard himself lasted only two years before defeat and death at Bosworth Field. If he had not died on the battlefield he would certainly have been killed on the instructions of the new king, Henry Tudor, whose own claim to the throne was tenuous.

It seems that although ready to order the murder of their predecessors, the new kings in all these instances did not wish to own their decision. The cause of death was left deliberately vague, hence the degree of uncertainty that still exists today. Few kings wished to begin their reign as an acknowledged regicide. Understandably so: it was in their interests to preserve the idea of the sanctity of monarchy, despite their own actions. They asserted that they had taken the throne in the interests of the country and for the benefit of others. They all emphasised their legitimate claim to the throne. The Tudors had a tough task on their hands if they were to establish themselves as the rightful rulers of England, let alone France, which Henry VIII in particular was keen to claim. Given this catalogue of violence towards the reigning monarchs it was little wonder that as late as 1646, when Charles I's situation was looking very insecure, the Dutch playwright of 'Mary Stuart or Martyred Mary' has Mary, Queen of Scots asking: 'Is't not the English custom, to hold the blood of kings of very little worth?'[4]

Other countries, of course, had their own challenges, though few gained such a reputation for the ruthless removal of failing monarchs. In France the Valois dynasty, whose throne was claimed by Edward III and successive English kings, was threatened by defeats at Crécy, Poitiers and Agincourt during the Hundred Years War. King Charles VI (1380–1422) experienced frequent psychotic episodes during which he needed to be secured in his apartments, sometimes refusing to bathe or change his clothes for months on end, and for a time believing that he was made of glass and had to be protected from contact with anything or anyone in case he shattered. During his reign various scions of the royal family and senior noblemen struggled for power in the vacuum left by the king. This sometimes became murderous, as witnessed by the assassinations of the king's brother Louis, Duke of Orléans, in 1407 on the orders of his cousin John of Burgundy, and then John's own assassination on the orders of the king's son, Charles, in 1419. Despite all this Charles VI was never deposed, and given these circumstances the main question would seem to be: why not? In 1420 he signed a treaty which made Henry V of England, who married his daughter Catherine, his successor rather than his own son, Charles. However, on his death in October 1422 he was not succeeded by Henry V, but by Charles. The English king had died two months earlier, leaving a nine-month-old heir, Henry VI, who proved to be as unfortunate a monarch for England as Charles VI had been for France.

Similar examples can be found in the history of most countries, with disputes, rivalries and civil wars, all of which sometimes culminated in the killing of the monarch. It is impossible to investigate every individual instance: there are simply too many and each has its own unique circumstances. However, by asking key questions about a number of cases in the sixteenth and seventeenth century it is possible to gain an understanding of the complexities involved and reveal some underlying common factors. Who were the people that carried out the killing? Was it the action of a single individual, a small band of conspirators or a much larger group? What were their motives – personal, financial, political, religious? How was it possible to kill an individual who might reasonably be expected to have good protection? Was it long in the planning or a spontaneous act taking advantage of an unexpected opportunity? What were the consequences of the death of the monarch? How were the regicides regarded by their contemporaries and by history? Did they succeed in achieving their wider aims? What impact did the killing have on the state and its inhabitants?

One striking feature of the political structure of Europe in the sixteenth and seventeenth century was the variety of entities that existed. The idea of the nation state headed by a monarch was more a construct of nineteenth-century historians than the reality of the time.[5] Dynasty was a more significant concept than nation, certainly at the start of the period. Our view of English, French and other monarchs as the leaders of their nations must be tempered by the fact that these monarchs frequently laid claim to other lands outside their 'nation' on the basis of hereditary rights. Thus, Henry VIII claimed the French throne, while French kings tried to assert their ancient rights in Naples. The dynastic empire of the Habsburg family reached its peak under Emperor Charles V. When he was elected Holy Roman Emperor in 1519 he had already inherited the Low Countries, Spain, territories in central Europe and much of Italy as a result of dynastic marriages by his grandparents and parents, and the early deaths of other family members. On his abdication in 1556 he divided his territories between his son, Philip (Spain, its American empire, lands in Italy and the Low Countries) and his own younger brother, Ferdinand (lands in central Europe and the Holy Roman Empire). The Holy Roman Empire itself consisted of over 300 separate principalities, duchies, free imperial cities and other territories ruled by princes, dukes, counts, bishops and city councils, headed by an elected emperor, always a Habsburg from the mid-fifteenth century onwards.

Of the hereditary monarchs, which we mistakenly tend to think of as being the norm, some dynasties were long established, such as the Valois in France, the Stuarts in Scotland and the Rurikids of Russia. The Ottoman Empire, ruled by sultans descended from Osman I in the early fourteenth century, had expanded into south-eastern Europe, the Middle East and North Africa during the fifteenth and early sixteenth century, taking Constantinople in 1453 and reaching the gates of Vienna in 1529. Others dynasties, though, were more recently installed, such as the Tudors in England in 1485, and the Habsburgs in the Spanish kingdoms in 1516. Denmark and Norway were ruled by the members of the House of Oldenburg from the mid-fifteenth century, and they also ruled Sweden for a short time before being replaced by the native Vasa dynasty in 1523. Differences existed in the way in which the hereditary principle was applied. It was usually the eldest son who inherited, but this was not the case in the Ottoman Empire, where all sons initially had an equal claim to succeed their father. Everywhere sons took precedence over daughters, but whereas in some countries a woman could become the monarch, in others that was ruled out. In France even a claim through a female line of inheritance was unacceptable.

Not all monarchies were hereditary. There were also elective monarchies, where representative bodies, usually dominated by the nobility, chose their kings, such as in Poland (later the Polish–Lithuanian Commonwealth), Bohemia and Hungary, although during the sixteenth century the Habsburgs came to regard the crown of the latter two as part of their patrimony. In Poland during the last thirty years of the sixteenth century, despite pressure to select the Habsburg Holy Roman Emperor, those elected were the French prince, Henry of Valois, who abdicated after becoming King Henry III of France, the Prince of Transylvania, Stephen Bathory, and then Sigismund III of the Swedish house of Vasa. The Papal States of central Italy were ruled from the Vatican City by popes elected by the conclave of cardinals. Many popes, such as those from the de'Medici and Farnese families, furthered their own family ambitions as well as the interests of the Church. Both hereditary and elected monarchs were concerned with the continuation and extension of their dynasties, though during this period as the people of certain areas increasingly came to see themselves as a 'nation', the rulers sought to use the concept to build up support, especially against an external enemy.

Not all states had a monarch. There were city states in Switzerland, such as Geneva and Zurich, and in Germany and in Italy, where some, like Florence, became hereditary duchies. There were also the maritime republics, Venice and Genoa, with extensive coastal territories in the Mediterranean stretching as far as the Black Sea. All of these had their own systems of government, though they were usually dominated by a wealthy oligarchy. The various provinces of the Low Countries, which had been part of the Duchy of Burgundy and came under Habsburg control, each had their own political structures, with provincial assemblies and an Estate-General where representatives of the various provinces met together. The rebellion of seven provinces against Habsburg control in the late sixteenth century eventually resulted in the creation of the United Provinces, usually known as the Dutch Republic.

Most political entities, however, did have a sovereign ruler, although they might be counts, dukes, archbishops, or have various other titles, and not a monarch in the sense of a king, queen, emperor, or sultan. The concept of monarchy which royal dynasties wished to propagate was one of divinely sanctioned rulers, associated with the idea that all lawful authority was derived from God. In order to emphasise this point, the ceremonial performance of coronations, first regularly adopted in France, was developed during the early Middle Ages as a means of sanctifying the monarch. Although the new monarch became king or queen on the death of the previous monarch, *'Le Roi est mort, vive le Roi'*, the coronation ceremony was an effective way of projecting the image of the monarch as God's chosen ruler. The idea spread throughout Christian Europe as monarchs recognised the advantage of such a ceremony.

Although the details of ceremonies varied from state to state, the main features can still be recognised on the few occasions in the present day when a coronation takes place. First came the acclamation of the monarch by the assembled subjects and clergy. This was followed by the traditional oath, taken by the monarch, to rule following the customs of his predecessors and to maintain and defend the traditional rights of his subjects and of the Church. Then came the most sacred part of the whole ceremony: the anointing of the monarch with consecrated oil by senior clergy. The monarch would then be enthroned, handed the orb, the sceptre and other symbols of power, and finally crowned. Those present would then pay homage to the monarch, pledging allegiance and loyalty. It is easy to see why a new monarch was keen to arrange a coronation, as it provided both temporal and spiritual authority. The drawback was that when things went wrong a monarch could be accused of failing to uphold their coronation oath and therefore to have forfeited their right to rule, as happened in late sixteenth-century France to King Henry III and in mid-seventeenth-century England to King Charles I.

The idea was developed that just as a physical body which grows from an embryo is regulated by one head, so there comes from the people of the kingdom, which exists as the body politic or *corpus mysticum* [mystical body], one man or head – the monarch – to govern them.[6] With the monarch at the summit everyone had their place in a hierarchical structure, from the nobility down through society to those who worked the land and owned next to nothing. Although there was certainly no uniform social structure across Europe, this concept was generally accepted as the basis for a stable society. Every individual was expected to know his or her place, and thus benefit from the reciprocal relationships that were assumed to exist. In its simplest form the nobility controlled large landholdings on behalf of the monarch and the most important of them had a place in the royal council. In return they provided money, advice and military service. The peasants worked the land owned by the lords, producing food and payment to the lord in the form of labour, taxes and sometimes military service. In return the lord provided protection and security for the peasant. When this was accepted by all groups a stable community existed, in which loyalty to one's overlord was rewarded.

From early medieval times societies developed in different ways so that no two states, or even regions within larger states, were the same. At the top of the hierarchy, power was gained through both formal and informal means. The formal political structure of a royal council and officers of state went alongside the informal, in which attendance at court and thus access to the monarch, friendship and personal contacts, played an important role in gaining influence and rewards.[7] Increasingly in some countries, as government became more complex, specialists in the law and finance were needed. These often came from outside the traditional elite and thus the power and influence that they sometimes gained created much jealousy among the nobility. At the other end of the hierarchy, the powers that landowners had over those who worked on the land and therefore the level of freedom experienced by large numbers of people, varied considerably from state to state. In some it was very little. As a result of these developments the societies of England and France had significant differences and those that existed in Russia and the Ottoman Empire were different again.

All this tends to give the impression of a reasonably stable, though very varied, political and social situation. Nothing could be further from the truth. Not only were there rivalries and conflicts between many of the states, but each had its own internal problems. These could be personal feuds and jealousies within the ruling family, an over-powerful nobility and factional disputes at court, or economic difficulties and social discontent. Such issues could lead to social and political instability and ultimately violent conflict. Much depended on the qualities of the monarch in order to achieve the desired calm and stability. To build up the confidence of the political elite and the population as a whole a monarch needed to be even-handed, to be seen as fair in dealings with all factions and individuals, and not to favour one group over another. This required consistency. People had to know what to expect from their monarch, whether it be on great matters of policy or adjudicating on minor issues. However, there was also the need for ruthlessness when it was required. Subjects needed to know that the monarch could deal with emergencies and to have reason to fear the consequences if they plotted or conspired against their monarch.

There was no shortage of advice available in the sixteenth century to young rulers and much of it stands the test of time. Perhaps the most famous tract was Machiavelli's 'The Prince', written for Lorenzo de'Medici, the Duke of Urbino, in about 1513. Even though it was not published in printed form until 1532, five years after the author's death, its ideas were already well known in much of Europe by then. For a ruler to be called 'Machiavellian' is rarely intended to be a compliment, carrying with it the suggestion of being unprincipled, but it might also have an element of grudging respect or perhaps fear. His advice was certainly based upon the brutal realities of power and politics at the time, but he also recognised many of the qualities that we still admire today. Machiavelli proposed that rulers should act courageously, confidently and decisively; to know when to fight and when to negotiate; to honour good citizens and ruthlessly punish troublemakers in order to discourage others. However, he did not always expect rulers to have a clean pair of hands if they were to prosper. Another work written in the 1510s, by the humanist philosopher Erasmus of Rotterdam, was perhaps more idealistic. *'The Education of a Christian Prince'* was dedicated to the young Charles of Burgundy, soon to become Emperor Charles V. Erasmus believed monarchy to be the best form of government, but emphasised that the sovereign must not forget that 'a large part of authority depends upon consent of the people', and that it was important to avoid tyranny. He stressed the virtues of peace and the importance of not being a slave to one's deficiencies and passions. He also advised: 'Conduct your own rule as if you were striving to ensure that no successor could be your equal, but at the same time prepare your children for their future as if to ensure that a better man would succeed you'.

Given human nature, not all monarchs, perhaps not many at all, would be able to achieve such standards. Few countries experienced the long-term peace and tranquillity that was wished for by most monarchs and subjects alike. The challenges faced by rulers were often daunting. The accession of some monarchs was not straightforward. Family disputes were frequent and it was not uncommon for there to be a challenger for the throne. Some monarchs inherited a troubled state, where lawlessness was widespread or where the established religion was under threat. Poor harvests, starvation and poverty were frequent and unpredictable; most monarchs could do little about them. The personal failings of a monarch were also an unavoidable feature of the system. If a monarch had obvious favourites who were given honours and positions that others believed them to be unworthy of, or if a monarch was inconsistent or wavering in his decisions, jealousies and rivalries could get out of hand. This could lead to plots, rebellions, murders and civil conflict. Often those who were discontented with the way in which their country was being governed held back from challenging the monarch directly by blaming ministers and advisors.

On some occasions monarchs were deposed and perhaps exiled, but at other times the final step was taken – to kill the monarch. It might be expected that the violent removal of the 'head' of the 'body politic' (in its simplest sense) was likely to result in a large-scale upheaval. This happened in some cases, but by no means in all. The nature and magnitude of the changes brought about by the killing of a monarch depended on the particular circumstances in the country, the motives of the killers, the qualities or failings of the monarch killed, and who or what replaced the dead monarch in the government of the country. These are what will be investigated in the following chapters.

'Lady Jane and her heirs male.'

The amended wording of the key part
of Edward VI's 'Devise for the Succession'
naming Lady Jane Grey as his successor
in the event of his dying childless

━━━◆═◊◦◊═◆━━━

It will *'teach you to live and learn you to die.'*

Lady Jane Grey on the value of the New
Testament in her final letter to her
sister, Katherine

━━━◆═◊◦◊═◆━━━

*'Although I accepted that of which I was not worth,
I never sought it.'*

From Lady Jane Grey's writings in
the days before her execution

CHAPTER 1

'MY SOUL WILL FIND MERCY IN GOD' – EXECUTION

O n 12 February 1554 the sixteen-year-old Lady Jane Grey, briefly Queen Jane, often known as 'the Nine Day Queen', was beheaded on Tower Green within the grounds of the Tower of London. At her trial, in November 1553 at the Guildhall, she was charged with having 'falsely and treacherously assumed and took up for herself the title and power of the Queen of the kingdom of England'. She had pleaded guilty along with her husband, Guildford Dudley, Thomas Cranmer, the archbishop of Canterbury (who had initially denied the charges against him), and two of her husband's brothers, Ambrose and Henry Dudley. The men were sentenced to be hung, drawn and quartered, while the former queen was to be 'burned alive on Tower Hill or beheaded as the Queen should please'[1]. They were reported to have taken the sentence calmly,[2] because although the sentences were expected, the prisoners probably believed that they would not be carried out.

Archbishop Thomas Cranmer was held captive for another two years before being burnt at the stake in Oxford on 14 March 1556 after another trial had found him guilty of heresy. However, the Dudley brothers were released from the Tower late in 1554. Henry died at the battle of St Quentin in 1557 fighting for Spain, England's ally at the time, against the French. Ambrose survived that battle, had a successful military career, was created Earl of Warwick and then appointed to the Privy Council by Queen Elizabeth. Their brother, Robert Dudley, also sentenced to death at a separate trial in 1554, later became Elizabeth's favourite and was created Earl of Leicester. How was it, then, that the young Lady Jane Grey, along with her husband, was executed, and why was she on trial in the first place?

Jane had been proclaimed queen and given a formal entry to the Tower of London, as was the tradition for a new monarch, on Monday 10 July

1553, four days after the death of King Edward VI, the son of Henry VIII. This all came as a surprise to her. She had only been informed that she was to be queen on the previous day and at first she protested that 'the crown is not my right and pleases me not. The Lady Mary is the rightful heir'.[3] Indeed 'the Lady Mary', daughter of Henry VIII and Catherine of Aragon, had already asserted her claim to the throne. Members of the Privy Council and senior officials rebuffed this claim, writing to Mary that Jane was 'possessed with the just and right title' to the throne by both 'good order of old and ancient laws',[4] and the will of King Edward. They continued that the divorce of her parents meant that she had no claim and that she should be 'quiet and obedient'. Even more remarkable, then, that some of those very same privy councillors were calling for Jane's death only months later.

During the evening of Wednesday 7 February, three months after her trial, Jane was informed that she was to be executed two days later. By then she knew that recent events, completely beyond her control, had made this outcome increasingly likely. She received the news calmly, determined to show the same courage and dignity that she had displayed at her trial. Queen Mary had reluctantly agreed to Jane's death and had commuted the usual gruesome punishment for treason to the more merciful beheading. But the queen still wanted to save Jane's soul by getting her to abandon her Protestant beliefs. She sent her personal chaplain, Dr John Feckenham, to the Tower to talk to Jane. He was familiar with the place having been held prisoner there for almost six years through most of Edward VI's reign. When he reported to Mary that he was hopeful that he could persuade Jane to return to the Catholic faith, it was decided to give him three additional days to complete his task. He did not succeed, though it is believed that Jane enjoyed their debates.

When not with Dr Feckenham, Jane spent her last days writing to her family, whom she had not seen for six months since her status had changed from that of queen, firstly to that of prisoner and then to that of condemned traitor. In her letters, and later on the scaffold, she intended that her words would reach a wider audience among those who shared her faith. To her father, Henry Grey, Duke of Suffolk, who had been returned to the Tower as a prisoner on 10 February and was to be executed two weeks later, she wrote in the prayer book. This would be passed to him after her execution. In it she forgives him for the misfortunes that he has brought upon her. She beseeches him to 'trust that we, by losing this mortal life have won an immortal life and I for my part as I have honoured your grace in this life, will pray for you in another life.'[5]

The forgiveness demonstrated in this message can be contrasted with a very different tone in parts of another letter supposedly written by Jane to her father at this time. It appeared in the second edition of Foxe's *Acts and Monuments* (1570). In this she complains that 'it hath pleased God to hasten my death by you, by whom my life should rather be lengthened'. She then accepts that although it was the result of the persuasion and insistence of others, 'in taking the crown upon me, I seemed to consent, and therein grievously offended the queen and her laws'.[6] However, it seems likely that this letter was a forgery, produced shortly after her death, based on words in a different statement in which Jane wrote that it was a 'lack of prudence for which I deserve the greatest punishment' and 'although I accepted that of which I was not worth, I never sought it'.[7]

To her thirteen-year-old sister, Katherine, Jane sent her personal copy of the New Testament in Greek, which she informed her sister had 'more worth than precious stones'[8] and that it would 'win you more than you should have gained by the possession of your woeful father's lands'. Moreover, it would 'teach you to live, and learn you to die'.[9] Probably reflecting on her own situation, Jane told Katherine that youth did not necessarily 'lengthen your life' because God called both young and old. As to her own death, she told her sister 'to rejoice as I do... that I shall be delivered of this corruption', repeating that she would 'win an immortal life'. She sought to provide guidance to Katherine, whom she considered to be more headstrong and rather less committed to the religious life, urging her to be strong in faith and 'Rejoice in Christ as I trust I do and seeing that you have a name of a Christian, as near as you can follow in the steps of your master, Christ'.[10]

There is no evidence of a letter to her mother, Frances Grey, the granddaughter of King Henry VII from whom Jane's place in the succession was derived, and with whom she always had a difficult relationship. Michelangelo Florio, Jane's Italian tutor, suggested that she wrote such a letter,[11] intending to console and comfort her mother, but if so it has not survived. Did Frances destroy it, either because it was too painful a reminder of Jane's fate, or because she wished no further misfortune to fall upon her other daughters through any connection with Jane?

Nor does Jane appear to have written a letter to her husband, who was to be executed on the same day as her, during the months that he had also been held in the Tower. The account of the papal envoy Giovanni Commendone mentions that Guildford requested a meeting with Jane 'to embrace and kiss her for the last time',[12] and that Queen Mary was agreeable to them saying goodbye. However, Jane refused, saying that it would be upsetting for them both and that she would rather delay it as 'they would meet shortly elsewhere and live bound by indissoluble ties'.[13] There must be some doubt as to whether these discussions took place at all. There is little evidence of any strong bond between Jane and Guildford; neither had wished for the marriage in the first place, their life together had been a matter of days, and even in that time there had been significant disagreements.

Her letters written, Jane now composed her own epitaph, taking pleasure in her skill in languages. She wrote three epigrams: one in Latin, the second in Greek and the third in English:

'If Justice is done with my body, my soul will find mercy in God.

Death will give pain to my body for its sins, but the soul will be justified before God.

If my faults deserve punishment, my youth at least, and my imprudence were worthy of excuse; God and posterity will show me favour'.[14]

These lines were probably preserved by Dr Feckenham, with whom Jane had a good relationship despite their failure to agree on doctrinal matters.

Executions usually took place early in the morning and as dawn broke on Monday 12 February it was cold and frosty, with a mist coming off the river. Guildford, it had been decided, would be executed first. But as the authorities wished for a substantial crowd to see his death, it was not until 10am that he was led out of the Beaufort Tower, across the precincts to the outer gate, watched by Jane from the house of Nathaniel Partridge, the Gentleman Gaoler, where she had her rooms. He was handed over to the sheriff of London, the officer responsible for arranging the execution, and escorted on the short walk to Tower Green by guards and a number of well-wishers known to him. There was no priest present since he had been denied his request for a Protestant one.

Arriving at the spot where just months earlier his father John Dudley, Duke of Northumberland, and forty-three years before that his grandfather, Edmund Dudley, had been executed, Guildford made a short speech. What he said is not known: either no one heard it or no one thought it worth recording. His end was swift. One blow of the axe, his body and severed head wrapped in a cloth, then rapidly thrown into a cart and taken back to the Tower. The return of his body was watched by Jane despite the efforts of her ladies to distract her. She might have murmured 'Oh Guildford, Guildford' and made a comment about the bitterness of death, but certainly not what was reported by Florio, who claimed that she spoke about the executions being the *antepasto* to a heavenly feast.[15]

Now it was Jane's turn.[16] She was to die privately on Tower Green in front of a small invited audience. There would be no crowd such as had attended the beheading of Anne Boleyn nearly eighteen years before. She stepped out of Partridge's house escorted by Sir John Brydges, her two attendants, Mistress Elizabeth Tylney and Mistress Ellen, and Dr Feckenham. Dressed all in black, she carried her prayer book, which it had been agreed would be passed on to her father, and then, after his execution, kept by Brydges. She carried herself with dignity though her attendants 'wonderfully wept'. Brydges had asked that she write something in the prayer book for him and she did so, referring to him as a good master lieutenant and a friend, ending with the words: 'for as the preacher sayeth there is a time to be born and a time to die and the day of death is better than the day of our birth. Yours as the Lord knoweth as a friend, Jane Dudley.'

Once on the scaffold Jane asked Brydges if she could speak her mind and he assented. She started by following the convention that those about to be executed accepted the legality of their punishment. 'Good people, I am come hither to die, and by the law I am condemned to the same; the fact indeed against the Queen's Highness was unlawful and the consenting thereunto me.' But she continued 'touching the procurement and desire thereof by me or on my [be]half, I do wash my hands thereof in innocency before the face of God and the face of you good Christian people this day.' She then asked those assembled to 'witness that I die a true Christian woman and that I do look to be saved by no other mean, but only by the mercy of God, in the merits of the blood of his only son Jesus Christ... now good people, while I am alive, I pray you to assist me with your prayers'. She was declaring for the final time her dedication to the reformed religion by emphasising her belief in salvation by faith alone and her rejection of the Catholic tradition of prayers for the dead.

Jane knelt to pray, reciting Psalm 51 in English, while Dr Feckenham joined her in Latin. Jane then rose and embraced Feckenham, thanking him for his company over the past few days. She removed her gloves, handed them to Mistress Tylney and gave her prayer book to Brydges. She allowed her companions to assist her in removing her gown, headdress and collar. The executioner knelt and asked her forgiveness, to which she replied 'most willingly', and he assured her that he would dispatch her quickly. He moved her onto the straw around the block and when she asked 'Will you take it off before I lay me down' he assured her that he would not. She tossed her hair so as to bare her neck and was handed the blindfold. Having secured it, she knelt to place her head on the block but it was beyond her reach. She cried out 'What shall I do? Where is it?' The execution party froze and a bystander had to step up to guide her into place. Having laid her neck on the block she uttered: 'Lord, into thy hands I commend my spirit', and the axeman carried out his task with a single blow. Her blood spurted out over the scaffold, soaking the surrounding straw and soiling the clothes of some of those chosen to witness her death. The executioner completed his job by holding up her head with the traditional words: 'So perish all the Queen's enemies! Behold the head of a traitor!' However, accustomed as they were to violent deaths, the bravery and spirit of the sixteen-year-old Jane had won the sympathy and respect of most of those present, many of whom must have known that this was an undeserved death; more a case of judicial murder than a justifiable execution.

Despite this, Antoine de Noailles, the French ambassador, reported that Jane's body remained on the scaffold for several hours after the spectators had departed. He also remarked on the extraordinary amount of blood from so small a body.[17] Why she was not moved immediately was a result of uncertainty as to what to do with the body of a heretic. No one was willing to take responsibility until they had official authority to take her body to the chapel of St Peter ad Vincula in the grounds of the Tower. There she was presumably placed alongside her husband, Guildford Dudley, her father-in-law, John Dudley, and two other headless queens, the executed wives of Henry VIII, Anne Boleyn and Katherine Howard. No memorial stone has ever been carved for Jane. When the chapel was undergoing restoration in Victorian times the floor of the chancel collapsed before the bodies of either Jane or Guildford had been found. As a result, a simple slab was placed on the floor of the chancel with an inscription saying that Jane and others were believed to be buried there.

CHAPTER 2

EDWARD VI'S 'DEVISE FOR THE SUCCESSION'

The death of a monarch can be a time of great danger for any country. If there are rival claimants to the throne there is always the risk of civil war. People are forced to take sides and only the most skilful, politically nimble or lucky can avoid the consequences of the changing fortunes of the leading participants to whom they are allied. Before 1553 Lady Jane Grey had never been involved in politics at any level and she lacked the good fortune to be able to make the crucial decisions for herself. What was responsible for her death, as one biographer makes clear in her subtitle, was a 'deadly inheritance'.[1] She could do nothing about her lineage. She was the eldest daughter (with no brothers) of Henry Grey, Marquess of Dorset, a descendant of Elizabeth Woodville and her first husband before she married Edward IV, and his wife, Frances Brandon, the daughter of Mary Tudor, Henry VIII's sister, and Charles Brandon, a close companion of Henry VIII whom he created Duke of Suffolk. In 1551 the death of Brandon's teenage sons by his final marriage after the death of Mary Tudor meant that Jane's parents became Duke and Duchess of Suffolk. Jane was the great-granddaughter of Henry VII and great-niece of Henry VIII. Being born related to the ruling family could often be a death sentence if circumstances turned against you.

The explanation for the events of 1553 that has been widely accepted for the last 450 years is that John Dudley, Duke of Northumberland, having been the leading figure in ruling England since 1549, during the minority of Edward VI, was determined to hold on to power at all costs because he feared for his life if the Catholic Mary became queen, and because of his great ambition. He therefore plotted to prevent Mary's accession. He married his son, Guildford Dudley, to Lady Jane Grey, and then used her membership of the Tudor family to have her proclaimed queen on the young king's death. Thus, he would be able to control both Jane and Guildford, and the Dudley family would become the ruling dynasty. He was able to achieve this by using his position of power in the country and influence with Edward VI to make members of the Privy Council fear for their lives if they did not agree to his plans. The 'Black Legend' which developed around Dudley claimed that these plans had guided his every action since the death of Henry VIII in 1547. He was blamed for all of England's problems, for the removal of his rivals on the Privy Council and even for poisoning Edward VI to expedite matters.

This account of the events leading up to the execution of Lady Jane Grey suited many people, both at the time and in following centuries. When Mary did become queen, everyone involved wished to divert attention from their own culpability by finding a scapegoat. Northumberland was the obvious candidate. After Mary's own death, future Protestant rulers and the public at large found that this account of Jane as the innocent victim of the 'evil Duke' and a 'martyr' for the Protestant cause fitted the view of history that they wished to believe. There is some evidence that can be used to support this account, but it also depends upon a great deal of speculation, especially regarding Northumberland's motivation and the malleability of Edward VI. Discerning the thinking behind the actions of any individual is always difficult. At a distance of 450 years, it becomes even more so, but that is part of the fascination of history. In recent decades more nuanced accounts have been written which challenge some of the assumptions of the traditional story.[2]

Fifteenth-century England experienced the prolonged internecine Wars of the Roses between the houses of York and Lancaster. Two kings, Henry VI and Edward V (one of the princes in the Tower), were murdered, another, Richard III, was slain on the battlefield, and there was a high rate of violent death in the Plantagenet family and among the English nobility generally. In addition, the wars resulted in thousands of retainers and others pressed into military service dying in battles, large and small. Although estimates of casualties are difficult, and reports at the time were certainly exaggerated, the Yorkist victory at Towton, fought over ten hours on Palm Sunday, 29 March 1461, probably resulted in 10,000 dead out of the combined armies of 50,000, making it the bloodiest battle on English soil.

Henry VII, the victor over Richard III at Bosworth Field in 1485, had established the Tudor dynasty and his son, Henry VIII, was determined to continue the line. By the mid-1520s he was desperate for a male heir. His various manoeuvres to secure a succession to his liking provide the background to the crisis in 1553 which eventually resulted in Lady Jane Grey's execution. Henry's six marriages are well known, but the problems caused by the legislation associated with them are less so. After almost twenty years of marriage, Henry and Catherine of Aragon had one child, Mary. Catherine's other known pregnancies had produced one short-lived son, Henry, and the miscarriage or stillbirth of two sons and two daughters. She was now beyond childbearing age; her last pregnancy had been in 1518. When Henry developed a passion for Anne Boleyn and she resisted his efforts to make her his mistress, he decided that he could solve both problems at once. If Pope Clement VII were to annul his marriage to Catherine, he could marry Anne and hopefully she would bear a healthy boy, who would be a legitimate heir.

The pope's delaying tactics and eventual refusal to grant Henry an annulment had major consequences. First, Cardinal Wolsey, who had been instructed by Henry to obtain the pope's agreement, was dismissed and charged with treason, dying on his way to London for his trial. Then Henry took the momentous decision to end the pope's authority in England and make himself head of the church in England. He was helped to achieve this by his chief minister, Thomas Cromwell, and the newly appointed archbishop of Canterbury, Thomas Cranmer. The First Succession Act of 1533[3] declared that Princess Mary was illegitimate and that the children of Henry and Anne were to be the legitimate heirs to the throne. It also demanded that his subjects, when requested, take an oath to accept both the Succession Act and the subsequent Act of Supremacy which made Henry and his successors Supreme Head of the English Church. The refusal to take the oath was regarded as treason and resulted in the execution of Sir Thomas More and others.

When Henry ended his marriage to Anne Boleyn after three years, she was beheaded on Tower Green and their child, Princess Elizabeth, was also declared illegitimate by the Second Succession Act (1536). This left Henry without any legitimate offspring and so the Act also gave him 'full and plenary power and authority' to choose who would succeed him by naming his successor in letters patent or his last will, if he died without an heir of his body. When his third wife, Jane Seymour, gave birth to Prince Edward in October 1537 Henry at last had his desired male heir who could be expected to continue the Tudor line. In a Third Succession Act (1543/44), Mary and Elizabeth were returned to the line of succession behind Edward, although in his will Henry added the proviso that they could not marry without the approval of the Privy Council. Nor were they restored to legitimacy, so they would become monarch not on the basis of inheritance, but on the power given to Henry to nominate his successors. If all of Henry's children were to die childless then the next in line would be the children of his niece Lady Frances Grey, the eldest of whom was Lady Jane. Frances herself was excluded from the succession, probably because Henry had no high opinion of her husband, Henry Grey, and did not intend to allow him access to power. Such was the confused situation that was at the heart of the disputes of 1553.

Edward VI was only nine years old when he became king in 1547. Henry had appointed a Regency Council of sixteen to run the country during his minority. However, the Council immediately agreed to appoint the new king's uncle, Edward Seymour, Earl of Hertford, as the Lord Protector of the Realm and Governor of the King's Person. He was created Duke of Somerset and most of the council received new titles or lands. Somerset proceeded to rule with little reference to the Privy Council, which was used merely to approve his actions. Edward's accession might have been peaceful, but his reign was one of controversy: over the powers of the Lord Protector as against those of the Council; about the extent of religious reform; and over foreign policy.[4]

Somerset's rule of two and a half years did not go well. His plan to marry King Edward to Mary, Queen of Scots, angered the Scots, who subsequently betrothed their young queen to Francis, heir to the French throne. The introduction of further religious reforms was unpopular, particularly in the West Country. These issues, together with Somerset's inability to deal with England's ongoing economic problems, particularly rapid inflation, led to widespread social unrest. In July and August 1549 protestors against enclosure in East Anglia took control of England's second city, Norwich, in what became known as Kett's Rebellion. Somerset's initial response was to placate the protestors, but that failed to end the uprising and lost him the support of many of the gentry and large landowners. The rebels repelled royal troops under William Parr, Marquess of Northampton, before being crushed by a stronger army commanded by John Dudley, the Earl of Warwick. Taking advantage of England's internal problems Henri II of France declared war and besieged Boulogne, which had been captured by the English in 1544.

These failures resulted in Somerset's removal as Lord Protector. Although often referred to as 'the good Duke' by many of the poor, who believed that he was sympathetic to their problems, they were not able to save him. Somerset's support within the Privy Council rapidly dwindled and he was taken to the Tower of London, charged with 'ambition, vain glory and entering rash wars… following his own opinion and doing all by his own authority'. Although released and restored to the Privy Council the following year, partly as a result of the intervention of his old friend John Dudley, his continued scheming resulted in his rearrest. Found guilty of plotting against fellow council members, though innocent of treason, he was executed in January 1552.[5]

The new dominant power in the council was John Dudley, Viscount Lisle, Earl of Warwick, now the Duke of Northumberland, who was to play a major role in the events leading up to the arrest and trial of Lady Jane Grey. He rejected the title of Lord Protector and became Lord President of the Council, aiming to involve the council more in the decision-making process than the autocratic Somerset. He also became the Grand Master of the Household, which enabled him to appoint members of the king's Privy Chamber, such as Sir John Gates. He was able to develop a close relationship with the young king. Having taken the leading role at a difficult time Northumberland adopted firm policies to restore peace and prosperity to the country. He enforced strict law and order measures and worked hard to put right the parlous state of the royal finances, ending the debasement of the coinage. He withdrew troops from Scotland and ended the war with France, agreeing to return Boulogne for 400,000 crowns. He proved to be an effective caretaker as Edward progressed towards maturity, though at the cost of widespread unpopularity.

Northumberland, like Somerset, had strong sympathies with the introduction of evangelical reforms in the Church. King Edward was brought up to be committed to the reformed religion. His tutors, such as Richard Cox and John Cheke, a friend of the renowned scholar and teacher, Roger Ascham, who tutored Princess Elizabeth, were well disposed to such ideas. This was something that he had in common with Lady Jane Grey, who was born a few months before the young king in 1537.

This was not universally popular and was opposed by the more conservative members of the council. It was strongly resisted by the king's sister, Princess Mary. In her youth she had a loving relationship with both her mother and father, had an excellent education, and developed into a kind, gentle character, with a love of fine clothes and dancing, who inspired affection in those close to her. However, after Henry put aside Catherine of Aragon, she was disinherited and deemed to be illegitimate. Henry refused her permission to visit her mother, even when Catherine was on her deathbed. A devout Catholic, Mary at first refused to accept the royal supremacy, only giving way after the death of her mother and the execution of Anne Boleyn in 1536, in order to 'save friends' who might otherwise have suffered on her behalf. She was allowed to return to court, often acting as hostess between her father's marriages. However, she received very little instruction in the art of government and despite many marriage negotiations linking her with European royalty, none came to fruition. Henry's last wife, Katherine Parr, is often credited with having Mary and Elizabeth restored to the succession.

With Edward as king, considerable pressure was put on Mary to conform in matters of religion, first by Somerset and then by Northumberland. This increased as her brother reached an age at which he wished to become involved. However, she insisted that she and her household should continue to be permitted to celebrate mass. She replied to Edward that although he was advanced for his years 'it is not possible that your Highness can at these years be a judge in matters of religion' and that she therefore assumed that the demands being made came from others. If the permission that she had been previously granted to celebrate mass was removed then 'rather than offend God and my conscience, I offer my body at your will and death shall be more welcome than life with a troubled conscience'.[6] During her father's life Mary had received support from Emperor Charles V's long-time ambassador in England, Eustace Chapuys. She now looked to the emperor himself, her cousin, for help and advice, writing to him in 1550 that 'after God, I take [you] as the father of my soul and of my body in all spiritual and temporal matters'.[7]

Mary's refusal to back down and her encouragement of others to resist resulted in sharp words between the king and his sister, though they were at times temporarily reconciled. She was granted properties in East Anglia, such as Framlingham Castle, and visited Edward at Greenwich in June 1552. Then on 6 February 1553 she entered London with a large retinue, welcomed by Northumberland's son, son-in-law, and many others from the king's household. After a delay of four days, a large procession involving many of the leading nobles went from her house in St John's, Clerkenwell, to Westminster, where she was greeted by Northumberland and numerous earls before being received by Edward. Northumberland later sent Mary a blazon of her full arms as princess of England.[8] She was being treated as 'the second person in the kingdom'.[9]

The reason for the delay of four days before Mary went to Westminster was that Edward was ill. He is often described as having a weak constitution, but there is little evidence to support this claim. Reports from his early years suggest normal childhood illnesses, and he was dangerously ill from quartan fever, a form of malaria, at the age of four, but he had no known ongoing health problems. He might reasonably have been expected to have a good lifespan, but in the sixteenth century life could be cut short at any time, even for the most privileged. He was well educated, took a keen interest in religious matters and had been gradually introduced by Northumberland to the concerns of government. At the end of 1552, aged fifteen, Edward attended and fully enjoyed the antics of the Lord of Misrule, the juggling, mock jousts and plays of the Christmas and New Year festivities at Greenwich.

Edward's illness in early February 1553 was described at the time as a chill or feverish cold, but it gave rise to concerns. Not only was Mary's visit to him delayed, but a play that he had requested to be performed was also postponed. Doubts were raised as to whether he would be able to attend the opening of parliament on 1 March, and he was only able to do so because the ceremony was moved to Whitehall Palace. There then followed an improvement. At the end of March he attended the dissolution ceremony and on 11 April he was well enough to travel along the Thames to Greenwich.[10] However, by early May his condition had deteriorated. He was never to recover. The accounts of his illness come mainly from the reports sent to Emperor Charles V by the Imperial ambassador, Jean Scheyfve. His information came from a medical student whose father was a minor official in the king's household. There were always accusations of poisoning when members of a royal family were very ill or died. In this case it was rumoured that Northumberland was behind it, but this can be discounted.

Diagnosed at the time as tuberculosis, it has more recently been suggested that Edward was suffering from a suppurating pulmonary infection,[11] which damaged the lungs, causing abscesses from which oozed pus. He developed a constant cough which produced a foul-smelling, greenish-yellow and black sputum. He had a fever and his body wasted away. General septicaemia set in and the toxins attacked other organs, such as the kidneys. He had difficulty speaking and breathing, his skin changed colour and there was swelling of his feet, lower legs and hands. By this stage, without modern antibiotics, the illness was fatal. Although there were some optimistic reports of improvements in his condition, by the end of May it was clear that Edward had weeks not months to live.

At some point in April 1553, probably after his arrival in Greenwich, Edward gave some thought to the succession in the event of his death, although this was not yet expected. In any case it would be some time before he married and then there was no guarantee of the immediate arrival of a child. He wrote his 'devise for the succession', a document that eventually had a number of alterations, additions and crossings out, indicating Edward's thought processes. It was to be of great importance in the events that immediately followed his death. The document makes clear some of the key ideas in Edward's thinking. He does not include either of his half-sisters, Mary or Elizabeth, in the line of succession. As they had both been pronounced illegitimate in the Second Succession Act, and this had never been repealed, he regarded their claims to the throne by inheritance as invalid, despite his father restoring them to the succession in the Third

Succession Act. Also, the elder of the two, Mary, had resisted all efforts to turn her away from the Catholic Church and if she became queen the religious reforms of both Henry and Edward would be abandoned. Denying Mary the crown on the grounds of illegitimacy was a way of avoiding this, but it meant that Elizabeth's claim would have to be denied as well.

Edward's 'devise' followed his father's ideas in two fundamental ways. Firstly, a female monarch should be avoided if at all possible. Secondly, that the Scottish line descended from Henry's elder sister, Margaret, who had married James IV of Scotland in 1503, should be excluded in favour of descendants of Henry's younger sister, Mary, who had married Charles Brandon, Duke of Suffolk, in 1515. Edward realised that as things stood, if he were to die then his sister Mary would succeed him. This initial 'devise' was the means by which he intended to prevent a Catholic and a woman from taking the throne.

The first part of the initial draft of the document read as follows.

> 'My Devise for the Succession.
> For lack of issue of my body: to the Lady Francis's heirs male; for lack of such issue, to the Lady Jane's heirs male; to the Lady Katherine's heirs male; to the Lady Mary's heirs male; to the heirs male of the daughters which she [Frances] shall have hereafter; then to the Lady Margaret [Clifford]'s heirs male; for lack of such issue, to the heirs male of the Lady Jane's daughters and so forth till you come to the Lady Margaret's daughters heirs male.
>
> If, after my death, the male heir had reached the age of 18 then he was to have the whole rule and governance.'

In other words, Edward's plan was for the crown to go to a son born to Frances, Duchess of Suffolk, or failing any such son, the sons of Frances's daughters in order of seniority – Lady Jane Grey, Lady Katherine Grey and Lady Mary Grey – and if they had no sons, to the sons of Lady Margaret Clifford (Frances' niece, Lady Jane Grey's cousin) and failing that the grandsons of these ladies. Other clauses outlined what should happen if there was no male heir at the time of his death, an elaborate scheme stating who should be regent until an heir was born and reached the age of eighteen.[12] As a plan to settle the succession if he were to die in the near future it was hopelessly inadequate. The youngest child of Lady Frances Grey, the Duchess of Suffolk, had been born in 1545, eight years previously, and so Frances was unlikely to conceive again. Of her children, Lady Jane

Grey was the eldest at barely fifteen years old, followed by Katherine aged twelve, and Mary aged seven. If Edward were to die soon, there would be no male heir and the succession could turn into a race between the sisters to give birth to the first son! For any straightforward succession from Edward to an adult male heir the king would have to live at least another eighteen years and if there was a young heir there was bound to be conflict about the regency.

There is little doubt that this 'devise' was Edward's own work. As his ill-health continued he was keen that his plan for the succession be given the force of law and be accepted by his Privy Council and leading officials. The important questions, to which we do not have definite answers, are: when did he show it to Northumberland and the Privy Council, and who was responsible for the various alterations that were made? Would Edward have discussed such matters unless he thought that he might die soon? If not, then the answer would most likely be in late May or early June. By then the king's life was in real danger and Northumberland was faced with a dilemma. Would he follow the king's clear intentions and make the original 'devise' workable and risk putting himself and his family in serious jeopardy if the plan went wrong, or would he simply pay lip service to the plan until the king died and then facilitate Mary's accession? Northumberland's whole career had been based on his wish to demonstrate unquestioning loyalty to the sovereign, perhaps the result of his not coming from the old aristocracy, and therefore the former choice was most likely.

By far the most significant change made to Edward's 'devise' was the addition of just two words after the name Lady Jane. The words 'and her' were added, so that it now read: 'Lady Jane and her heirs male'. This acknowledged that Lady Jane was the immediate heir, to be followed by any male children that she might have. This, of course, went against Edward's wish not to have a woman on the throne, but it did cut through all the uncertainties about which of Lady Frances's daughters would produce the first son and, most importantly for Edward, meant that a Protestant and not a Catholic would be on the throne. It does seem suspicious that Lady Jane Grey was married to Northumberland's only remaining unmarried son, Guildford Dudley, in late May 1553, just as it came to be recognised that Edward's illness was probably terminal. The change in the 'devise' to make Jane the heir was almost certainly made after this marriage. Northumberland was obviously aware of the personal benefits of the plan for him and his family, but also of the dangers involved. It is impossible to say at this distance of time whether he was simply assisting the king to achieve his wishes or using the situation to his own advantage; quite possibly both. Nevertheless, even if the changes were Northumberland's, then Edward certainly endorsed them, as he had the marriage of Lady Jane to Guildford Dudley.[13]

On 12 June the law officers were summoned by Edward and instructed to turn the amended 'devise' into a legal document. When they pointed out that they were being asked to break the law and, in their view, commit treason by ignoring the Third Succession Act which placed Mary and then Elizabeth in line before the Greys, Northumberland stormed in and berated them. Only after they had been ordered to appear before the king again on 15 June, and asked why they had not carried out his orders, was the document produced. Members of the Privy Council, the secretaries of state and the law officers were required to sign it, in effect promising to implement Edward's wishes after his death. Some needed to be persuaded, either with grants of land or promises of future rewards. Archbishop Cranmer, who had clashed with Northumberland over the independence of the Church, only agreed when he was reassured by lawyers that it was legal. Another document was produced to be signed by the king, and then by leading nobles, churchmen, courtiers, officials and other notables to endorse his wishes. Yet nobody told the new heir to the throne, Lady Jane Grey.

Born in 1537, Jane had spent her early years at Bradgate House in Leicestershire. Early in 1547 she was sent to the household of Henry Grey's friend Thomas Seymour, brother of the Lord Protector, the Duke of Somerset. Such moves were not unusual; children were often placed in the households of their social equals or superiors – a kind of sixteenth-century finishing school. Seymour saw that Jane was a valuable asset and had persuaded her parents that as the king's uncle he would have sufficient influence to bring about Jane's marriage to the new king. Seymour was ambitious and jealous of his brother's position, not satisfied with a seat on the Privy Council and being made Lord Admiral. He soon caused a scandal by marrying the dowager queen, Katherine Parr. This was a benefit for Jane and for eighteen months, until her death in childbirth, Katherine was to be an important figure in Jane's life. Also in the household for a time was Princess Elizabeth, with whom Seymour shamelessly flirted. She later summed him up as a 'man of much wit and very little judgement'. After Katherine's death, Jane returned briefly to Bradgate, but Seymour, not wishing to lose a valuable asset, persuaded her parents to send her back. However, Seymour's political intrigues resulted in his arrest two months later and he was executed in March 1549. As a close ally, Henry Grey had to work hard to distance himself from Seymour. He was interrogated on five occasions and eventually offered Jane as a bride for Lord Protector Somerset's son, Lord Edward.

Jane is usually described as being short of stature, thin though prettily shaped, attractive and gracious. More significantly, all accounts regard her as an exceptional student. Her father was in many respects a weak man, easily led, a gambler, who failed to impress in any official appointment. However, he was well read, keen for his daughters to be educated and a strong advocate for the Protestant faith. He financially supported like-minded scholars in England and Europe, and employed several chaplains of note, including Thomas Harding (the Regius Professor of Hebrew at Oxford), James Haddon (a founding fellow of Trinity College, Cambridge) and John Aylmer, later Bishop of London under Queen Elizabeth, who was Jane's tutor.[14] By the age of fourteen Jane spoke or read French, Italian, Latin and Greek, and had started to learn Hebrew. She too was fully committed to the reformed religion and was prepared to challenge anyone who followed the old beliefs and traditions. She flourished while with Katherine Parr and Thomas Seymour but, although still encouraged in her studies, found the regime at her parents' home rather more restrictive.

In *The Scholemaster*, published in 1570, Roger Ascham describes a visit that he made to his friend John Aylmer at Bradgate in 1550. Jane had probably already met Ascham when he was tutor to Princess Elizabeth. While at Bradgate he came across Jane reading Plato in Greek while the rest of the household was out hunting. He reported her as saying that hunting was but 'a shadow to the pleasure that I find in Plato. Alas, good folk, they never felt what true pleasure meant'.[15] When he asked how she came to this realisation, she compared the gentle approach to learning taken by her tutor, Aylmer, to the constant demand of her parents that she did everything perfectly, according to accepted etiquette.

In April 1553 Jane was informed of her impending marriage to Guildford Dudley. Despite Northumberland's efforts, he had been turned down as a husband for Margaret Clifford, Jane's cousin, the previous year. Although she must have been aware that her marriage was likely in the near future, some reports suggest that she strongly objected to the plan, and claimed that she was already betrothed to Somerset's son Thomas, Earl of Hertford. Many biographers accept that she was forced to accept the union 'by the urgency of her mother and the violence of her father'.[16] It all happened quickly. In splendid celebrations that lasted from 21 to 25 May they were married in a triple ceremony at Northumberland's main London residence, Durham Place. Along with Jane, her sister Katherine married Henry Herbert, son of the Earl of Pembroke, and Katherine Dudley (Northumberland's daughter) married Henry Hastings, son of the Earl of Huntingdon. King Edward had given his blessing and sent magnificent clothes and expensive jewellery as gifts. Were these marriages part of the routine aristocratic alliances common at the time, or part of a plot to promote Guildford Dudley to the throne? Jane and Guildford's marriage was not consummated immediately. Guildford, along with others, suffered from food poisoning and Jane returned to her parents' mansion in Chelsea. However, at the insistence of their parents, she did go to Durham House for a few days in late June, where she slept with Guildford. The marriage was now binding.

Jane was unwell and back in Chelsea when on 9 July Mary Sidney, Northumberland's eldest daughter and wife of Henry Sidney, who was King Edward's companion in his final days, arrived and told her that she had to accompany her to Syon House, one of the Dudley family's residences, 'to receive that which had been ordered by the king'. There they were joined by Northumberland and the earls of Northampton, Arundel, Huntingdon and Pembroke. In Jane's account of this meeting, written in a letter to Queen Mary in August, she says that she was at first puzzled as to why some of the earls knelt before her, until Northumberland, realising that she was confused, called in his wife and Jane's mother and announced that Edward had died three days earlier and had named Jane as his successor.[17] All then knelt to Jane saying that they were bound by oaths to Edward to uphold his intentions.

Jane is said to have burst into tears[18] and questioned her right to the throne, only to be persuaded by her father and husband (who had both just arrived) as well as her mother that it was her religious duty to obey both Edward's wishes and theirs. She eventually gave way and prayed that if the crown was rightfully hers then God would 'grant me such grace and spirit that I might govern it to his glory and service and to the advantage of this realm.' The next day she was proclaimed queen in London and a procession of barges took her and her family to the Tower, though there was little display of public enthusiasm for the new queen. She remained there for the rest of her life, first as queen, then as prisoner. Later that day, in a discussion about her coronation, it was mentioned that another crown would need to be made for her husband. It became clear to Jane that Guildford knew all about Edward's will and had not told her. At this she announced that she was willing to make him a duke but not king. Guildford was furious, as was his mother, and he petulantly announced his intention to leave the Tower, saying that he would not sleep with Jane until she exerted her authority as queen and ordered him to stay.

CHAPTER 3

THE RIGHTFUL QUEEN RESTORED

Mary had been kept informed of her brother's deteriorating health, first by Northumberland and later by her own informants, while at Newhall in Essex and then at Hunsdon, in Hertfordshire, both a day's ride from London. On 7 July, the day after Edward's death and before it had been announced, Northumberland's younger son, Robert Dudley, was sent with about 300 mounted guards to escort her to London.[1] On his arrival at Hunsdon, Robert discovered that Mary had already left. Her actions strongly suggest that she had prior knowledge both of Edward's imminent death and of his will that would exclude her from the succession. Too many people knew of Edward's 'devise' for it to remain a secret, especially as some of them were not happy with it. So, probably on 4 July, Mary rode north to Sawston, near Cambridge, where she rested for a few hours, and then moved on to her house at Kenninghall, Norfolk, where supporters awaited her. She might have been intending to flee to the Continent, where she would have requested support from Emperor Charles V. Had she succeeded she would have become a constant thorn in the side of the new regime, although such a flight could well have been seen as an abdication of her claim to the throne.[2] When they heard of the failure to secure her the Privy Council ordered six ships to the east coast to prevent her escape. However, with her many estates in East Anglia, Mary realised that she could rely on considerable backing. From Kenninghall she issued a letter to the Council claiming the throne and demanding allegiance, and messages were sent throughout the country to rally support. She did not make the Catholic religion her rallying cry and drew support from many who believed her to be the rightful queen regardless of their religion, as well as those who had grievances against Northumberland and the existing government. She then moved on to Framlingham Castle in Suffolk, a much stronger base for military action.

If there had been a well-planned plot to deny Mary the throne then the obvious move would have been for Northumberland to seize Mary earlier. This, however, was fraught with difficulty. If Mary was taken too soon, before Edward's death, then it could well provoke strong opposition.

Much better that the country was faced with a *fait accompli*. However, it was impossible to know exactly when the king would die, and in any case Mary was clearly being kept well informed of the situation. While the French were keen to prevent her from becoming queen, Emperor Charles V was very much in favour of her accession, as a Catholic, his cousin and someone who looked to him for advice. However, most observers, including the imperial ambassador, believed that Mary had little chance with the whole Tudor state ranged against her and the Privy Council in control of London. For much of her life she had given in when faced with a major decision, but this was the biggest one of all and she showed her mettle. Northumberland, known as an effective man of action, faltered at this crucial stage, possibly under-estimating Mary, perhaps doubtful as to the legality of his actions. It has also been suggested that he had been worn down by the heavy responsibilities of office – he had frequently absented himself from court because of illness – and wished for nothing more than a peaceful retirement. If Northumberland was the ruthless conspirator of the 'black legend' or had expected serious resistance from Mary, then he would have prepared more thoroughly. He had neither summoned existing troops to London nor made financial plans to pay for the rapid recruitment of new troops.

With Mary quickly gathering forces at Framlingham, the Privy Council in London realised that things were going to be more difficult than they had expected. Nevertheless, they were still slow to react. They issued a statement pointing out that if Mary became queen she would marry a foreign prince and England would be subject to foreign domination, but military action was now required. It was initially thought that Jane's father, the Duke of Suffolk, would lead a force into East Anglia, but both Jane and the duke opposed this. Northumberland was by far the most experienced commander available and he decided to take to the field. There was some difficulty raising enough soldiers, and so it was not until 14 July that he left the capital. He was obviously concerned as to whether he could really trust the Privy Council members to see the plan through when he left London. He urged his fellow councillors to remember their oaths to Edward and received the reply: 'My Lord, if you mistrust any of us in this matter your grace is far deceived; for which of us can wipe his hands clean thereof?' Many of them were soon to do so!

By the end of 15 July Northumberland had reached Cambridge, where he rested for a couple of days before marching on to Bury St Edmunds. By this time discouraging news was beginning to arrive. Northumberland had witnessed considerable hostility as he marched: he was the hated 'evil Duke' who had killed hundreds as he crushed Kett's Rebellion in 1549 and was blamed for the execution of the 'good Duke'. Mary's support had grown rapidly and her troops now outnumbered his estimated 3,000 men, and although Mary had no acknowledged commander, some experienced noblemen were joining her. The captains and crew of the ships sent to guard the coast had joined Mary, taking their artillery from the ships to bolster her army. With reinforcements arriving and effective leadership, Northumberland could still prevail, but it had to be very soon.

The news from London was now even worse for Northumberland. Signs of resistance to Jane's accession were growing in areas immediately west of the capital and as Mary's position grew stronger, support for Queen Jane and Northumberland drained quickly away. When the earls of Pembroke and Arundel were asked to raise and lead troops against opposition in the Thames valley they would not do so. Fear of retribution took hold of the Privy Council. It became a case of every man for himself in their efforts to distance themselves from Northumberland. On 18 July Arundel and Pembroke led the Privy Council in their decision to support Mary's claim. The following day Suffolk informed his daughter that she was no longer queen, at which she expressed her relief. Suffolk and his wife left the Tower, the duchess intent on begging for mercy from the new queen, with whom she had long had a good relationship. Meanwhile Northumberland returned to Cambridge, where on the afternoon of 20 July he received the Privy Council's proclamation. He summoned his men, pointed out that everything that he had done had been on the orders of the Privy Council, and declared Mary the rightful queen. He was arrested along with his closest associates, escorted to London by Arundel, and lodged in the Tower.

For a queen who has been widely referred to as 'Bloody Mary', Mary was surprisingly lenient during her first months as monarch. For those implicated in the attempt to deny her the crown – most of the administration – much depended on good contacts and luck. It suited her to graciously listen to their hurriedly prepared excuses and pleas for mercy, before allowing them to buy pardons and then restore them to positions of influence alongside her long-time, usually Catholic, supporters. These were men who had survived Henry VIII's shifting policies and were adept at adjusting their loyalties to the changing circumstances. Indeed many of them soon discovered that they had been Catholics all along. If Mary had sought to punish all who had been involved in the recent events few among the nobility of England would remain. Of those put on trial in the immediate aftermath, only Northumberland, Sir John Gates[3] and Sir Thomas Palmer[4] were executed. Jane herself remained in the Tower, but her father was released. Others, such as Northumberland's eldest son, were sentenced to death but were reprieved.

On 18 August Northumberland stood trial in Westminster Hall charged with treason. He pleaded not guilty. Many of those who sat in judgement had weeks before been members of the Privy Council. They were not there to decide upon his guilt or otherwise, but to ensure that he was convicted and executed for actions in which they themselves had participated. He was the scapegoat. His defence was that as he had only acted on the authority of the monarch [meaning Edward] and the Council he could not be guilty of treason. He followed this up by questioning whether those who were equally responsible for his actions had the right to pass judgement on him. The court deliberately misunderstood the first point by replying that Jane Grey was a usurper and stated that as long as his judges had not been charged with any offence they could not be challenged. Found guilty, he requested that he die as a nobleman, be beheaded not hung, drawn and quartered, and that mercy be shown to his family. His death was set for the morning of 21 August and thousands had gathered on Tower Hill before it was announced that it was to be postponed. Northumberland had agreed to hear mass in the chapel of the Tower. On the scaffold the next day he told the crowd that he believed in the Catholic Church and that the country had erred for the last sixteen years. This, unlike the show trial, was the propaganda coup that Mary had hoped for. Was this a genuine change of heart or a wish to make peace with the new queen in order go to his death with a clear conscience and perhaps help his family? Northumberland cannot have hoped for his own life to be spared.

Jane remained a prisoner, but by the end of the year she had been given the freedom to walk in the grounds of the Tower. Her father had been pardoned and her family were free. Mary did not believe that Jane bore any responsibility for the events of June/July 1553. However, Jane remained loyal to her faith, and was appalled when she was told that not only Northumberland, but also the former chaplain at Bradgate, Thomas Harding, and even her own father, though almost certainly with no sincerity, had converted to Catholicism. Although many of the queen's supporters, such as Stephen Gardiner, Bishop of Winchester, and the representative of Emperor Charles, Simon Renard, regularly advocated further executions, including Jane's, the queen resisted. What brought about Jane's death was the reaction to Mary's intention to marry Philip of Spain, the emperor's son and heir.

As the first queen regnant in English history,[5] Mary was expected to marry and produce an heir. At the age of thirty-seven there was considerable urgency. She showed no inclination to marry the only surviving English Catholic with royal heritage, Edward Courtenay, the 26-year-old son of the Marquess of Exeter (executed in 1541) who had spent the previous fifteen years in the Tower. She asked Emperor Charles for advice and he suggested his son, Prince Philip, whose first wife had died several years before. There was considerable opposition from her own inner circle, but Mary was determined that the marriage should take place. When Parliament requested that she marry within the realm she was furious. There had already been unrest about the repeal of Edward VI's religious laws and the reintroduction of the Mass. If Mary expected her subjects to rejoice with her, she was mistaken. Spanish representatives sent to finalise the arrangements had snowballs hurled at them in the streets. The marriage treaty was made public in January 1554, with the ceremony due to take place that summer.

By then a plot to prevent the marriage, involving Jane's father, was already in motion. While he would raise a force in the Midlands, Sir Peter Carew would do so in the southwest and Sir Thomas Wyatt, son of the diplomat, poet, and early admirer of Anne Boleyn, would do so in Kent. However, the conspirators' organisation and security was poor and their plans soon became known. Wyatt succeeded in leading 3,000 rebels towards London. Driving back a royal force at Rochester, they reached Southwark on 3 February, but were prevented from taking London Bridge. They crossed the river further west, at Kingston, and headed for London. By 7 February they had advanced along Whitehall and the Strand but were held at the heavily defended Ludgate. They had expected widespread support but few Londoners joined them: although they did not like the marriage, they were still mainly loyal to Queen Mary. Faced by superior forces the rebels rapidly dispersed and Wyatt was taken prisoner. The other conspirators, including Jane's father, were rounded up and taken to the Tower.

Mary was not going to be so merciful this time. She considered that her initial clemency had been abused. Gallows were erected at every London gate, as well as several in Southwark, on London Bridge, Cheapside, Fleet Street and Charing Cross. They were well used; those who had marched against the queen were to die and as many as 200 were hanged. Of the leaders, Carew managed to escape abroad and, although arrested in Flanders two years later, escaped with his life. The Duke of Suffolk's foolhardy involvement had not only signed his own death warrant but Jane's as well. She had nothing do to with the plot. Indeed, had the rebels succeeded in removing Mary, it was Elizabeth who would have been made queen. The princess was taken to the Tower and had to convince her interrogators that she had no part in the rising. Even though Jane was equally innocent, she always remained a possible focus for future rebellions. Within days she was dead: queen for just a few days, never anointed, never crowned, but still a threat. Of all the monarchs killed during the age of the Tudors and Stuarts she had done least to deserve her fate.

MARY STUART,
QUEEN OF SCOTS
The Unwanted Monarch

*'I will be plain with you, the religion which I profess I take
to be the most acceptable to God: and, indeed, neither do
I know, nor desire to know, any other.'*

Mary, Queen of Scots to Nicholas Throckmorton, English
ambassador to France, before her departure
for Scotland in 1561

———◆———

'In My End is My Beginning.'

The motto embroidered by Mary, Queen of Scots, in
her cloth of state while in England

———◆———

*'As a queen and sovereign, I am aware of no fault or offence
for which I have to render account to anyone here below.'*

Mary at her trial in England in October 1586

CHAPTER 4

A QUEEN WITHOUT POWER

Mary Stuart's birth, on 8 December 1542 at Linlithgow Palace, came as a disappointment to her father, King James V of Scotland. His French wife, Mary of Guise, had given birth to boys in 1540 and 1541, but both had died in April 1541. Although he had several children by various mistresses, he was desperate for another legitimate son. Two weeks earlier James had suffered a major setback when an ill-prepared Scottish army was crushed by a much smaller English force at Solway Moss. Not consoled by the birth of his daughter, he now feared not just the loss of his throne, but also the end of the Stuart dynasty, even of an independent Scotland. Henry VIII was in a position to invade his country, and even if his daughter were ever to become queen she would be married to a foreign prince and Scotland would become part of that prince's lands. A despondent James, although only thirty years old, died just six days after the birth, leaving Mary as the infant queen and James Hamilton, Earl of Arran, the heir presumptive, as regent. Her father's fears were never realised, but Mary's life, and death, played a significant role in the history of Scotland, England and France in the second half of the sixteenth century.

Arran initially favoured a pro-English policy and signed the Treaty of Greenwich with Henry VIII. This established peace between England and Scotland and began arrangements for the future marriage of Mary to Henry's son Prince Edward. However, hostility to England resulted in the Scottish parliament eventually rejecting the treaty six months later. Arran switched his support to the traditional 'auld alliance' with France, coming to terms with Mary of Guise. Arran led Scottish resistance to England's efforts to bring about Mary's marriage to Prince Edward in the 'War of Rough Wooing'. A French marriage planned for Mary by her mother was then agreed. Fearing for Mary's safety after defeat by English forces at the Battle of Pinkie in September 1547, Arran supported the decision of the Scottish Parliament that the now five-year-old Mary should be sent to France. He was rewarded by being created Duke of Châtellerault and French assistance was given to Scotland against the English.

Scotland had plenty of recent experience of child monarchs. Just one of the previous four kings, James IV, had acceded to the throne when more than ten years old and managed to reach the age of forty. James V himself had become king at seventeen months. These young kings had all been brought up in Scotland and came to know their country well. When married to foreign princesses their spouses came to live there. Mary, though, was to be brought up with her husband-to-be, Francis, the eldest son and heir of King Henry II, at the French court, where she arrived in August 1548. There she received the education of a French princess, being taught languages, learning to play musical instruments, and developing skills in embroidery, dancing and riding. She was generally popular, becoming friends with Elizabeth of Valois, Francis's younger sister and the future wife of Philip II of Spain. Mary developed into a tall, vivacious, attractive young woman. As a Catholic and strongly influenced by French culture, she was not so different from her father and grandfather. However, unlike them, Mary learnt little about Scotland and, it has been argued, had little real interest in it, eventually to become its 'reluctant ruler'.[1]

Mary's mother, Mary of Guise, remained in Scotland to look after the interests of both her daughter and France. After the treaty of Boulogne in March 1550, which brought peace between England and Scotland and removed all English troops from Scotland, Mary of Guise travelled to France. She visited her daughter for what would be the last time, her brother, the influential Francis, Duke of Guise, and the French court. On her return journey she travelled through England and in October 1551 she was given a grand reception at Whitehall Palace, where King Edward VI presented her with a diamond ring. Princess Mary did not attend, but Lady Jane Grey and her mother played a prominent role. In 1554 she was appointed as the regent in Scotland. She faced numerous problems over the next few years with the rise of Protestantism and growing conflict with the 'Lords of the Congregation', a group of Protestant noblemen who wished to push through the reform of the Church in Scotland and end the French Catholic influence in the country.

Events moved quickly in the late 1550s. In a magnificent ceremony Mary Stuart married the Dauphin, Francis, at Notre-Dame de Paris on 24 April 1558. Prior to the service Mary had signed documents agreeing that Francis would become king of Scotland, and that if they were childless on her death the crown of Scotland would revert to France. There then followed four deaths, all of which were to have significance for Mary. In November 1558 Queen Mary of England died and was succeeded by her sister Elizabeth, whose parliament soon passed legislation to establish a

Protestant Church in England. The French king provocatively declared Francis and Mary to be the rightful king and queen of England. He was asserting Mary's claim to the English throne as the senior, legitimate descendant of Henry VIII, whose eldest sister, Margaret, was the wife of James IV of Scotland, mother of James V and grandmother of Mary. This claim was based on the belief that Henry VIII was never properly married to Anne Boleyn and that Elizabeth was therefore illegitimate. Much to Elizabeth's anger this was reflected in the coat of arms adopted by Mary and Francis, which quartered their coats of arms with that of the royal arms of England. Although Henry II had no intention of invading England at this point, as his wars against Spain had emptied the coffers, the claim would always be useful in negotiations and could be pursued more vigorously in the future, especially if Elizabeth were to die childless.

Then, in July 1559, King Henry II died after a jousting accident and Mary's husband became King Francis II at the age of just fifteen. Mary's relations, the Guise family, in the form of her uncles, Francis, Duke of Guise, and Charles, Cardinal of Lorraine, dominated the young king's government. They wished to use Mary to extend their power to Scotland, where their sister, Mary of Guise, was under increasing pressure from the Lords of the Congregation who demanded the end of her regency. The Protestant theologian, John Knox, returned to Scotland in 1559, adding to her problems. He had worked in England during the reign of Edward VI but had left for Europe on the accession of the Catholic Queen Mary. After a brief visit to Scotland in 1556, when he offended Mary of Guise by encouraging her to support the Reformation, he was based in Geneva. There he had anonymously (although it became widely known that he was the author) published *The First Blast of the Trumpet against the Monstrous Regiment of Women*, attacking the rule of women as being unnatural and against the will of God. Aimed particularly against Queen Mary in England and Mary of Guise in Scotland, it naturally angered the new English queen Elizabeth and Mary, Queen of Scots.

The struggle between the pro-English and pro-French parties in Scotland intensified. French troops were sent to support Mary of Guise, based in Edinburgh Castle. By now most Scots regarded her and the French troops as foreign oppressors, just as they had regarded the English occupiers ten years earlier. In October 1559 the Protestant Lords deposed Mary of Guise and set up a council of twenty-four nobles in her place.[2] The regent withdrew to the heavily fortified port of Leith and requested more French reinforcements. The Protestant Lords signed the Treaty of Berwick with Elizabeth in February 1560. An English fleet was sent to blockade Leith and, if they were needed, troops were promised to help remove the French. Mary of Guise, already ill, died in June 1560. Her daughter Mary, having last seen her nine years earlier, was distraught when told the news. However, her death opened the way for the Treaty of Edinburgh the following month between the Scottish Lords, the representatives of Elizabeth I, and those of the French king, Francis II. It was agreed that both English and French soldiers and naval forces would be removed from Scotland. This effectively ended the 'auld alliance', established a new Anglo-Scottish understanding, and empowered the Scottish Lords to push the establishment of the Protestant church in Scotland though parliament. They ended papal powers and banned the use of the Mass. Mary's opinion had not been asked by either the Scottish or the French leaders, but neither had she taken the initiative. She had not returned to Scotland to impose her authority, or insisted on her right as queen to be involved in deciding who ran the country in her absence and the terms of any treaty signed in her name.

The fourth significant death within thirteen months was that of the young French king Francis, Mary's husband. After only seventeen months on the throne, the sickly boy succumbed to an ongoing infection of the middle ear which resulted in an abscess in the brain. He died on 5 December 1560 and Mary became the dowager queen of France shortly before her eighteenth birthday. Francis's 10-year-old brother became the new king, Charles IX, with his mother, Catherine de'Medici, as regent. After a period of official mourning, Mary spent time with her Guise relations, aware that she was faced with two major decisions: whether to remarry, and if so, to whom, and whether she should return to Scotland, a country which she had left twelve years previously and knew little about.

Mary seemed keen to remarry. This gave the unfortunate impression that she would prefer to be queen consort in France or Spain rather than queen regnant in Scotland. There were many prospective marriage candidates, including Don Carlos, the 15-year-old son of Philip II of Spain, Archduke Charles of Austria, the son of the Holy Roman Emperor, and the young Earl of Arran, son of the sometime regent of Scotland, descended from James II of Scotland. The possible benefits of any of these matches were outweighed by the concerns of rival countries, who recognised the threat that any such marriage could pose to them. Mary was certainly not a free agent in these marriage plans. Catherine de'Medici was hostile to the idea of her marrying Don Carlos as the match would strengthen Spain's international position. It was clear that her mother-in-law, now regent in France for the young Charles IX, had no place for Mary in her plans as she rapidly removed the Guise family from power. Consequently, even as talks were taking place,

Mary used contacts in Scotland to ease the path for her return to the country of her birth, perhaps believing that she would have more independence of action there.

As far as relations with her cousin Queen Elizabeth were concerned, Mary regularly claimed that she wished for harmony and 'sisterly love', as did Elizabeth. However, there were significant obstacles. The Treaty of Edinburgh had required Francis and Mary to stop using the symbols of the English monarch in their coat of arms. Both before and after Francis's death Elizabeth's representatives were sent to France to persuade Mary to ratify the treaty. Mary was not willing to agree to the removal of these symbols, as it would be seen to signal the end of her claim to be heir presumptive to the English throne (if not the rightful queen, as some, and occasionally she, would have it). She played for time, at first stating that she would be guided by her husband and then, after Francis's death, by saying that she could not ratify the treaty without first consulting her council in Scotland.

During 1561 Mary met two Scottish delegations. The first, led by John Leslie, Bishop of Ross, who was later to become Mary's envoy and staunch defender, represented Catholic, pro-French opinion. He advocated her return to the north of Scotland where Catholic earls held sway, promising that an army of 20,000 could be raised to defeat the Lords of the Congregation and re-establish Catholicism. The second was led by her half-brother, Lord James Stewart (Stuart), the illegitimate son of James V, born in 1531. He had become a leader of the Protestant Lords of the Congregation and had good relations with Elizabeth's chief adviser, William Cecil, whom he visited on his way to France. He asked Mary whether she would adopt the Scottish Protestant faith. She refused, but agreed to return to Scotland without any demands other than that she would be allowed to follow her own faith in private. An understanding was reached, and Mary decided to return to Scotland on those terms, somewhat to the surprise of James Stewart and his supporters.

CHAPTER 5

RETURN TO SCOTLAND –
MARRIAGES AND MURDERS

As she left Calais in August 1561, having lived in France for thirteen years, Mary's last tearful words were 'Adieu France. It's all over now. I think I'll never see your shores again.' She was right, but although she did not know it she was leaving a country that was soon to slide into the chaos of the Wars of Religion that were to last the rest of her life. The two ships taking Mary, her companions and staff to Scotland took only five days to reach the port of Leith, landing in thick fog. They were followed more slowly by ten other vessels carrying the possessions of the queen and her household: tapestries, furniture, clothes, paintings, gold plate, bed linen, horses and mules.[1] Elizabeth had initially refused to give a promise of safe conduct, which Mary had requested in case storms in the North Sea might necessitate taking refuge on the English coast, on the grounds of the non-ratification of the Treaty of Edinburgh. Mary wrote to Nicholas Throckmorton, Elizabeth's ambassador to France, about Elizabeth's 'unkindness' and informed him that 'I am determined to adventure the matter, whatsoever come of it'. She continued that if she did have to land in England 'the Queen, your Mistress, shall have me in her hands to do her will of me; and if she be so hard-hearted as to desire my end, she may then do her pleasure, and make sacrifice of me... In this matter God's will be fulfilled'.

Elizabeth's belated change of mind came after Mary had set sail. The English queen's indecision on this matter was perhaps an early example of the difficulties that she generally experienced when dealing with the Scottish queen. The over-riding issue was Mary's claim to be heir presumptive. If the as yet unmarried and childless Elizabeth acknowledged Mary as such, this might encourage plots to remove Elizabeth. If she dismissed Mary's claim, who else would be the heir? Elizabeth did not like any of the alternatives. Elizabeth also recognised that Mary was an anointed and crowned monarch and did not wish to do anything that would be seen to undermine the rights of such a monarch; any precedent set might be turned against her.

Mary's arrival in Scotland was met with mixed reactions. The majority of the population was pleased to have their queen return, and her understanding with her half-brother, James Stewart, generally held. John Knox, as might be predicted, was condemning. He remarked that 'All men lamented that the realm was left without a male to succeed', and wrote, with reference to the fog on her arrival, that: 'The sun was not seen to shine for two days before, nor two days after. That fore-warning gave God unto us; but alas, the most part were blind'. There were noisy demonstrations outside Holyrood Palace on the first Sunday when Mary attended Mass. Mary needed to issue a declaration that she had no intention of changing the religious settlement to reassure the Protestants. She announced that she would make no attempt to impose Catholicism on Scotland. The members of the Privy Council that she appointed were essentially those lords who had been running the country before her arrival. James Stewart became her chief adviser, being created Earl of Moray in September 1561. There was continuing opposition to her holding Catholic services, especially from Knox, whom she summoned on a number of occasions to answer for his regular criticisms, especially when Catholic services were held outside the royal palace. He was typically forthright in his views. He informed Mary that if monarchs exceeded their lawful powers then it was the duty of their subjects, however humble, to resist, even by force. When he spoke out against her possible marriage to Don Carlos of Spain and Mary asked what her marriage had to do with him, he responded that every subject had the right to warn of dangers to his country.

Mary was still only eighteen years old and though tall, attractive, vivacious, intelligent and regal in bearing, she was inexperienced in government. She encouraged a revival of Scottish court life, often so vibrant under her predecessors, with music, dancing, masques, playing cards, riding and hunting, much to the horror of men like Knox and his supporters. She dressed fashionably and expensively, her rooms were made comfortable with wall hangings and cushions made of gold and silver cloth, and her furniture displayed fine plate and glassware.[2] Most of her time was spent in the company of members of her household, many of whom were French or had been with her for years in France. Despite this Mary often felt lonely, without many close friends to whom she could confide her innermost feelings, and she was prone to illness and depression.

What she found most difficult was the continual infighting of the Scottish lords and the frequent criticisms of her lifestyle. In her experience the French nobility might well have been seeking to gain favour and position in competition with others, but they rarely displayed the open hostility to each other, and even the monarch, that the Scots did. However, the issues that she was expected to deal with were no worse than those of other rulers. As Nicholas Throckmorton, the English diplomat, told her: 'Madam, your realm is in no other case at this day, than all the other realms of Christendom are; the proof whereof you see verified in this realm (France).'[3] The problem was that Mary showed little interest in political matters unless it concerned her relationship with Elizabeth and her right to the succession in England. She rarely took the lead. Mary's attendance at council meetings was irregular. Between August 1561 and December 1562, she attended seventeen out of fifty-five such meetings; in 1564 five out of fifty; and in 1566 twelve out of sixty-two.[4] When she did attend it was often when she wished to discuss matters of personal interest rather than issues of importance to the nation as a whole. A critical consideration of her performance as a monarch concluded that 'She had a very high sense of what was due to her as a queen. What was apparently lacking was the recognition that there was something fundamental due from her'.[5] She largely relied on others to rule the country. Until 1565 it was her step-brother, Moray. His advice, although in his own interests, aimed to maintain the status quo and peace with England. He kept Elizabeth's representatives regularly informed of events north of the border. Increasingly other noblemen resented his influence and sought to advance their own power at court or extend their landed interests.

What finally upset the delicate balance was Mary's marriage. Unlike her cousin Elizabeth, whose decision not to marry caused her advisers such consternation, Mary wished to take another husband. England was hostile to a match with a foreign prince, whether Spanish, French, or from the Holy Roman Empire. Such a power on its northern border would be seen as a serious threat. Mary understandably recognised the dangers of marrying a Scottish nobleman given their internal rivalries, and in any case she regarded this as beneath her. She still had hopes of marrying Don Carlos, the son of Philip II, until the Spanish king himself ended hope of such a match early in 1564, citing his son's mental instability. This was not a false excuse. Philip had serious concerns about his son and Carlos was to die in 1568, probably as a result of a hunger strike, six months after his arrest and imprisonment on the orders of his father.

Elizabeth wished Mary to marry a loyal Englishman to ensure that the pro-English policies of Moray would be continued. In 1564, when Mary asked directly who that might be, Cecil and Elizabeth informed her that they had in mind Lord Robert Dudley, soon to be created the Earl of Leicester. While not immediately rejecting the idea, Mary was less than impressed. Dudley had no royal links and as yet no noble title. Both his father, the Duke of Northumberland, and his grandfather had been executed for treason. He had been romantically linked with Elizabeth for years and the death and possible murder of his wife had been a scandal across Europe. But Mary wished to see if she could benefit, namely by gaining recognition of her right to succeed Elizabeth. When Elizabeth finally refused this demand early in 1565 and Dudley made clear that he had no wish to move to Scotland, Mary responded that she did not wish to marry Elizabeth's cast-off. The plan collapsed.

A new candidate, Henry Stewart, Lord Darnley, rapidly took Dudley's place. Three years younger than Mary, one of the few men taller than Mary herself, and regarded as handsome, he was the son of Matthew Stewart, Earl of Lennox, descended from King James II of Scotland and Margaret Douglas, the daughter of Margaret Tudor, Henry VIII's sister, by her second marriage. Such close royal ties had an obvious appeal to Mary and had the added benefit of strengthening her claim to the English throne. Certainly any child they had would have the strongest claim to the thrones of both England and Scotland. The fact that his mother was a Catholic made him an even more attractive match in Mary's eyes. His parents had married in 1544 after Lennox's exile from Scotland and lived in England where Darnley had been born. Lennox received permission to return to Scotland in 1564 and Darnley followed him in February 1565. He met Mary and by April a marriage looked likely. Elizabeth let Mary know her displeasure but was told that it was not her fault that the previous plans had failed and that as a queen she had every right to choose her own husband.

The marriage took place on 29 July even before the papal dispensation that had been requested, because Mary and Darnley were cousins, arrived. By then Mary's chief adviser, Moray, had left court to signal his strong disapproval, though to most people at the time it looked as though he objected to the loss of political power. He refused to return to court and was declared an outlaw. Mary skilfully built up a strong coalition of Protestant and Catholic noblemen and, faced by superior forces, Moray fled to England but received no military support from Elizabeth. By the end of the year Mary was pregnant, perhaps the only useful service that Darnley performed for her. With an heir on the way and her rival exiled she was seemingly at the height of her powers, no longer having the need to gain Elizabeth's favour. She appointed new members to the Privy Council, including more

Catholics and James Hepburn, the Earl of Bothwell, Lord High Admiral of Scotland.

However, Mary was soon to realise that she had made a massive misjudgement in her choice of husband. When she announced that Darnley would rule jointly with her, without consulting either parliament or the Lords, she lost the backing of many of the nobility who had previously supported her. Darnley, handsome and charming on the surface, showed his true nature: vain, arrogant, jealous, aggressive, over-ambitious and unreliable. He was soon demanding the crown matrimonial, which would give him the right to make decisions independently of the queen and to become king in his own right if Mary were to die. Her refusal to grant this added to the rows that they were having about personal matters, appointments and the royal prerogative. By early 1566 the marriage was already breaking down, despite Mary's pregnancy. She also further alienated many of her previous supporters. She was making increasing use of her household servants, particularly her private secretary, the Italian David Rizzio, who had considerable influence. Some believed, almost certainly incorrectly, that he had become her lover. Mary refused to pardon Moray, who many thought should be allowed to return to Scotland. She seemed to have plans to allow freedom of conscience in worship to Catholics throughout the country and was believed to be in contact with the papacy, France and Spain, raising a fear of foreign invasion to impose Catholicism. She put peace with Scotland's southern neighbour at risk by declaring that she was the rightful queen of England.[6]

A conspiracy developed, headed by Darnley, the earls of Morton (Mary's Chancellor) and Ruthven, and Moray, still exiled in England. Their plan was that Moray would be pardoned, and Darnley handed the crown matrimonial. They would then reassert the dominance of Protestantism and remove foreigners from Mary's household. As a first step Rizzio was to be murdered. Darnley insisted that this should be done in front of Mary. On the evening of 9 March 1566 Mary and close friends, including Rizzio and the Countess of Argyll, were having supper in a private room in Holyrood Palace adjacent to her bedroom. Having led Ruthven up the private staircase from his rooms on the floor below, Darnley joined them while Ruthven crossed Mary's bedroom and audience chamber to open the door to let in eighty armed men, including Morton. They then burst into the supper room, threatened Mary and dragged Rizzio away.[7] They had agreed that each one was to strike a blow, just as Julius Caesar's killers had done. They would all be responsible for the murder. Safety in numbers: could they all be accused of the crime? Rizzio was found later with at least fifty-three stab wounds and Darnley's dagger left in his body. Some of Mary's remaining supporters, whom the rebels would have liked to have captured, including the earls of Huntly and Bothwell, managed to escape. Mary herself was held captive.

The upheavals of the next eighteen months, involving more murder, intrigue, rebellion, and ever-changing allegiances, were as dramatic as any in British history. They show both the strengths and weaknesses of Mary's character and judgement. She first used her considerable charm and persuasive abilities on Darnley to get him to betray his erstwhile friends and engineer their escape together from Holyrood. She gathered supporters and returned to the capital, though this time to the stronghold of Edinburgh Castle. She then pardoned those lords not directly responsible for Rizzio's murder, including Moray, and restored them to her council. The actual murderers, including Morton, fled to England. Mary seemingly patched up her relationship with Darnley. On 19 June 1566 she gave birth to a son. However, after the confinement Mary and Darnley neither slept nor ate together. She was rightly distrustful of her husband, and he continued to attempt to undermine her authority, being resentful and jealous of her friendships, particularly with Bothwell. In early December Darnley failed to make an appearance at their son James's christening. The queen's closest advisers assured her that he could be dealt with, either by annulment, divorce or 'other means', though Mary made clear that they should do nothing that would damage her reputation or be prejudicial to her son. She probably believed that pressure would be brought to bear on her husband, even the possibility that he might suffer a beating given the frequent violence among the Scottish nobility, but did she anticipate or even have knowledge of what actually happened?

Queen Elizabeth had sent her congratulations on the birth and indicated that she would never do anything to undermine Mary's place in the succession, though she was clearly not going to recognise it publicly. Mary for her part was persuaded, against her better judgement, to pardon Morton and others who had fled to England and to permit their return. Morton wanted revenge for Darnley's betrayal. He plotted the king's murder, along with Bothwell, William Maitland, the queen's secretary, and many others. Darnley, having moved to his Lennox family stronghold in Glasgow for security after the pardons, was ill, probably with the symptoms of secondary syphilis.[8] At the beginning of February 1567, in order to keep watch on his activities, Mary cajoled him to move into a residence at Kirk o' Field in Edinburgh, supposedly by the promise of a reconciliation, which he understood to mean renewed sexual relations and the restoration of his political power. She spent much time with him that week, spending some nights in a separate bedroom.

On the evening of 9 February she visited him again, accompanied by a group of nobles, though they all left at about 11pm in order to attend a wedding masque at Holyrood. It was planned that Darnley would join Mary there the next day. At 2am there was a huge explosion and the house at Kirk o' Field was blown up. At dawn rescuers discovered the body of Darnley, along with that of his valet, in the garden. It was first thought that they had been killed in the explosion, blown out of the building by the force of the blast. However, it soon became apparent that their bodies had no marks consistent with either burning or a heavy fall. They had been strangled. There are still unanswered questions about how the murder was carried out. If they were murdered in the house and their bodies then moved to the garden, why was there the need for an explosion that failed to disguise the real cause of their deaths? An explosion could possibly be explained away as an accident; strangulation could not. The most likely scenario was that Darnley was intended to be killed in the explosion but heard suspicious movements in the house and while attempting to escape with his valet was caught and killed in the garden. At the same time the plotters who caused the explosion lit the fuse, not knowing that Darnley had fled. There may even have been two separate plots, though it would have been a major coincidence for them to be carried out on the same night. The exact details will never be known, but a king, even one not yet crowned, had been murdered and as the news spread much of Europe was horrified.

Mary at first believed that she had been the target of the explosion. This is not impossible, as she had originally been planning to stay overnight at Kirk o' Field. However, those later held responsible for the murder would have been aware that she had left for Holyrood. Even allowing for her apparent shock at the murder, Mary's actions over the following days and weeks again demonstrated poor judgement and later came to be used against her. If she had behaved in a more fitting manner, she could have continued to rule with the advantage that she would be free of the problems caused by her husband. However, although she decreed that there should be the traditional mourning period of forty days, she failed to observe it herself, attending a wedding feast just two days after the death. Soon after that she left court to go to a country retreat. She also failed to give Darnley the state funeral that was expected for a king. She did little to ensure that a proper investigation took place. Many of those involved had the power to hinder such work. Bothwell, for instance, was the Sheriff of Edinburgh. The failure to apprehend those responsible fell short of public expectations and resulted in scathing criticism not just from Darnley's father, Lennox, but more widely in Scotland and abroad.

Rumours soon focused on Bothwell as the main culprit and as Mary spent some time in his company only a couple of weeks after the murder, the possibility of her own involvement was raised. She might have found it difficult to believe that someone who had been so loyal to her would have been involved in Darnley's murder. In Edinburgh, however, posters suggesting as much, and worse, were displayed, perhaps as part of a propaganda campaign by Lennox. At first they consisted of Bothwell's likeness with the words 'Here is the murderer of the King'. Very soon they implicated Mary as well. In one, the initials MR and JH (James Hepburn, i.e. Bothwell) were accompanied by a sword and a mallet, while in the most provocative, a mermaid with the initials MR, holding a net and a large sea anemone, which represented the female genitalia, was portrayed about to catch a hare, prominent in Bothwell's heraldic arms, surrounded by seventeen swords, a direct reference to his love of duelling but which could also be seen as phallic symbols.[9]

The public mood turned against Mary. Elizabeth wrote expressing her horror at the murder and warning her 'you must preserve your reputation. I must and I will tell you that people for the most part are saying that you will look through your fingers at this deed rather than avenge it, and that you don't care to take action against those who have done you this pleasure', going on to exhort, counsel and beg 'that you will not fear to touch even him whom you have nearest to you if he was involved'.[10] In response to Lennox's accusations, a private trial of Bothwell was arranged by the Privy Council. Held on 12 April, it was a travesty of justice. Lennox set out for Edinburgh with 3,000 retainers only to be told that he could take just six into the city. As a result, he dared not enter to present his evidence. Bothwell, on the other hand, took with him several hundred musketeers to clear the streets and then surround the court to allow in only his supporters. He seemed unconcerned, as well he might, because Argyll and Huntly, two allies of his at the time, were in charge of proceedings. After sitting for eight hours, with most of the time spent debating a proposal made by Lennox's lawyers to postpone the trial so that he could participate, Bothwell was acquitted. Only four days later he performed a leading role in the opening of parliament and provided the armed guard for the queen. Bothwell, Morton, Huntly and Argyll all received confirmation of their titles and lands. Mary also finally agreed to ratify the Acts passed in 1560 by the Reformation Parliament. It looked as though she was paying off the plotters and seeking to placate public opinion.

With Bothwell's growing power and influence over Mary, he had come to believe that he could marry her and become the next king. By persuasion and bullying he gained the signatures of numerous lords on the 'Ainslie Tavern bond', which declared that for the good of the nation Mary should marry a native Scotsman, namely him. Bothwell then proposed to Mary, using the bond to demonstrate that this was the wish of her leading subjects. The queen, perhaps to his surprise, refused him, explaining that there was too much scandal around the death of her husband. Bothwell was not one to readily accept this decision, despite the fact that he was still married. In late April, having visited her son in Stirling, Mary was travelling back to Edinburgh with a small party of about thirty servants. Near Linlithgow she was intercepted by Bothwell and several hundred armed men. He informed her that it was too dangerous for her to go to the capital and insisted that she accompany him to his castle in Dunbar. She was in no position to resist and, declaring that she wanted no bloodshed, she agreed to go.

Twelve days later Mary arrived in Edinburgh with Bothwell and their forthcoming marriage was announced. It went ahead on 15 May. What happened at Dunbar Castle is subject to much speculation. Was this a plan in which Mary was a willing accomplice? It was pointed out that she put up no resistance when Bothwell intercepted her party. However, his men completely outnumbered hers. Was she then seduced by Bothwell and taken in by his claims of affection? She had experienced emotional turmoil for many months and was perhaps vulnerable to such declarations. Or did Bothwell force himself upon her with the result that she then felt obliged to marry him? It was not unknown for rape to be used in this way: the demonstration of power over a woman to force her obedience. Such an action would certainly fit with what is known about Bothwell's character and outlook. Mary's own explanation of the events, given later to the Bishop of Dunblane, does nothing to clarify the issue, perhaps deliberately. 'Bothwell awaited us by the way, accompanied with a great force, and led us with all diligence to Dunbar... Albeit we found his doings rude, yet were his words and answers gentle'. It is sometimes argued that she could have escaped from Dunbar, as Bothwell was certainly not there for the whole of the twelve days, because he appeared in Edinburgh to arrange his divorce from Lady Jean Gordon, whom he had married only fourteen months earlier. But if Mary had been abused it is possible that she was in such a disturbed state that she lacked the strength to act decisively. However, if force was involved in securing the marriage, Mary showed a surprising degree of loyalty to Bothwell over the next three months, though many at the time would have expected such loyalty once they were married.

We will never know exactly what happened at Dunbar, but the consequences of Mary's marriage to Bothwell proved disastrous for her. There was open rebellion by many of the leading lords, Morton to the fore, claiming that their aim was to rescue the queen from Bothwell's captivity. Mary had lost any control that she ever had of the situation. Previously loyal lords and the officers of state would not fight for her. Even Pope Pius V criticised her behaviour and wrote that he wished to have no further communication with her. On 15 June 1567 Mary and Bothwell's small army took up position on Carberry Hill, south of Musselburgh, and was confronted by the rebels. They called upon the queen to give up Bothwell but she refused, saying that many of the lords had agreed to the marriage by signing the Ainslie Tavern bond. Next it was proposed that Bothwell meet Morton, or a proxy, in single combat, but this was forbidden by Mary. She perhaps knew that she was in the early stages of pregnancy and did not wish to have another fatherless child. During these talks much of her army drifted away and she was left with no alternative but to negotiate: in effect, capitulate. She agreed to surrender with the understanding that she would be well treated and in return Bothwell was given safe conduct away from the site.

After being taken to Edinburgh, where she was jeered and insulted in the streets, the queen was imprisoned in the castle of Lochleven near Kinross. Her jailers were a cousin of Morton's and Lord Lindsay, who had been one of the murderers of Rizzio. She miscarried twins and, while still in a state of great distress, on 24 July was presented with a document of abdication. When she at first refused to sign it, Lindsey threatened violence, and even to cut her throat, thus forcing her to sign. Mary no longer ruled Scotland and the crown passed to her one-year-old son, James, who was crowned five days later, with Knox preaching the sermon at the ceremony. The deposition of an anointed monarch was a radical step, which would horrify Elizabeth in England and other European rulers. Moray, who had once again managed to be out of Scotland when the crucial action occurred, returned, visited Mary at Lochleven to lecture her about her failings, and became regent. Mary never accepted the legality of the abdication document.

Moray and his associates took the initiative by promising to find and punish those responsible for the king's murder. Since most of them had been either directly or indirectly involved themselves, they had every intention of pointing the finger at Bothwell and Mary. They wished to make her deposition appear to be not merely the seizure of power for political reasons, but also the inevitable consequence of the murder and moral outrages committed by Mary. They unleashed an extensive propaganda campaign against her, claiming that they had irrefutable evidence of her guilt. It has been argued that they had very personal motives for deposing her. Mary was soon to be twenty-five, the age at which in Scottish law the monarch had the right to review all titles and land she had previously issued. But it must be doubtful whether Mary ever had the power to deprive them of their lands. As for Bothwell, he fled via the Orkneys and the Shetlands to Norway, then ruled by Denmark. He was captured and until his death in 1578 remained a prisoner of the Danish king, who initially hoped to use him as a bargaining counter to restore the northern islands to Danish/Norwegian rule.

Mary's time at Lochleven was in some ways a foretaste of her years in England. Having recovered her health and nerve, in the spring of 1568 she unrealistically asked Catherine de'Medici to send French troops to assist her. Even without such help she was planning to escape. The first attempt failed, but in May, with the help of young men susceptible to her charms and hopeful of advancement, she succeeded. She raised a sizeable army, attracting some of the nobility who still supported her as the rightful monarch and some whose loyalty might be questionable but who considered themselves inadequately rewarded by those now in power. However, this army was crushed by Moray's smaller force in a short battle at Langside, just outside Glasgow, and Mary fled south into Galloway. Describing this time to her uncle in France, Mary wrote: 'I have endured injuries, calumnies, imprisonment, famine, cold, heat, flight not knowing wither, ninety miles across the country… then I have had to sleep upon the ground and drink sour milk, and eat oatmeal without bread, and have been three nights like the owls'.

Although her supporters advised against it, Mary made the fateful decision to cross the Solway Firth to England and ask her fellow queen, Elizabeth, for assistance. In France she had estates, money, and a powerful family who could take her side, even though they were fully committed to the troubles at home and despite Catherine de'Medici's opposition. In England she had none of these things. Her only relations were her mother-in-law, the Countess of Lennox, who disliked her, and Elizabeth, with whom she seemed to have great hopes of a positive relationship, despite evidence to the contrary. This was another unfortunate decision and one that Mary would have plenty of time to regret.

The instability in Scotland continued even in Mary's absence in what is often referred to as the Marian Civil War. Her now leaderless supporters upheld her cause. They drew strength from the knowledge that Mary had international backing as the rightful queen, though little overseas assistance was ever provided, and from the endemic rivalries between the Scottish nobility. Involving mainly skirmishes and sieges, the queen's party rarely had the upper hand, though after Sir William Kirkcaldy of Grange, the keeper of Edinburgh Castle, switched sides to the queen's party in 1571, it took more than two years and the intervention of English troops to bring about his surrender, thus ending the war. Kirkcaldy was hanged for his disloyalty.

A number of the leading figures in the king's party, those in power during the minority of James VI, suffered violent deaths. The first was the regent Moray, Mary's step-brother, long the careful schemer, having knowledge of numerous plots but rarely getting his hands dirty. He has the dubious distinction of being the first head of state to be assassinated by use of a firearm, something that became all too common in later centuries. In January 1570 he was shot by James Hamilton from a window of Archbishop Hamilton's house in Linlithgow using a 104cm-long match-lock carbine with a rifled barrel. The killer had been in Mary's army at Langside, as were many of the Hamilton family, and after the shooting he fled to France, where he offered his services to the Guise family in the Wars of Religion. His uncle, the archbishop, was arrested and hanged for complicity in the murder. Moray was succeeded as regent by the Earl of Lennox, Darnley's father. He died in 1571, shot in a skirmish at Stirling. In 1572 Morton became regent and remained so until 1579. Shortly after his removal as regent he was accused of the murder of Darnley, found guilty and executed in June 1581. At last, after managing to point the finger elsewhere for so long, one of those really responsible for the regicide paid the price, but many others avoided punishment.

CHAPTER 6

FELLOW QUEEN OR DANGEROUS CONSPIRATOR? MARY AND ELIZABETH

Mary, in borrowed clothes and with her shorn hair covered by a hood, landed at Workington on the evening of 16 May with twenty companions after a four hour crossing on a fishing vessel. Word was soon out that the Scottish queen was in the town. She was taken to Carlisle Castle by armed soldiers, to guard her more than to protect her. While still in Scotland she had written to Elizabeth requesting help and she now wrote again asking for either an army to regain her throne or if that were not immediately possible the permission to travel to London to meet with the queen and make her case. Mary reasoned that her abdication was invalid because she had signed it under duress. Elizabeth's councillors, with William Cecil to the fore, argued that given the scandals around Mary's relationship with Bothwell and her involvement in Darnley's murder, the queen could not possibly meet her cousin until she had been cleared of these charges and her reputation restored. As a result, after being held at Carlisle for six weeks, Mary was moved to the rather more comfortable Bolton Castle in North Yorkshire under the custodianship of Lord Henry Scrope. There she would be secure, but there would be no immediate royal meeting.

Mary's arrival in England created a major problem for Queen Elizabeth. On the one hand her instinct was to provide assistance to her cousin and fellow queen. She had been outraged at the deposition of an anointed monarch, saying that the Scottish lords had 'no warrant nor authority by the laws of God or man to be as superiors, judges or vindicators over their prince and sovereign'. Acceptance of the removal of their monarch could one day put her own position in jeopardy. But now Mary was in England Elizabeth had to take into account both the safety of the country and her own security on the throne when deciding how to handle the situation. There were a number of possible courses of action but most had serious drawbacks. She could raise an army to support Mary in fighting for her restoration, as the Scottish queen requested, but this would mean war with those who had been England's allies in Scotland, who had driven out the French and established the Protestant faith. Alternatively she could hand Mary back to the Scottish Lords, who would then have to decide how to deal with her. Mary might then be imprisoned or they might even get rid of her, either by quasi-legal means that few would accept as legitimate or by more nefarious means which would certainly draw widespread disapproval. Elizabeth's hands would be reasonably clean but her conscience would not be if Mary were to die. If Elizabeth allowed her to leave England for France or Spain, Mary might then try to persuade their rulers to become involved in a Catholic crusade against both England and Scotland. If she were to be permitted to live freely in England, then there was the risk that Mary could use her religion, together with the fact that the English queen had not assisted her militarily, to build up Catholic support against Elizabeth. All options were fraught with danger. For the time being Mary would remain in England: not as a welcome guest and free agent, but isolated and secured where her actions could be closely monitored.

The Scottish Lords had spent the previous year justifying the removal of their anointed queen and their takeover of the running of Scotland. The public were told that Mary was directly involved in the murder of Darnley, and had committed adultery with Bothwell before his divorce and their own marriage. There were frequent references to her 'moral turpitude' and to her 'furious love' for Bothwell, intended to show that she had no control over her emotions and was thus totally incapable of ruling the country just as John Knox had previously argued. The most blatant anti-Marian tract was written by George Buchanan on behalf of the Lords. He was careful to date the start of her affair with Bothwell as not earlier than the birth of her son, James, but before Darnley's death. He did not wish to throw any doubt upon the boy's legitimacy. James was, after all, to be brought up as a Protestant and their king by the Lords. Buchanan showed little regard for factual accuracy; what mattered to him was blackening Mary's name. He provided dubious details of the meetings between the queen and Bothwell, at which Bothwell had 'abused her body at his pleasure', his access to Mary's bedroom supposedly being facilitated by Lady Reres. [In fact she was one of Bothwell's former mistresses who was so angry when discarded by him that she was ordered to leave court.] According to Buchanan, Mary had arranged Darnley's move to Kirk o' Field from the safety of his Glasgow stronghold, and had given her excuses to leave him late on the evening of his murder, in full knowledge of the plot. Her reaction on being told of his death had been not one of sorrow; she could scarcely hide her delight. She had been a willing participant in her supposed abduction to Dunbar where the couple 'spared no time to fulfil their ungodly appetite, yet somewhat to cover her honesty she pretended to be ravished'.

To back up these accusations the Lords at first hinted at the existence of evidence which would confirm Mary's guilt. This eventually turned out to be eight letters written by Mary to Bothwell, the so called 'Casket Letters', found under Bothwell's bed. They provided the only evidence that Mary was party to the plot to kill Darnley. The Lords used their supposed knowledge of the letters to justify their removal of Mary from the throne. However, there seems to have been no mention of them until after her deposition. Also, questions were raised at the time, and have been ever since, about their authenticity. If they were genuine, then Mary's guilt in both adultery and murder was certain. But as the originals were last seen in the 1580s and we now only have copies, and copies of copies, the debate continues. Is it conceivable that Mary would have written such incriminating letters? Why did the Scots at first seem reluctant to publish them? On the other hand, if they were forgeries it would have been difficult to produce all of them so quickly and so expertly. A solution might be found in the suggestion that letters written by Mary, originally quite innocent, were doctored, with additional material added, words taken out of context, or simply with a change of date, to present a damning final version.[1]

These letters became central to the conference set up in England to investigate the motives for the Lords' rebellion and to come to a conclusion as to how valid the charges against Mary really were. Elizabeth favoured such a process as it meant that Mary would not be put on trial, as the trial of a monarch would be completely unacceptable, given her view that a monarch answered only to God. It was agreed that Moray would present the Lords' case and Mary would send representatives, headed by John Leslie, Bishop of Ross, to defend her. Elizabeth intended that if Mary was found to be blameless she would return to Scotland as queen but with limited powers and Moray would remain in charge of the government. If not, then Mary would remain in England under guard. Elizabeth's chief minister, William Cecil, argued strongly against Mary being restored and wanted to see the end of any chance of her ever succeeding to the English throne.

The conference opened at York on 4 October 1568 presided over by Thomas Howard Duke of Norfolk, his cousin Thomas Radcliffe, the Earl of Sussex, and Sir Ralph Sadler, who had long experience in Scottish affairs. Both sides delivered their opening statements. Moray privately showed the Casket letters to the panel, but before presenting them formally he wanted Elizabeth to commit to supporting his government and abandoning Mary if he was able to prove his case. Undecided, Elizabeth ordered an adjournment and the inquiry shifted to London. In late November it was decided that the letters would be accepted as evidence and immediately Leslie demanded that Mary be allowed to attend in person to deal with the accusations. Upon the refusal of this request Mary's representatives withdrew from the conference. The letters were presented and discussed by a larger group of Privy Councillors at Hampton Court. However, without Mary's defence being presented the tribunal decided that it was impossible to make a definitive final judgement. In January 1569 the case against her was declared not proven. Moray was to rule Scotland and given a small loan, though he had not achieved his main aim of Mary being handed over and taken back to imprisonment in Scotland. She would remain in England.

Mary's degree of freedom and the number of household servants that she was permitted over the next nineteen years fluctuated depending on how much of a threat to Elizabeth she was perceived to be at any given time. She spent time in a number of castles and stately homes, often in properties owned by George Talbot, the Earl of Shrewsbury, her custodian for fifteen years between 1569 and 1584, and his wife, Bess of Hardwick. Security around her tightened during the sitting of the tribunal. At its conclusion Mary was moved from Bolton Castle, where Lady Scrope, the sister of the Duke of Norfolk, was considered too sympathetic to her, to Shrewsbury's supervision at Tutbury Castle in Staffordshire. After a visit to Mary there, the Irish lawyer, Nicholas White, recommended to Cecil that she be allowed very few visitors because with her 'goodly personage, alluring grace, pretty Scottish speech and searching wit, clouded with mildness'[2] she might well gain considerable sympathy and support. However, after complaining about the cold, damp and ill-furnished rooms at Tutbury, Mary was permitted to spend time at the more comfortable Wingfield Manor and Chatsworth House in Derbyshire. On occasions she was allowed visitors, to send and receive letters, and to walk and ride in the grounds, though never out of sight of her guards. While in Shrewsbury's custody, mainly at Sheffield Castle from 1570, she was generally treated well, though he came to resent the cost and inconvenience of his responsibility. Mary spent much of her time engaged in embroidery, often with Bess of Hardwick. The monograms, MA (Mary) and ES (Elizabeth Shrewsbury), can be seen on their work. Many examples still remain – in the Victoria and Albert Museum, the Royal Collection, Oxburgh Hall, and Hardwick House. Some of her embroidery reveals the frustration at what she regarded as her captivity – the caged bird with a hawk hovering nearby and the large ginger cat studying a small defenceless mouse. Mary also embroidered a phoenix in the flames representing regeneration (her mother's symbol) and her French motto *'En ma fin est mon commencement'* ['In my end is my beginning'].

Elizabeth and her councillors were always conscious that Mary could become the focus of plots to replace her and re-establish the Catholic Church. The first manifestation of this threat was the ill-planned Northern Rebellion of 1569 led by the Catholic earls of Northumberland [Thomas Percy] and Westmorland [Charles Neville]. Mary was apparently aware of their plans but told them not to rebel. Nevertheless they went ahead. In November 1569 they occupied Durham and then Barnard Castle, but when faced by troops loyal to Elizabeth they fled north, the leaders escaping to Scotland. Several hundred followers were executed. Northumberland was taken prisoner in Scotland and over two years later was sold back to England and on 22 August 1572 publicly beheaded in York. Westmorland evaded capture and fled to relative safety in Flanders. In an effort to assist the rebellion and encourage further attempts to remove Elizabeth, Pope Pius V issued the papal bull *'Regnans in Excelsis'* in February 1570. This declared 'the pretended Queen of England and the servant of crime' to be a heretic, releasing her subjects from any allegiance to her, and that 'whosoever sends her out of this world with the pious intention of doing God's service, not only does not sin but gains merit'.

Further difficulties were caused by suggestions that Mary should marry Thomas Howard, the Duke of Norfolk, who had just been widowed for the third time. The ambitious Norfolk, a Catholic sympathizer though brought up a Protestant, the senior nobleman in the country and cousin to Queen Elizabeth, believed that he was not given the status that he deserved. Although very much aware of the discussions about his marriage to Mary and having knowledge of the plans of the northern earls, he did not become involved. Indeed he had been sent to the Tower of London shortly before the earls rebelled and was held for several months, though he was not charged. Shortly after his release he became involved in the Ridolfi Plot.

Roberto Ridolfi was a Florentine banker who had been an agent of the pope in 1567. With the aim of overthrowing Elizabeth, expediting the marriage of Mary and Norfolk and establishing them on the throne, he set about organising and helping to finance a plot. He recognised that a foreign army would be needed for the plan to be successful. Having gained the backing of John Leslie, the Bishop of Ross, Mary's chief adviser, and then Mary and Norfolk, he travelled to Rome, Madrid and Brussels, winning the support of the pope, Philip II of Spain and the Duke of Alba, who was to lead an invasion of Spanish troops from the Netherlands after Elizabeth's removal. The Elizabethan intelligence network showed its efficiency. Messages were intercepted, servants arrested and tortured until the whole plan was exposed. Although Ridolfi remained safely abroad, Norfolk was arrested, tried and executed, just as his father had been in the final days of Henry VIII's reign. As for Mary, although involved in the plot she was not its instigator. She admitted that she wished for her freedom and her restoration in Scotland, but always denied any intention of deposing Elizabeth or seeking to impose Catholicism on England. Nevertheless her position in England was seriously damaged. Elizabeth now permitted the publication of the Casket Letters and the case against her made by the Scottish Lords. Many members of parliament wished her executed and a bill was drawn up excluding Mary from the succession and to make it treasonable to discuss her marriage or her claim to the throne. Elizabeth did not wish the bill to become law and announced that she would give it her consideration in the future.

Given these events it is hardly surprising that Mary was regarded with suspicion. However, during the 1570s Mary must have recognised that the chances of her restoration to the Scottish throne were declining. In 1573 the final stronghold of her supporters in Scotland, Edinburgh Castle, was lost. In 1579 her son James officially came of age and he began to take effective power four years later. Mary had hopes of his eventually agreeing to them ruling jointly but this was never a realistic outcome. Hope of overseas help for plots in England faded as France became ever more engulfed in the Wars of Religion and Spanish resources were taken up dealing with the revolt in the Netherlands. Mary, however, was still complaining of her treatment to Elizabeth. In 1582 she wrote of how everyone sought to prevent good relations between them, of how she was treated worse than any prisoner because she was held captive without any charge against her despite being 'a royal sovereign, your closest relative and legitimate heir'.[3] Such language was likely to anger Elizabeth and raise once again the threat of plotters. For the unmarried Elizabeth the problem of the succession remained. By 1583 she had reached the age of 50 and it was clear that she would have no children. Those keen to see Mary inheriting were likely to be encouraged.

Elizabeth was still reluctant to take any further action against Mary, who, in efforts to gain Elizabeth's favour, promised that she would do nothing to challenge Elizabeth as the reigning monarch or encourage religious changes in England. Even so, William Cecil and other senior councillors continually pressed the queen to declare that Mary should never inherit the English throne and, if she became involved in other plots, be executed.

Such pressures became stronger after the Throckmorton Plot. The queen's spy-master, Francis Walsingham, now had a well-developed network of observers and informants. They were aware of contacts made between Mary and Mendoza, the Spanish ambassador. Late in 1583 Walsingham had Francis Throckmorton arrested. Found in his house were coded letters bound for Mary, the identity of leading Catholics in England willing to support a foreign invasion, a list of safe harbours where such an invasion could land, and copies of anti-Elizabethan propaganda from abroad.[4] Throckmorton had been in contact with the French and Spanish ambassadors, and the Duke of Guise in France. Under torture he admitted to encouraging an invasion by Philip II and his French ally, Guise. Throckmorton was executed and Mendoza expelled from the country.

The anti-Catholic, and thus anti-Marian, mood in England was not helped in July 1584 by the murder of William of Orange, the leader of the Dutch rebels against Spanish rule. He was shot by Balthasar Gerard, who considered him to be a traitor to King Philip and to the Catholic religion. If one Protestant leader could become the victim of a Catholic plot what was to stop another? The Throckmorton plot had been thwarted but there could well be others. Coincidently, Bess of Hardwick's accusations, later withdrawn, that her husband, Mary's custodian Shrewsbury, had been influenced by Mary's natural warmth of character and ability to charm, and consequently, been too lenient with her, made matters worse. Mary was moved to the custodianship of Sir Ralph Sadler at Wingfield Manor. After a few months he took pity on her situation and admitted to Cecil that he had taken her hawking with him. He was replaced by Sir Amyas Paulet, and Mary was moved to the inhospitable Tutbury Castle.

In this heightened atmosphere of conspiracy and fear, the Privy Council drew up the 'Bond of Association', whose signatories would pledge to kill anyone who might benefit from Elizabeth's assassination, even if the attempt was unsuccessful. In other words, Mary could be put to death without trial if there was any plot to murder the queen. It also included the heir of a beneficiary, in other words, Mary's son James. Thousands signed the bond but when it was brought to parliament Elizabeth objected. She insisted that anyone considered a beneficiary of such a murder attempt [Mary] should be tried before a tribunal and that the heir [James] should not be prevented from succeeding to the throne unless it could be proved that he had known about the plot. With these amendments, the Act for the Surety of the Queen's Person was passed at the end of 1584. The statute declared that once someone was found guilty of such a crime they could be lawfully killed.

Under the supervision of Paulet, a strict uncompromising Puritan, with very strong anti-Catholic views and immune to her undoubted ability to charm, Mary's freedom of action was severely limited. She was largely confined indoors, could not send letters, all incoming post was opened and read, there were regular searches made of her rooms, and she was prevented from making her traditional giving out of alms to locals for fear that she might be buying their assistance in some way. She had never been so cut off from the outside world. She called Paulet 'one of the most zealous and pitiless men I have ever known'.[5] Her unrealistic hopes of her son James helping her were dashed when he informed her that although he would always respect her position as Queen Mother, he would never allow her to return to Scotland, let alone as joint ruler. He was looking after his own interests, in particular being accepted as heir to the English throne. Nevertheless, she believed that her complaints about the conditions at Tutbury had been listened to when in December 1585 she was moved from Tutbury to Chartley Hall. There, however, she was subjected to the same regime.

Mary was therefore delighted when two letters were smuggled in to her by being hidden in the bunghole of a beer keg. A local brewer was willing to assist Gilbert Gifford, who was introduced to her, in one of the letters from Mary's agent in Paris, as someone she could trust to organise secret correspondence. A code was devised and letters exchanged. John Ballard, who had trained as a Catholic priest in France and returned to England under the false identity of Captain Fortescue, contacted Anthony Babington, an English Catholic with good connections. Babington was to arrange Mary's escape from Chartley, the murder of Elizabeth and a foreign invasion. He gave Mary full details of the plot in a letter received by her on 14 July 1586. She would be rescued by one hundred men, while six men would be sent 'for the dispatch of the usurper, from obedience of whom we are by the excommunication of her made free'. Mary was desperate to escape her captivity and despondent when James signed a treaty of friendship with England earlier that month. Although advised by her secretary not to reply, she recklessly responded to Babington's letter three days later.

What she and her fellow conspirators did not know was that every letter sent via the beer kegs was opened, decoded and reported to Walsingham. Gifford was a double-agent and the whole system had been set up to incriminate Mary. Her reply did just that. She wanted her rescue to be effected before the 'six gentlemen' carried out their work, she had great 'praise' for a foreign invasion and promised to reward those who worked 'for her delivery'. The decoder, Thomas Phelippes, indicated that he believed there was sufficient here to convict Mary by drawing the picture of a gallows on the seal of the copy that he sent to Walsingham. Before he returned Mary's letter to the beer keg for delivery to Babington he forged a final section asking Babington for the names of the 'six gentlemen'.[6]

The deception was complete. In reality there was no threat to Elizabeth but it did reveal the extent to which Mary was willing to go in order to gain her freedom. It all unravelled quickly. Gifford went back to France, not wishing to be involved in the arrests and trials. Walsingham's men moved in and arrested the known plotters. Babington, having realised that all had been uncovered, fled, only to be captured ten days later. No doubt under torture, he soon confessed and was hanged, drawn and quartered, along with six others, at St. Giles Field, in September. Mary was not immediately informed of the discovery of the plot. On 11 August she was surprised when Paulet suggested that they go out hunting. While her party was setting off she saw a group of horsemen galloping towards them. She might have briefly imagined that these were her rescuers, but was soon to be disabused. Their leader spoke to Paulet and then informed Mary that she was to be arrested. He told her that 'The queen finds it strange that you ... should have conspired against her and the state, a thing which she could not have believed had she not seen the proofs of it with her own eyes and known it for certain'.[7]

Elizabeth, appalled at Mary's involvement, was again troubled about what to action she should take. She knew that her subjects, especially her closest advisers, would demand the death penalty. Even though Elizabeth accepted that Mary posed a real threat, she still had qualms about putting a fellow monarch on trial, let alone executing her. She was concerned about the precedent of a royal execution authorized by a law (The Act for the Surety of the Queen's Person of 1584) passed by parliament, how foreign powers would react, and how posterity would judge her. Mary, for her part, expected that she would suffer the ultimate punishment and started to prepare for a martyr's death. She wrote to her cousin, the Duke of Guise, saying that she was 'resolute to die for my religion'. She, too, wished to influence how history would remember her.

On 21 September she began the four day journey from Chartley Hall to Fotheringhay Castle, in Northamptonshire, where it had been decided that her trial would take place. Elizabeth had rejected using the Tower of London, not wishing to have Mary in the capital. The trial date was set for 14 October. Mary initially refused to accept the court's jurisdiction. She said that she had come to England of her own free will after receiving promises of help from Elizabeth and that she was not a subject but an 'absolute prince and not within the compass of your laws'. She was then told that the trial would go ahead without her if she did not appear. The following morning she reluctantly agreed to defend herself against just one charge, that of conspiring to murder Elizabeth. The law required that there should be at least twenty-four lords and privy councillors appointed to hear the case. In fact, thirty-one attended as well as five senior judges. Cecil let it be known that anyone who avoided being involved would be regarded with suspicion. Every detail of the trial was meticulously planned. The courtroom was to be the sixty-nine-foot-long presence chamber on the first floor, divided by a waist-high rail, behind which there was space for a limited number of selected observers. At the front of the room there was a chair on a dais beneath a cloth of state, representing Elizabeth's throne, which would remain empty as she was not going to attend. Benches were placed around the other three sides for the commissioners, with a central table for the lawyers. Mary was provided with a high-backed, red velvet covered chair at the side.

The trial lasted two days. As Mary entered the courtroom, dressed in black velvet with a white cap and veil, the commissioners removed their hats. She was to be given the respect due to her. She was accompanied by her doctor, Bourgoing, who was later to write a detailed account of the trial and her last days[8], her steward, Melville, and three ladies-in-waiting. Mary had little idea of the evidence that Walsingham had put together. She did not yet know that her letters had been intercepted and decoded. She knew nothing of Babington's confession, or about the written statements of her two secretaries, who did all that they could to avoid any blame. Her defence, even in the face of this damning evidence was that she never ordered or agreed to Elizabeth's assassination. She argued that she had the right to call upon others to help her escape from illegal imprisonment and if they decided to depose the queen then it had nothing to do with her, saying: 'I do not deny that I earnestly wished for liberty. In this I acted from a very natural wish ... Can I be responsible for the criminal projects of a few desperate men, which they planned without my knowledge or participation'. She challenged the depositions of her secretaries and demanded that they appeared in court to be questioned. She attempted to win sympathy by explaining how ill she was, rheumatism and lack of exercise meant that she had difficulty walking. She also made the point that she had no representation: 'I am alone without counsel, or anyone to speak on my behalf. My papers and notes have been taken from me, so that I am destitute of aid, taken at a disadvantage'. On the second day she was pressed on the issue of a foreign invasion and the transfer of the crown to Philip II of Spain. Mary responded by saying that she 'desired nothing but my own deliverance'. Towards the end of the day she demanded to be heard by the queen in person or by a full parliament. She then left the hall with impressive dignity.

Before a verdict was reached Elizabeth sent an order to Cecil to suspend the proceedings for ten days. On 25 October the commissioners met again, this time in Westminster, and interviewed Mary's secretaries, who confirmed their statements. Mary was then unanimously found guilty and condemned to death. It was another five weeks before Elizabeth issued the proclamation declaring this outcome. She had come under pressure from both those who wished for a stay of execution and those who wished for swift action. Mary's disrepute amongst Catholic rulers in the late 1560s was forgotten. Foreign monarchs argued Mary's case, especially Henry III of France, who argued that she was 'exempt from human jurisdiction and subject only to the judgement of God'[9]. He wished to deflect the heavy criticism that he was receiving in France for failing to protect Mary, his sister-in-law, a fellow Catholic and a former queen of France. Her son, James VI, sent representatives from Scotland and a personal letter to Elizabeth imploring that the life of his mother be spared, particularly emphasising how her death would undermine the whole concept of monarchy. Given the public outcry in Scotland it is possible that he was more concerned with saving his face there rather than saving his mother's life in England.[10] He had no wish to irreparably damage his chances of being Elizabeth's successor. Parliament and the Privy Council, however, wanted an immediate execution. There was little sympathy for Mary in their discussions. The Puritan M.P. for Warwick, Job Throckmorton, called her: 'the daughter of sedition, the nurse of impiety, the handmaid of iniquity'. He continued that she was 'Scottish of nation, French of education, papist of profession, a Guisian of blood, a Spaniard in practice and a libertine in life'.[11] Elizabeth responded by asking them to consider whether there was another way in which Mary could be dealt with, especially as she, as monarch, had to consider the reaction of other states to Mary's execution. As Mary herself had pointed out, the theatre of the world was wider than the little realm of England. The parliamentarians quickly rejected any alternatives.

The queen ensured that her reluctance to carry out the sentence was publicised, and told foreign diplomats that she had only issued the proclamation because of the pleading of her parliament. She also sought to avoid direct responsibility by privately hinting that it would be helpful if someone who had signed the 'Bond of Association' in 1584 kept their word and killed Mary, thus saving their queen from the need to sanction a fellow queen's death. Walsingham wrote to Sir Amyas Paulet suggesting that he facilitated such an action, but the high-minded Paulet refused to 'make so foul a shipwreck of my conscience'[12]. Elizabeth's equivocations and delays lasted well into the New Year. She did not sign the death warrant until 1 February, when rumours of plots and even a foreign invasion, quite possibly started by those who wished a swift end to Mary, might have finally persuaded her that Mary had to die. Even then she handed it to her junior secretary William Davison and told him to keep it secret, except from Walsingham, who was ill at the time. Nevertheless, once Walsingham was informed, word of the signed warrant got out. On 3 February Cecil arranged a meeting of leading council members and it was decided that they would act upon it without troubling the queen further. They were afraid that she might change her mind. They instructed Robert Beale, the clerk to the Privy Council, to take the warrant to Fotheringhay. He arrived on 7 February, accompanied by the earls of Kent and Shrewsbury, her long-time custodian, who had been given the responsibility of overseeing the execution.

The final chapter of Mary's life now took place with remarkable speed. Everything had been prepared for weeks and so there was little more to do except the work of the executioner. While Elizabeth had been agonising over the decision, Mary had been awaiting her fate. She refused to admit her guilt despite Elizabeth's demands and Paulet's urging, maintaining that she was an innocent victim, dying for the cause of her religion. To her cousin, the Duke of Guise, she wrote that 'we, both men and women, may be ready to shed our blood to maintain the fight of the faith'.[13] She had heard the sound of what she thought must be the construction of the scaffold on which she was to die, and had already asked Elizabeth that her body be taken to Reims to be laid alongside that of her mother, not wishing to be buried in heretic soil.

On the evening of 7 February Shrewsbury informed Mary that she would be executed the following morning and Beale read out the warrant. Mary thanked them for the news, claiming that she would be very glad to leave this world. Her servants later reported that she told them that she would now be 'freed of all her sorrows and troubles'[14]. She asked that her chaplain be allowed to give her communion and hear her confession, but was told to her dismay that she would receive consolation and instruction from Richard Fletcher, a Protestant, the Dean of Peterborough, and later Bishop of London. She refused to see him. Her requests that she be buried in France, and that her papers and accounts be brought to her so that they could be put in order and she could write her will, were also refused. Her last evening was spent eating a brief meal with her servants, to whom she gave her few remaining possessions as gifts, followed by writing and praying. She did not write to Elizabeth but at two o'clock in the morning began her last letter, to Henry III of France, her 'royal brother'. She wrote of her treatment by Elizabeth 'at whose hands I have suffered so much for almost twenty years', and of how she was being executed for 'the Catholic faith and the defence of my God-given right to the English throne.[15] She asked Henry to find a place for her chaplain, to pay her doctor and her faithful servants the wages due to them, and to have prayers offered to God for her soul. She wished him to know all that had happened to her at Fotheringhay but because she did not have enough to time her servants would be able to give him a full account later.

After a short, fitful, night, disturbed by the sound of the guards marching outside the chamber, she rose at 6 o'clock the next morning. Attended by her maids, she dressed carefully in a black satin gown and a white veil, beneath which was a beautiful auburn wig. She asked Dr. Bourgoing to read out her will, which she then signed, and having said her farewells, Mary knelt to pray. A short time later Shrewsbury, Kent and Sir Thomas Andrews, the sheriff of Northamptonshire arrived to escort her on her final walk. At the door she was told that Elizabeth had ordered that she should die alone because her servants might cause trouble and attempt to dip their handkerchiefs in her blood to keep as a relic. She questioned whether this could be so, saying that other gentleladies had been accompanied to their deaths and that if she were not, the executioner would have to take off her outer garments which would be unseemly. The earls decided that a few others could go with her as long as they gave their word not to cause a disturbance.

She entered the hall, carrying a crucifix and a prayer book, supported by Melville, Bourgoing and two female companions, Jane Kennedy and Elizabeth Curle. Over 100 local gentry and other dignitaries were gathered in front of the scaffold, which was twelve feet square, stood two feet high, and was completely covered in black cloth, as was the block[16]. Mary made a short speech to those nearby. She asked them to 'tell my friends that I died a true woman to my religion, like a true Scottish woman and a true French woman, but God forgive them that have long desired my end and thirsted for my blood'.[17] Dean Fletcher then started prayers for her soul, which she ignored and loudly said her own prayers first in Latin and then in English.[18] Her ladies helped to remove her outer clothes revealing a red bodice and a red petticoat, the colour of blood and of Catholic martyrdom. Mary quietly reminded her servants of their promise not to cry out. The executioner from the Tower of London, referred to as 'Mr. Bull', who was to be paid £10 for these duties, made the traditional request for forgiveness, which she granted. Jane Kennedy then tied a white veil around her eyes. She knelt on the cushion in front of the block, recited the Thirty-First Psalm, and then carefully placed her neck on the block, with the words 'Into your hands O Lord I commend my spirit'. The executioner's axe swung down. The first blow cut into the back of her head and Mary was heard to cry out. A second blow was needed to sever her neck, all but a small sinew which was then cut with the axe. As the executioner went to hold up her head the wig came off in his hands and her head fell to the floor in front of the stunned audience. As 'Mr. Bull' bent to pick up the head, Dean Fletcher shouted: 'So perish all the Queen's enemies', just as the executioner of Lady Jane Grey had done some thirty-three years before. It was a different queen, who had a different religion, and although both had shown reluctance to approve the beheading of their rival, both would be more secure as a result.

As the hall emptied, with Mary's body still on the raised stage, the executioner found beneath her petticoats her small dog, covered in blood, which had somehow hidden there as Mary had left her rooms. All her belongings were taken and destroyed, as was the blood-stained block and cloth covering of the scaffold, to ensure that nothing could be retrieved and used as a relic, thus enhancing Mary's status as a martyr. Her heart and other organs were removed and buried deep within the building. Her body was then embalmed, wrapped in a waxed cloth and placed in a lead coffin. It remained at Fotheringhay for over six months, until it was interred at Peterborough Cathedral. It was moved to Westminster Abbey in 1612 by her son, James, by then the king of England.

Despite celebrations in London, with bonfires and the ringing of church bells, when news of the execution spread, Elizabeth knew that it would unleash a storm of protest across Europe. Ports were closed for three weeks in an effort to delay the news reaching foreign capitals. Mary's servants were held in England and not permitted to return to France or Scotland until the autumn when the immediate furore had died down. Elizabeth attempted to distance herself from direct responsibility. When informed of the execution she appeared to be at first shocked and then angry. She went into mourning, declaring that although she had signed the warrant she had not ordered that it should be delivered to Fotheringhay. She publicly berated her ministers. Cecil, the driving force behind the execution, was banished from court. However, he had worked with her for long enough to know that it would only be a matter of time until she relented. He was right; by March he had resumed his duties in full. The main scapegoat was Davison who was accused of over-stepping his authority and sent to the Tower of

London. Although he was held for over a year and given an enormous fine, his salary continued to be paid, which the fine never was.

None of this deflected the vitriolic criticism to which Elizabeth was subjected. Many abusive publications were produced, especially in France and Scotland. In Scotland there was much anger and wild talk of attacking and burning down Newcastle in retaliation and much written about the Jezabel, that English whore, responsible for murdering 'our Queen', despite the fact that she had fled the country in fear of her life nineteen years earlier. James publicly grieved, though was reported to have said privately that 'Now I am sole king'. He did not break diplomatic relations with England, an act which would have seriously threatened his relations with Elizabeth and the English establishment, jeopardising his hopes of succeeding her.

However, it was in France where Mary's execution had the greatest impact with serious consequences for its king. There were mass demonstrations in Paris, and preachers portrayed Mary as a Catholic martyr, just as she intended, and Elizabeth as a she-wolf, an incestuous bastard and treacherous public whore. The English ambassador, Stafford, reported that 'truly I find all men here in a fury' and that the manner of her death was detested by people of all ages and religions.[19] Gruesome illustrations of her death were displayed and visited by thousands. For King Henry III the execution was a personal, political and diplomatic humiliation. He was genuinely appalled by Mary's death and organised a requiem Mass for her on 12 March. Stafford was denied entry to the French court and he was told by Walsingham to stop reporting to Queen Elizabeth just how widespread the anger in France was. Despite this, Henry's opponents in the Catholic League headed by the Guise family and encouraged by Mendoza, now Philip II's ambassador in Paris, used Mary's death to whip up further hatred of the king for his failure to save her and defend the faith. The execution was used to argue the case that he should end any toleration of Protestants in France. Calls for revenge were widespread. Within a year books praising Mary and her heroic death, such as Blackwood's *'Histoire de la Martyre de la Royne d'Escosse'*, were being published and selling in large numbers. Internationally Henry III could not risk a complete break with England for fear of strengthening Spain's position. On the other hand, Philip II could not only increase his backing for the Catholic League in France but was provided with the justification that he needed for his planned invasion of England. If successful, there was the added advantage that he might now take the English throne himself, claiming that this was Mary's wish, rather than having Mary on the throne as his proxy. The stage was set for the sending of the Armada the following year.

Mary, Queen of Scots achieved little of lasting significance in her lifetime, though she was to become the ancestor of all subsequent British monarchs. Although queen of Scotland almost from her birth until she was twenty-four, her personal rule only lasted five years. However, her close family ties with the Tudors and the Guise family meant that her very existence was the cause of considerable friction both within and between Scotland, England and France, and had a significant influence on the policies of their rulers and leading figures. Her life, and death, has been the subject of heated, often partisan, debates over the last 400 years. These have concentrated on whether she was complicit in the murder of her second husband, Darnley, on her alleged moral failings in her relationship with Bothwell, and on the level of her involvement in plots to bring about the overthrow and death of her fellow monarch, Elizabeth.

Mary has been portrayed as the innocent victim of the actions of others and as a Catholic martyr cruelly mistreated and betrayed by the cousin to whom she appealed for help against those who deposed her. She has also been seen as a murderer and devious schemer who received her just desserts at the hands of the English queen whose crown she coveted. These judgements may well be different if she had been a man. Her affair with Bothwell and the debate about the 'Casket letters', which brought about her deposition in Scotland and then disgrace in England, would be seen in a very different light if this had been a king with a passion for someone other than his wife.

If the focus is turned more onto Mary as a ruler, it can be argued that she was never fully committed to actively ruling Scotland. She enjoyed her early life as a princess and then the queen consort in France, and many of her later actions suggest that her real interest was in gaining the English throne. In Scotland she has be seen as a monarch trying to achieve a degree of religious tolerance at a time when such toleration was unusual, with the stability of her country undermined by the ambitions of an internecine nobility. However, a strong case can be made that she was a weak ruler, too dependent upon others, who made disastrous decisions about who to marry and then, having been deposed in Scotland, misjudged how she would be received by Elizabeth. Once in England there can be little doubt that she played a significant part in the events leading to her eventual execution. She allowed herself to be drawn into plots which threatened the very existence of Protestant England and its queen.

VALOIS AND BOURBON

Regicide and Changing Dynasties in France

'The reign of a heretic could never be accepted.'

From the Declaration of Peronne, issued by the
Catholic League in March 1585

———— ◆═◆◇◆═◆ ————

*'What do you think you have done? You have killed two men
who have left a lot of friends.'*

Catherine de' Medici to her son King Henry III in December
1588, on hearing the news of the murder of Henry, Duke of
Guise and his brother Louis, Cardinal of Guise

———— ◆═◆◇◆═◆ ————

'Paris is worth a Mass.'

Attributed to Henry IV. He is claimed to have said this to a
friend on 25 July 1593, the day he was publicly
received into the Catholic Church

CHAPTER 7

THE FRENCH WARS OF RELIGION

T he execution of Mary, Queen of Scots had such an impact in France largely because of the remarkable reversal of fortunes experienced there since the mid-sixteenth century. For much of the first sixty years of the century, an increasingly united and prosperous France was a major power on the international stage. Francis I challenged Emperor Charles V for dominance in Europe, and successfully resisted the claims of Henry VIII to both the lands once ruled by the kings of England and the French throne itself. In 1558 his son, Henry II, captured Calais, England's last foothold in France. The prestige of the monarchy in France under these effective rulers remained high. However, during the following decades the country was riven by violent internal disputes, usually referred to as the Wars of Religion. A weakened monarchy was unable to reconcile the religious divisions that existed in the country. When the nobility took the lead as protectors of either Catholic or Huguenot (French Protestants who belonged to the Reformed Church of France in the Calvinist tradition) communities, and religious sentiment became linked to the political ambitions of the leading aristocratic families, the outcome was civil war. As well as inflicting all the horrors of such wars on the country – economic collapse, political chaos, violent death, starvation and homelessness – large numbers of the nobility were killed in battle, assassinated or executed and, eventually, two monarchs were murdered. No king had previously met this fate in France, unlike its northern neighbour, England.

By the time of the killing of Henry III in 1589 France had been in turmoil for almost thirty years. He was stabbed by a Dominican friar, Jacques Clément, while at St. Cloud, outside Paris, making final preparations for an attack on his own capital. He died of his wounds within twenty-four hours. Twenty-one years later Henry IV was killed by François Ravaillac who took his opportunity when the king's coach was held up by congestion in the Les Halles district of Paris. Both murderers insisted, even under torture, that they had acted alone, without any assistance from friends or group of conspirators. At the time few people believed these claims, but no wider conspiracy was ever proved in either case. However, even if this was the case, there is no doubt that the prevailing religious and political beliefs of the time had a major influence on the decision of these individuals to attempt the murder of the king. To understand the strength of feeling in late sixteenth and early seventeenth century France it is necessary to consider the key events and changing attitudes since 1559.

On the death of Henry II in July 1559, from injuries sustained ten days earlier in a jousting incident, when splinters from his opponent's shattered lance entered his forehead, the Valois dynasty looked secure. He and his wife, Catherine de' Medici, had ten children, five sons, the eldest Francis, followed by Louis, who died in infancy, Charles, Henry (originally christened Alexandre-Edouard but renamed Henry at his confirmation in 1565) and Hercule (who later changed his name to Francis on the death of his oldest brother), and five daughters, Elizabeth, Claude, Margaret, and twins Joan (stillborn) and Victoire, who died in infancy. Though Francis was only fifteen and not in good health at the time of his accession, he was already married to Mary, Queen of Scots, and there was no reason to suppose that he would not produce an heir and reign for many years. Even in the event of his early death without a son (daughters could not inherit) there were three brothers in place to succeed him.

However, it soon became clear that the regime needed monarchs like Francis I and Henry II, who had the capacity to appear all-powerful and gain the loyalty of the leading noble families. As it turned out none of Henry II's sons were able to accomplish that. Three of them became kings of France, but none of them were long-lived. Francis II died after only seventeen months on the throne in December 1560, resulting in Mary, Queen of Scots' departure back to Scotland. Charles IX, only ten on becoming king, died in May 1574, aged 23, to be succeeded by Henry III. Hercule (Francis), by then the heir presumptive, died in 1584, aged 29, and only Henry survived into his thirties, murdered at the age of 38. Most significantly, none produced a male heir, a fact that was to play a major part in the events leading up to Henry's assassination.

Although Francis II's reign was short, the problems that he faced were those that his brothers also had to deal with over the next thirty years. The two central issues were not new but they required strong and secure leadership to prevent them from getting out of control. Firstly, rivalry between the leading noble families – Guise, Bourbon and Montmorency. From which of these families should the king appoint those entrusted with the key positions of power? Secondly, the rapid spread of Protestantism during the 1540s and 1550s. The doctrines and organisational skills of John Calvin and his supporters exploited the weaknesses of an unreformed Catholic Church to gain many adherents, especially in the towns and amongst many of the lesser nobility who held political power in rural areas. Should this threat be dealt with by compromise or by persecution? During the 1550s Henry II had issued a series of edicts aiming to prevent the spread of Calvinist ideas and introducing severe punishments for heretics, but by 1560 there were perhaps two million Huguenots in France, including nearly half of the nobility. The question that faced his successors was should priority be given to uniformity of faith as insisted upon by many Catholics, a policy which became closely associated with the Guise family, or to freedom of worship as demanded by the Huguenots?

Over the following decades even these issues might have been resolved if the monarchy had taken a consistent approach. However, the changes of monarch, combined with their relative inexperience and lack of competence, resulted in vacillating policies. Patterns were repeated. The Guise family would be dominant, then temporarily out of favour at court, before being re-instated. The Huguenots fought to achieve limited rights of worship which would then be removed when Catholic zealots challenged royal power. The one constant figure, until her death, was the queen mother, Catherine de' Medici. She was determined to defend and if possible extend royal power, often by trying to find a middle way and take advantage of the divisions between the feuding nobility, but was never able to control the powerful forces of family ambitions and religious fervour.

In 1559 Francis, with his mother's agreement, handed power to the influential Guise family. Mary of Guise had married James V of Scotland, was the mother of Mary, Queen of Scots, Francis' wife, and the regent in Scotland. Her brother Francis, Duke of Guise, became Francis' military commander and head of the royal household, while their younger brother, Charles, Cardinal of Lorraine, controlled finance and justice. In February 1563 the duke was stabbed by a Huguenot assassin while besieging Orleans. He died six days later and his family and supporters took an oath promising to avenge his murder. His sons, Henry, the new Duke of Guise and Louis, the Cardinal of Guise, once they became of age, exercised considerable power. They believed that Admiral Gaspard de Coligny, a Huguenot political and military leader, a nephew of Anne de Montmorency, the aging Constable of France, was behind their father's murder. Montmorency, a Catholic loyal to the monarchy, opposed his nephew's leadership of the Huguenots, but defended him against such accusations, having no love of the Guises. Coligny was formally cleared of the charge but the Guises wished for revenge. The ensuing feud between the Guises and Coligny made peace even more difficult to achieve.

The Guises were often seen as the leaders of those Catholics who rejected any compromise on matters of religion even though at times, when it suited his political ends, Henry of Guise did advocate some moderation in the persecution of the Huguenots. Their power was resented by many in the country, like Montmorency, who regarded them as outsiders, not from the old French aristocracy, being from the House of Lorraine, which in the early sixteenth century was outside France. Claude of Lorraine, Henry's grandfather, distinguished himself commanding troops for Francis I and had been created Duke of Guise in 1527.

The other rivals of the Guises were the Bourbons. Three brothers were all significant figures in the events of the time. The eldest, Antoine of Bourbon, king of Navarre by virtue of his marriage to Jeanne d'Albret, was the first prince of the blood, who many believed should have become regent in 1559. He was side-lined by the Guises, but remained loyal to the monarchy. On the accession of Charles IX, he agreed to the regency of Catherine de' Medici. In return he was appointed Lieutenant-General of France. He commanded the royal armies in the First War of Religion (1562-63), dying of wounds sustained at the siege of Rouen in November 1562. His son, Henry of Navarre, born in 1553, was raised as a Protestant by his mother and married to the king's sister, Margaret of Valois, in 1572. He became King of Navarre and the leader of the French Huguenots in the later stages of the Wars of Religion.

Of Antoine's brothers, Charles entered the church, became the Cardinal of Bourbon and in the 1580s, became an ally of the Guises and the Catholic candidate to be the next king during the reign of the childless Henry III, in opposition to his nephew, Henry of Navarre. The youngest brother, Louis, Prince of Condé, was involved in a plot against the Guises in 1560, arrested, and then released by Catherine de' Medici on the death of Francis II. He became a leader of the Huguenot forces when the Wars of Religion broke out in 1562 and remained their commander until captured after defeat at the battle of Jarnac in March 1569. He was executed and his body paraded through the streets of Jarnac on the back of a donkey, probably on the orders of Henry of Anjou, who was to become King Henry III in 1574.

The French Wars of Religion were a series of conflicts, often merciless, of varying duration and geographical extent, over a period of more than thirty years, each concluded with a truce or peace agreement that settled very little and would soon be broken. Religion was an important causal factor, though it has been convincingly argued that the participants were fighting less over detailed theological doctrine but more to defend their own religious community, a 'body of believers'[1] and their own concept of a righteous society. While Catholics regarded the Huguenots as 'heretics', Huguenots considered Catholics to be 'superstitious idolaters'. These communities looked to their co-religionists amongst the nobility for political and military leadership. Most Catholics expected the monarch to rid the country of heresy, as kings were required to promise in their coronation oath. However, others who became known as the '*Politiques*' or 'United Catholics', believed the country required a strong monarchy that could rise above the religious divisions. Often higher officials who had traditionally worked for the monarchy, they were often anti-Guise, and were prepared to support the monarchy to achieve peace and national unity by granting Huguenots limited rights of worship in certain towns and communities.

At times both Catholics and Huguenots looked for support from foreign powers; the Catholics to Philip II of Spain and the Huguenots to their co-religionists in England, Germany and the Low Countries. Such agreements often conflicted with the crown's foreign policy objectives. Habsburg Spain was still considered a significant threat by many of the French nobility. For Philip II, a France weakened by civil war would be no position to interfere in Spain's problems in the Netherlands. On the other hand, any French alliance with England would provoke a strong reaction from Philip and increase his support for the Catholic pro-Guise faction. The details of the twists and turns of royal policy, frequently changing alliances, the national and local conflicts, the battles, assassinations, numerous peace agreements and betrayals of these years have been considered at length elsewhere[2] and here it is intended to give just a flavour of these events in order to cast light on the murders of two kings – Henry III and Henry IV.

In 1560 Francis II's death and the accession of the young Charles IX, with Catherine de' Medici as his regent, resulted in a sharp decline in the influence of the Guise family at court. In January 1562 Catherine attempted to bring about a compromise on the religious divisions in the country and avoid a civil war by issuing the Edict of St. Germain (Edict of January) which for the first time gave limited recognition to Huguenot worship. They held sway in much of southern and western France, although there were always significant Catholic enclaves ready to challenge them. The edict caused widespread unrest amongst Catholics, particularly in Paris, always a Catholic stronghold.

The Duke of Guise set off from his estate at Joinville to travel to Paris, with a considerable retinue, in order to increase Catholic pressure on Catherine. On the morning of 1 March, he attended mass at the local church in Vassy. Nearby, several hundred Calvinists were worshipping in a large barn. How the violence started is disputed, but the outcome was that the duke's soldiers fired on the unarmed worshippers, killing perhaps 50 and wounding 100 (the estimates vary considerably). The Duke was angered by the lack of discipline[3] and the unnecessary killing, but on his arrival in Paris he was cheered in the streets as the hero of Vassy. Meanwhile Huguenot leaders, led by Condé, announced their intention to defend their co-religionists and prepared for war. The first War of Religion had started.

As violence led to more violence, co-existence between Catholic and Huguenot communities became almost impossible. Already in 1562 Huguenots in Catholic towns started to be slaughtered and driven out, as in Tours and Sens. After Huguenots attempted to seize the *Hotel de Ville* in Toulouse, Catholic mobs took to the streets leaving 3,000, mainly Huguenots, dead. The Huguenots, not slow to respond, came to be viewed as violent heretics who had moved from image breakers to murderers of priests, likely at any time to carry out a massacre of Catholics. On capturing Lyons they destroyed all Catholic institutions in the city and killed anyone who attempted to stop them.

By the time Henry of Anjou became King Henry III in 1574 there had been four wars and the St. Bartholomew's Day Massacre, an episode that did even more to damage relations between the religious factions. During a period of relative peace following the third war, most of the leading Huguenot families had gathered in Paris for the marriage of Henry of Navarre and Margaret of Valois in August 1572. The marriage of the Huguenot leader and the daughter of Henry II and Catherine de' Medici was intended by Catherine to bring greater unity to the country. On 22 August, four days after the wedding, there was an unsuccessful attempt on the life of Admiral Coligny, a Huguenot leader, generally believed to have been instigated by the Guises. His supporters visited King Charles IX to demand justice, suggesting that they were prepared to take matters into their own hands if not satisfied. The following evening, fearing a violent Huguenot reaction, and later claiming that there was evidence of a Huguenot plot, Charles IX and his Council decided that they would end that threat by assassinating the fifty or so leading Huguenots then in Paris.

Before dawn on the following morning squads of soldiers were sent out to the houses where most of them were staying. One of the first to be killed, by a group led by Henry, Duke of Guise, was Admiral Coligny, whose body was thrown from a window, dragged through the streets and hanged on a public gibbet. The killing then turned into an unplanned general massacre of Protestants. The soldiers of Henry of Anjou, the king's brother, who had been posted to protect the Admiral and keep order in Paris, allowed Guise's men into the residence and made little effort to keep control elsewhere as mob violence swept through the capital, where perhaps 2,000 were killed. The violence spread to other towns and cities during the following weeks and many more thousands were murdered. Henry of Navarre, recently married to the king's sister, was only spared because he agreed to convert to Catholicism and remain at court. He renounced the pledge as soon as he was able to escape from Paris, over three years later. The Huguenot cause was seriously damaged by the loss of many leaders, though not destroyed. Their communities in the west and south of the country remained strong and prepared to defend themselves. The massacre had solved nothing except to diminish the moral and political reputation of the crown[4] and, in the eyes of the Huguenots, undermine the idea of a sacred monarchy.

With trust shattered, further wars could hardly be avoided. During the fourth war (1572–3) a large royal force led by Henry of Anjou failed to capture the city of La Rochelle, held by the Huguenots, in a siege lasting five months. This was followed by the death of Charles IX in 1574. Henry of Anjou, who had in the meantime been elected King of Poland and Grand-Duke of Lithuania, became King Henry III of France. He was deprived of his Polish-Lithuanian titles when he failed to return there after his coronation in France. Henry was unable to do any more than his predecessor to bring about a lasting peace, despite the efforts of his mother, Catherine de' Medici, to avoid further conflict. Fighting broke out with depressing regularity. Early in his reign the edict of Beaulieu (1576), signed on his behalf by Catherine de' Medici, made considerable concessions to the Huguenots, provoking a strong Catholic reaction, including the establishment of various leagues and associations which aimed to prevent the implementation of the edict. Henry himself believed that the concessions went too far and wished for a settlement that conceded less, though he would need to fight to achieve this. Even then many Catholics opposed any concessions at all. His wish for peace and religious unity, supported by moderates on both sides of the religious divide, had the effect of turning the more extreme factions on both sides in the conflict against him. However, starting in 1580, at the end of the seventh war, there was a period of relative peace.

This could not be expected to last and by 1585 hostilities were renewed, leading to the eighth war, which become known as the 'War of the Three Henrys'. The three Henrys involved were King Henry III, Henry of Navarre and Henry, Duke of Guise. The crisis was sparked by the death of Henry III's brother, Francis, of tuberculosis in June 1584. Since Henry's accession, Francis, who had succeeded him as Duke of Anjou though he was often referred to as '*Monsieur*', a formal recognition of his position as the second prince of the kingdom, had been the heir presumptive. Henry III had married Louise of Lorraine in 1575, two days after his coronation, but as yet they had no children. Although the king certainly had affairs in his early married life, the couple were close. Henry had for some time been desperately concerned for the future of the Valois dynasty. Was this divine punishment for his sins or his failure to eradicate heresy from his realm? He had undertaken pilgrimages and spiritual retreats in the hope that God would bless them with a child – to no avail.

Henry III's relationship with his younger brother had been difficult. Francis (or '*Monsieur*') frustrated by his lack of power, had caused problems for the king. He had headed the group of 'malcontents' at court, had been a suitor of the much older Queen Elizabeth I, had called for the removal of 'foreigners' (the Guises) from important roles in government, and agreed to support the largely Protestant rebels in the Low Countries against their Spanish rulers, defying Henry and Catherine de' Medici. However, Francis's death created a much greater problem. The new heir presumptive, according to the Salic Laws, was Henry of Navarre, the leader of the Huguenots. The principle of agnatic succession, a tenet of the Salic Laws, excluded females from inheriting the throne and forbade inheritance through a female line. Henry was directly descended from King Louis IX (1226-1270), often referred to as Saint Louis, through ten generations of the male line. Catholics throughout France were alarmed at this turn of events, the more so when Navarre refused to come to court and abandon his faith as requested by the king.

CHAPTER 8

THE DEATH OF A TYRANT? THE END OF THE VALOIS MONARCHY

In September 1584 Henry, Duke of Guise, his brothers, Charles, Duke of Mayenne and Louis, Cardinal of Guise, together with other Catholic grandees, founded a Catholic League, with the aim of preventing Henry of Navarre ever becoming king. Philip II of Spain also wished to prevent this outcome. His main objective was to prevent any French support for the Protestant rebels in the Spanish controlled Netherlands. Philip had to decide between three possible approaches – direct armed intervention, working with Henry III, or a secret deal with French Catholics. The former would be very expensive. Henry was regarded as unreliable, and so he chose the third option. By the end of the year the Treaty of Joinville had been signed with Henry of Guise, undertaking to defend the Catholic faith and destroy Protestantism in France and the Low Countries. The treaty also recognised Charles, Cardinal of Bourbon, Navarre's uncle, as the rightful heir to the throne, arguing that the coronation oath required the king to be a Catholic and that this, as God's law, took precedence over the Salic Law. It was understood that when the Cardinal of Bourbon became king he would follow a pro-Spanish foreign policy. Spain would provide substantial funds within six months of the start of an armed uprising, to be repaid once Bourbon was King Charles X.[1]

Henry III's actions had antagonised many of his subjects. Huguenots distrusted him for his leadership of royal armies against them in the earlier Wars of Religion and for failing to enforce the concessions granted to them. Many Catholics criticised him for failing to wipe out heresy. A large section of the nobility were angered by his giving increasing rewards, both financial and influence over government policy, to a group of young men, the *mignons*, who often came from the lesser nobility, at the expense of those of superior rank. *Mignon* originally meant companion, but it became a pejorative term when applied to Henry's favourites. He preferred to spend more time with them, sometimes leaving court to go to a country retreat with a selected few, and access to him was made more difficult, both to those at court and to the population as a whole by his unwillingness to be constantly on the move around the country as was traditional for the monarch. Rumours began to circulate, often initiated by those who considered themselves excluded from power, about the nature of his relationship with these young men, especially given his failure to produce an heir. In Henry's later years he increasing came to depend upon two of the *mignon*, Jean-Louis de La Valette and Anne de Joyeuse, Baron d'Arques, who became Duke of Épernon and Duke of Joyeuse, respectively, in 1581.

It came to be believed that his court was a place of extravagance and decadence, of licentious and debauched behaviour, tolerated and even encouraged by a king, who many considered to be weak, idle and luxury loving. There is no doubt that Henry did enjoy brightly coloured, extravagant clothes, jewellery, dancing, theatre, tournaments, fencing, tennis, cards and dice games, and that his behaviour could sometimes be regarded as odd, such as his insistence on wearing a bonnet in his apartments[2] and his love of lap dogs. Much the same could be said about many monarchs of the time, but in Henry's case such behaviour provided material for rumours and gossip that undermined his authority. He could be moody, proud, and vindictive but he had many positive qualities that are rarely mentioned either in writings at the time or in later histories. It is only recently that his reputation has been somewhat restored by historians who have pointed out that he was hard-working, witty, intelligent, cultivated, and a good public speaker. There is no substantive evidence of homosexual relationships – occasionally dressing up in women's clothing was not unusual amongst kings of the sixteenth century.

There were a number of ways in which Henry could deal with the problem created by Navarre becoming heir presumptive. He could attempt to persuade him to convert to Catholicism, he could side with the Catholic League, deny Navarre's right to the throne and declare war on the Huguenots, or he could ally with Navarre. Between 1584 and 1589 he tried all three approaches. His preference was to avoid war and for Navarre to abandon his Protestant faith. The Duke of Épernon was sent to Gascony in the early summer of 1584 and had several meetings with Navarre with no positive outcome. Henry's problem was that news of talks with their enemy, the heretics, inflamed Catholic opinion. By early 1585 supporters of the Catholic League were gathering weapons and mobilising troops. In the Declaration of Peronne, issued on 31 March 1585, they stated that 'the reign of a heretic could never be accepted', and called upon all Catholic noblemen, towns and communities to 'take arms so that the Holy Church of God should be restored to its place as the true and only religion'. They criticised the influence of the *mignon* and the *Politiques*, for 'diverting the King from his holy and most useful intention ... to reunite all his subjects to a sole Catholic religion' and for weakening 'the authority of the Catholic princes and lords' who should rightly be advising the king. They also called for the abolition of all new taxes since 1574.[3] While declaring their loyalty to the king, hoping that his 'descendants reign happily after him', the declaration was a serious challenge to Henry.

Henry III responded by arguing that he had been refused the necessary funds to be able to fight the Huguenots, that he had restored Catholic worship in several towns and that he objected to the succession being discussed as if he and the queen were of no importance. He claimed that he had made appointments on merit, and asked whether 'private interests ... should be the cause of troubling a whole estate, and replenishing the same with blood and desolation?' In other words, he all but accused Guise and his followers of putting their own personal interests above that of the country. He called upon them to 'withdraw themselves from all leagues and associations and to reunite themselves unto him' and exhorted 'the captains of the said risings speedily to disperse their bands.'[4]

His statement had little impact. The Catholic League soon had control of most of northern, central and eastern France with only areas in the south and west remaining loyal to the king. Henry hired Swiss troops who could move to defend Paris, a city whose loyalty was already in doubt, if it was attacked. When Catherine de' Medici began negotiations on the king's behalf, Guise made increasing demands as his position strengthened. Eventually, in July 1585, the treaty of Nemours was agreed. Guise took control of more towns and his supporters were rewarded. Henry even had to agree to pay for troops hired by his opponents. The subsequent edict on religion banned Protestant worship and gave Huguenots six months to abandon their faith or leave the country. In reply Navarre and Condé (the son of Louis, Prince of Condé, executed at Jarnac in 1569) affirmed their determination that Protestantism should be defended. They made an alliance with the moderate Catholics, led by Henry Damville-Montmorency, and renewed their promise to allow Catholics freedom of worship. Meanwhile Pope Sixtus V issued a papal bull which deprived Henry of Navarre, who was referred to as the enemy of the true faith and a notorious heretic, of any right to the throne, and stated that anyone showing obedience to him would be excommunicated. In October 1585 a further royal edict declared the Huguenots, and their allies, traitors and they were given just two weeks to convert or leave.

Outright war was now inevitable, even though King Henry was still hoping to avoid it. Catherine de' Medici sent her representative to meet Navarre in the Huguenot stronghold of La Rochelle over the summer of 1586 with little success. The Duke of Guise, the Cardinal of Bourbon and the Cardinal of Guise, decided that they would turn down any proposed peace settlement. Henry III realised that unless he led troops against the Huguenots he would never win over Guise and the Catholic League. In January 1587, at a meeting of princes, nobles and men of substance in Paris, he announced the failure of talks with Navarre, despite the unceasing work of his aging mother, and that he had decided to fight. This was met with 'cries of joy and acclamations' but when he continued that he would require a subsidy of 600,000 *ecus* from the Parisians they became angry.[5]

In 1584 Catholics zealots in Paris had formed a secret association. Its leaders became known as *les Seize* (the Sixteen), after the 16 districts of the city. Feeling was running high in the capital, other major cities, and indeed much of the country. The price of bread had increased rapidly during the previous ten years; taxes were rising; the depredations of war were being felt in many regions; justice was considered to be ineffective. Early in 1587 the Sixteen plotted to take control of key points of the capital, but the plan collapsed when the king was warned by a spy in their midst. Catholics throughout France were then outraged when news of the execution of Mary, Queen of Scots in England reached France. Numerous abusive pamphlets denouncing Queen Elizabeth and her Huguenot allies were circulated, Mary was seen as a martyr while King Henry was accused of failing to protect his sister-in-law, the former queen of France, or to avenge her death. His reputation sunk even further. For much of the year there were disturbances in the streets of Paris.

Henry was also facing an invasion of eastern France by a combination of German mercenaries, Swiss troops and some French soldiers, led by John Casimir, regent of the Palatinate, in support of the Huguenots. In July 1587 he met the Duke of Guise and they agreed to work together, even though Guise refused to make any concessions to the Huguenots and was reported to have commented to the Spanish ambassador that he regarded Philip II 'to be the father of all Catholics and of myself in particular'.[6] King Henry and his advisers devised a plan which he hoped would defeat the Huguenots and give him, rather than Guise, the glory. One army, with his best troops led by Joyeuse, would fight Navarre in the south-west. Guise would be given the role of harassing John Casimir's army in the east with insufficient troops, while Henry, with a large force, stationed himself on the Loire to prevent the invaders from linking up with the Huguenots. He expected success for Joyeuse and himself, while Guise would be seen to have achieved little.

It did not work out that way. In October, Navarre crushed Joyeuse's army at the battle of Coutras, with numerous royalist casualties, including Joyeuse himself and 300 noblemen. Navarre, however, failed to take advantage of the victory. Meanwhile, Casimir's army failed to cross the Loire and gradually disintegrated. The German troops, who had set off on their own, were defeated twice by Guise during the autumn. The duke was deprived of the chance to destroy them completely when in December they surrendered to Henry and agreed to leave France. The king also came to an agreement with the Swiss troops who he paid to return home. Although great celebrations were held in Paris, with Henry at their centre, it was said that the crowds had to be bribed to shout *'Vive le Roi'* and preachers praised the duke. Guise, to his anger, was excluded from the triumph. The king, showing no regard to popular sentiment, then appointed the hated Duke of Épernon not only to the posts previously held by the deceased Joyeuse, but also to the governorship of Normandy, usually handed to princes of the blood. These acts were said by the contemporary Catholic historian, Etienne Pasquier, to have lost the king more noblemen than on the battlefield of Coutras. Catholic League propagandists produced large numbers of pamphlets against Épernon and the king. It was hardly surprising that both Paris and Guise's base in Soissons became hotbeds of opposition to the king.

Paris was on the point of insurrection. In late April 1588 the king's spy in the Sixteen reported another plot to seize control of the city. Henry had already increased his personal bodyguard in 1584, when he appointed forty-five loyal young noblemen to protect him around the clock, fifteen on each shift. He now further strengthened security at the Louvre and ordered the Swiss troops in his pay to move to the Paris suburbs. He also forbade Guise to come to Paris. Guise wished to protect his supporters in the capital but to go to Paris would be nothing less than rebellion. Nevertheless he went and called upon Catherine de' Medici, declaring his wish for a reconciliation. On 9 May 1588 they visited the king together at the Louvre. At first angry, Henry was placated by his mother's reassurances. On leaving, Guise was greeted as a hero in the streets.

Talks continued with little progress, but the duke now had troops almost at the walls of Paris. The king ordered Swiss and French Guards into the city in a bid to control the situation, probably planning to round up Guise's supporters. This broke the long understanding that the Parisian militia would be responsible for their own defence and not have foreign troops stationed there. Large crowds began to gather and Catherine asked Guise to disperse them. He disingenuously replied that he had no power over them and that only the magistrates who controlled the militia could do so. On the night of 11–12 May the Parisians began to erect barricades of overturned carts, doors, barrels filled with sand or stone. The following day became known as the 'Day of the Barricades'. The king ordered his troops back to the Louvre but many were constrained by the barricades. Guise had to be asked to secure their safe passage, which he did, but at the same time ordered more soldiers of the Catholic League to come to Paris, all the while claiming that he was acting in the king's name. The next day he received Catherine de' Medici and demanded full-scale war against Henry of Navarre, immediate implementation of the decrees against the Huguenots, the dismissal of Épernon, and his appointment, along with other family members, to various governorships.

By the time that Catherine realised that there could be no agreement, Henry III, escorted by his Swiss troops, had already departed Paris using the only gate left unguarded, the Porte Neuve. He travelled to Chartres from where he could negotiate without danger of being held captive. Guise secured his control of Paris and nearby towns by appointing his supporters to key posts. Henry at first resisted Guise's demands but eventually, encouraged by Catherine, he signed the Edict of Union in August 1588. This gave Guise all he wished for, including his appointment as commander of the royal armies. Nevertheless, Henry still intended to regain the initiative. There were to be elections to the Estates-General, the national body representing the three social classes (estates) – nobility, clergy and commoners. He hoped that when those who were elected met in Blois in the autumn he would have enough backing to alter the situation. He was to be disappointed. The majority were League supporters and each estate selected a chairman who was loyal to Guise. The duke himself was the Grand Master, who sat immediately below the king.

Having arrived in Blois Henry proceeded to sack all his ministers, many of whom owed their position to Catherine de' Medici. He wished to demonstrate his independence and show that there could be a fresh start with Catholic men of experience and loyalty to him. His opening speech at the Estates-General on 16 October was combative, emphasising his authority. He said that he wished 'to extirpate heresy from the provinces of this kingdom, to re-establish good order, to relieve the poor people who are so greatly oppressed, and to raise up my own authority, which is now so unjustly abased...' He declared that all leagues and associations should have his permission and that 'subjects who do not leave them or get involved in them without my consent will be tainted and convicted of the crime of treason.'[7] He did, however, assure the assembly that he had no intention of allowing a heretic to succeed him if 'it should happen that God leaves us in such misfortune that I have no descendants'.

Despite this, the actions of the Estates-General provided very little reassurance for the king. The Third Estate (who paid most of the taxes) wished him to reduce his expenditure and would only agree small sums being granted to him. He once again argued that he was being asked to fight the Huguenots without being provided with the means with which to do so. He was offended when he was required to retake his oath to abide by the Edict of Union, implying that he couldn't be trusted. He had a number of conversations with Henry of Guise, after some of which he was said to have been furious. However, on 22 December after a stormy first meeting in the gardens of the chateau of Blois, a second one, in Catherine de' Medici's chamber, seemed to be more conciliatory. Henry asked Guise to attend a Council meeting the following day but explained that he himself would not be there as he was leaving for a day in the countryside. This turned out to be part of a carefully orchestrated plan to assassinate the duke.

Guise had received several warnings that an attempt might be made on his life but had dismissed them all, saying that if he took notice of all such threats he would never get anything done. Perhaps he did not believe that the king would dare to carry out such an act. If so, he was wrong. Henry III had been pushed too far. While the king waited in a neighbouring room, Guise arrived for the Council meeting early on the morning of 23 December. He was then quietly informed that the king wished to see him in his bedchamber. This, of course, meant that he had no guard with him as they were not permitted to enter the king's personal rooms. Awaiting him were some of Henry's bodyguard, the Forty-five, who immediately killed him. Meanwhile, in the council chamber Guise's brother, the Cardinal of Guise, was seized. Henry ordered his execution and he was hacked to death the following morning, after which both bodies were dismembered, burned and the ashes scattered to the winds.[8] The Cardinal of Bourbon, the League's chosen heir, other noblemen and some members of the Paris Sixteen in Blois at the time were imprisoned.

Henry claimed to the papal legate that these actions were in self-defence, necessary to foil a plot to depose and kill him, but was told that he had committed a very grave error. He then sought and received absolution from a confessor of his own choice. He told his mother what he had done saying that: 'I have forestalled him in the plot which he had conceived against me. I could no longer tolerate his insolence ... I wish to be king, not a prisoner or a slave as I have been since 13 May.'[9] She realised that the murder was unlikely to bring about peace, as was made clear in her last interview with her old friend, the Cardinal of Bourbon, still in captivity. He told her that her frequent negotiations and concessions had been responsible for the situation. She died on 5 January 1589, aged 69. Born in 1519 in Florence, married when 14 years old, queen consort of France between 1547 and 1559, she had for the last thirty years worked to support her sons as kings of France. She must have died a very disappointed woman. It was reported that she had told Henry: 'You have killed two men who have left a lot of friends'[10].

She was proved to be correct. Royal authority was widely flouted. The Duke of Mayenne, Guise's younger brother, became the commander of the League's army, along with the Duke of Aumale, who was appointed governor of Paris. They set about capturing towns held by royal forces and in other cities supporters of the Catholic League were able to seize control. Thus places such as Le Havre, Amiens, Rouen, Chartres, Orleans, Marseilles, Arles, Agen, and Poitiers, many of which had not supported the League before, were lost by the king. Although a considerable number of the conservative nobility still preferred Henry to what they regarded as the extremists of the League, they retired to their estates and the king's position deteriorated rapidly. He also faced the wrath of the Church for the murder of a cardinal. In May 1589 he received an instruction from Pope Sixtus V to free the Cardinal of Bourbon and other clerics within ten days, and appear in Rome (or send a representative) to explain himself within sixty days, on pain of excommunication.

Henry needed to take drastic action. His only remaining option was to come to terms with Henry of Navarre. The Huguenot leader explained his decision to support the king by announcing that as 'first prince of the blood and the first peer of France' he wished to defend the crown and the king's person, appealing to all Frenchmen to do the same.[11] In April 1589 they signed a pact, to last for one year, agreeing to join forces to fight 'those who violate His Majesty's authority and trouble his state', in other words, the Catholic League. It restored Huguenot rights that had been removed over the previous four years and gave them additional towns. Navarre promised 'not in any place through which he passes ... to change or permit to be changed anything concerning the Catholic religion' while Henry stated that he hoped that Navarre would convert to Catholicism soon. They planned a joint campaign to re-capture Paris. In July their forces advanced, aiming to cut off the city's supplies, with Navarre commanding the vanguard.

The atmosphere in Paris was violently hostile to King Henry. Fiery pamphlets were being produced and distributed in large numbers.

These, together with sermons and other tracts, were increasingly radical in nature. For centuries the kings of France had an almost sacred status. The coronation ceremony with the anointing and crowning of the monarch gave the king a unique position amongst men, demonstrating God's approval and demanding his subjects' loyalty and obedience. In some countries this had been undermined, such as in England which had witnessed the murders of Edward II, Richard II and Henry VI, but in France no such challenge existed until the mid-sixteenth century. The 'Most Christian King' received God's special favour because he promised in his coronation oath to remove heresy from his kingdom. He had failed to do so. The pope's condemnation of Henry III was widely publicised in Paris

Catholics now forcefully argued that Henry III had broken both his contract with God and that with his people. The king, they claimed, could not ignore the law. The idea that the people had the right to remove a tyrant was openly discussed. As early as 7 January 1589, the professors of the Sorbonne announced 'That the people of this realm are released and delivered from the oath of loyalty and obedience made to King Henry' and 'That this same people may legally and with a safe conscience be armed and united, gather funds and contribute for the defence of the Apostolic and Roman Church against wicked devises and efforts of the said King and his adherents'.[12] They were effectively calling for his deposition. The Duke of Guise's sister, Mme. de Montpensier, had her preachers in Paris openly declare King Henry a heretic and a tyrant. All kinds of insults and scurrilous rumours about him were spoken and printed. Many of them were unfounded but this did not prevent them stirring up Catholic opinion to a fever pitch. Public images and portraits of the king and queen were defaced or destroyed.

If the Huguenots had started the attack on the sacred right of the king to determine their faith, the Leaguers took things much further. In the spring of 1589 one of the founding members of the Sixteen, the influential preacher and Sorbonne theologian, Jean Boucher, was writing what became the best-known exposition of their arguments. He asked whether it was just and lawful for firstly the Church and secondly the people to depose Henry III, and followed this by asking whether it was just and lawful for the people to take up arms and even kill the tyrant before a formal act of deposition was received from the Pope. His answer to all three questions was a resounding 'Yes', as might be determined from the title of his work, *The Just Deposition of Henry III*. Individuals, he argued, were justified, even required, to take up arms to remove a tyrant who violated God's laws by permitting heresy, recognising a heretic as his heir and being responsible for the murder of the Guises.[13]

As Henry III and Navarre's joint army of over 30,000 closed in on the capital, anti-Valois sentiments increased as the hardships of the population grew. By the end of July food supplies for the population of 300,000 were running low. The militia, aided by volunteers who provided their own weapons, were responsible for manning the walls and guarding the fourteen gates, but would they be able to withstand a major assault even if backed up by the League's army, which had already failed to stop the king's advance? Calls for the killing of the Henry III, regarded by many as an agent of Satan, were frequently heard. The king himself was now based at St Cloud, just to the west of Paris, occupying a first-floor room in a large mansion, with his Forty-five nearby, while Navarre's headquarters were at Meudon, just to the south of St. Cloud. Not surprisingly there had been warnings of various plots to kill the king over the previous couple of months.

In late July Jacques Clément, who was studying at the Dominican order's house in the rue Saint-Jacques, whose members were therefore often called 'Jacobins', managed to contact a royalist army captain being held captive in the Louvre, Charles of Luxembourg, Comte de Brienne. Although regarded as eccentric and scatter-brained by his fellow students, Clément persuaded the captain that he wished to leave the capital and join the king's side. Brienne provided him with a pass of safe conduct that would allow him to travel to Orleans without being arrested by royal forces. On 31 July Clément left Paris and then walked to St. Cloud accompanied by some Huguenot soldiers. He made contact with Jacques de Guesle, one of the king's attorneys, and told him that he had an important document from royalist supporters in Paris to deliver to the king. This concerned plans to have one of the gates in the walls of Paris opened for the king's soldiers to enter. The details, he said, were for the king's eyes only. Under interrogation he convinced de Guesle of his sincerity.

The following morning he accompanied de Guesle to the royal headquarters and they were escorted upstairs to the king's apartment by Pierre du Halde, a member of the king's personal household. Henry was sitting on his close-stool (commode) as they entered. Clément requested a private word with the king. The others present withdrew and Clément approached the king and lent forward as if to speak quietly to him. He then drew out a dagger and stuck it into Henry's lower abdomen. Clément was immediately seized by the king's attendants who wished to capture him alive for interrogation, but as the guards rushed in he was cut down and killed. As a result it has been impossible to determine whether he had acted alone or as part of a wider conspiracy. Such was the febrile atmosphere around the country, especially in Paris, that it is perfectly believable that an unstable individual, influenced by the propaganda leaflets and outspoken sermons of the time, might wish to become a martyr and make an attempt on the king's life. On the other hand, such a person might also be easily manipulated, encouraged and aided by others to do so. The leaders of the Catholic League had not explicitly called for Henry's murder but they had created a situation in which someone might attempt it.

Initially it seemed that Henry might survive. Over the next few hours he dictated numerous letters to his wife, to foreign dignitaries and to close advisers. Navarre visited him during the late morning and, reassured that the wound was slight, soon departed. In some of his letters Henry states that it was God's will that he had survived. However, during the afternoon and evening his condition worsened. The stab wound had cut into the intestine and its contents had entered the bowel cavity, causing peritonitis. This may have been made worse by his doctors' decision to purge his bowels.[14] The king died early the following morning. Narratives of his last hours are inconsistent and unreliable because they were written to match the political standpoints of their authors. It is claimed in some accounts that one of his last acts was to name Henry of Navarre as his successor, though stating that he would only become king if he became a Catholic. Other accounts, however, make no mention of this. We will never know for certain. As he neared death it is said that his confessor at first refused to absolve him of his sins because he had yet to meet the pope's demands, but after Henry promised that he had always been a true Catholic, said that he wished 'to die in the bosom of the Catholic apostolic Roman church' and prayed 'My God, have pity on me and forgive my sins', he received absolution. His death brought to an end the male line of the House of Valois which had ruled France for over 250 years. What remained unclear was who would succeed him.

CHAPTER 9

HENRY IV AND THE NEW DYNASTY

lthough Henry III's murder was immediately recognised as having dramatically altered the political landscape, and few regretted the death of the king, no-one questioned the institution of the monarchy. In Paris, rather than shock at the murder, there were celebrations. There was widespread support for the Catholic League's proclamation of Charles, Cardinal of Bourbon as King Charles X, even though he was still being held prisoner in Chinon under the control of Henry of Navarre. In November the *Parlement* of Paris, the highest court of law in France, recognised Charles as king. They could not possibly consent to a Huguenot monarch, and argued that even if Henry did convert to Catholicism, it could not be accepted because he had done so once before in 1572 after the St. Bartholomew's Day Massacre and renounced his conversion as soon as he was free to do so, making him a lapsed heretic and thus beyond the pale. The publication of Boucher's '*The Just Deposition of Henry III*' was followed by many other pamphlets and sermons justifying Clément's actions. The assassination was presented as divine intervention to protect Paris and Clément was regarded by many as a martyr, dying to protect the Catholic faith.

Naturally not everyone agreed with this point of view. Queen Louise did not believe that Clément had acted alone and pressed Henry of Navarre to bring anyone involved in the plot to justice. The prior of the Dominicans in Paris, Francois Bourgoing, who had celebrated the murder from the pulpit, was seized and taken to Tours, the temporary royalist capital, to face trial. Although he denied encouraging Clément to kill the king he was found guilty and executed by being tortured, drawn and quartered in February 1590. Several other priests who had also praised Clément's murder of the king suffered a similar fate.

Henry of Navarre worked quickly to assert his claim to the throne. To his Protestant army he was now Henry IV, king of France and Navarre, the rightful heir under the Salic Laws and acknowledged as such by the former king. But Henry knew that he could only rely on the loyalty of less than a quarter of the country, mainly in the south. He needed the backing of those in the Catholic nobility and their followers who had remained loyal to Henry III. Although a Huguenot, if he was to be king of France, a largely Catholic nation, he would have to defend Catholic rights too. Even though he rejected the initial demands of the negotiators, that he immediately renounce his faith, ban all Protestant worship in France, and make only Catholic appointments, by 4 August an agreement had been reached. They accepted his assurances that he would protect the Catholic faith, take religious instruction with a view to conversion, punish those who were responsible for Henry III's murder, and ensure that all towns captured from the League would remain under Catholic control. He also agreed that they could send a representative to Rome in order to explain their decision to the pope. In return, they accepted the right of Huguenots to worship in places that they now held until a final settlement could be reached.

Not all of the former king's commanders and troops were willing to accept this arrangement. Some abandoned their posts and joined the League's army. Others, such as Epernon, who had gained favour and high office under the dead king, and were thus hated by the League, were not yet willing to trust the Huguenots and departed for their estates. Even some Huguenots left, dismayed by Henry's willingness to consider conversion and the readiness with which he came to terms with the moderate Catholics. Henry IV was left with a force of barely half the size of the original combined army which had besieged Paris and, unable to continue the siege, he withdrew to Normandy. The Duke of Mayenne, brother of the murdered Duke of Guise, led the League's army in pursuit. He was confident of victory and refused all offers of negotiation but his numerically superior army was repelled by Henry IV in September at Arques, near Dieppe and then heavily defeated at Ivry in March 1590. Henry himself was in the thick of the fighting, almost captured at Arques and at one point rumoured to have been killed at Ivry. These defeats of the League's army, though by no means bringing about its dissolution, made it less likely that those moderate Catholics who had so far remained out of the fray would respond to its call for support.

Henry then moved back towards Paris. He took towns to the north and east of the capital in order to block the main routes by which it was provisioned. This also meant that he would have troops in position to hamper any relief forces that Mayenne could bring in from the north or that the Spanish might send from the Low Countries. Henry's artillery was set up at Montmartre overlooking the city, flour mills were destroyed and there were reports of Henry's troops firing on women and children who risked their lives by foraging outside the walls. Food prices in Paris rose rapidly, despite rationing, and perhaps as many as 40,000 died of hunger or disease. By July Henry expected the city to capitulate but, despite the great hardships, the city would not surrender and Henry failed to break through its defences. Mayenne's troops and a Spanish army from the Netherlands led by Alexander Farnese, Duke of Parma, the nephew of Philip II, joined forces in late August and advanced on Paris. Henry IV, who was always struggling to pay his soldiers and the Swiss mercenaries that he employed, did not have sufficient troops to both continue the siege and fight the relief army. After the failure of a final assault on the walls he withdrew.

However, the League's position was seriously weakened by the death of Charles, Cardinal of Bourbon, their King Charles X, in May 1590 while still a prisoner. There was no plausible alternative candidate. Some argued for Charles, the young son of the deceased Duke of Guise, whose ancestry could be traced back to Charlemagne. Others preferred the experience of his uncle, the Duke of Mayenne, though he had already lost the confidence of many as a result of his defeats at the hands of Henry IV. Another group, encouraged by Philip II and his ambassadors, wished to have Isabella Clara Eugenia, Philip's daughter by his third wife, Elizabeth of Valois, Henry III's sister, on the throne. None of these gained widespread support and no strong candidate emerged.

Meanwhile the war continued with both sides calling in foreign assistance. The Spanish provided funds for the Catholic League and the Duke of Parma's army gave military support when required. Henry IV looked to England and the Protestant rebels against Spanish rule in the Netherlands. In 1591 Henry IV and Elizabeth I agreed to a joint attack on Rouen, with the Earl of Essex commanding the English forces. Elizabeth hoped that the capture of the city would mean that she would be able to recoup the substantial sums that she had already lent the new king. The initial assault failed and so from November 1591 Rouen was besieged. The population suffered greatly but the garrison held out until Parma's troops marched across northern France and relieved the city in April 1592. Henry was slightly wounded when the cavalry unit that he was leading came into contact with the vanguard of the Spanish army. When criticised for not pressing home his advantage and perhaps capturing the enemy leader, Parma is reputed to have commented that he believed that he was dealing with a general of an army not a 'mere captain of light horse, as he perceived the king of Navarre was'.[1] Parma's disdain for French commanders was not confined to his enemies. He had doubts about the wisdom of his instructions to leave the Netherlands, where his troops were already having serious problems against the Dutch rebels, in order to intervene in France. Of the leaders of the Catholic League, his allies, he commented that they had 'no other view but to enrich themselves and promote their own private interests without any regard for the public good'. Although the siege of Rouen had been lifted, his army was seriously pressed by Henry while returning to the Netherlands. Having previously taken numerous treatments at Spa for oedema, Parma himself suffered wounds that further damaged his already precarious health. He died in December 1592, aged 47, before receiving news of his dismissal as Governor of the Netherlands.

Throughout France the long-standing problems of a growing population and ever-increasing prices had been made worse by decades of civil war. Armies lived off the land, taking what provisions they required in the countryside and sacking towns, causing widespread distress. There was an increasing readiness to support anyone who could bring about peace. Although Henry IV was slowly making progress in securing more towns and areas of the country, he could not take Paris. Even there, though, divisions were becoming apparent. The Sixteen, fearing that the city would eventually be surrendered, attempted to secure it by carrying out a purge of anyone who they suspected of supporting Henry IV or even considering negotiations with him. Three leading members of the *Parlement* were hanged and a list of other possible victims was drawn up. These measures met with the disapproval of the nobility and the population as a whole. Mayenne returned to Paris and took action. Four leaders of the Sixteen were hanged and other fled.

With an open rift in the Catholic League, widespread social disorder, and uprisings caused by the harsh economic conditions in several parts of the country, many had come to the conclusion that the wars must end and Henry IV be accepted as king. The stumbling block remained his religion. Although back in 1589 he had agreed to take instruction with a view to conversion, he had not yet done so, claiming that he wished to be seen to be doing so of his own free will rather than as a result of the coercion of his enemies. By early 1593 events slowly started to move towards a conclusion. Mayenne summoned a meeting of the Estates-General in Paris in order to choose a new monarch and asked Catholics who supported Henry to send representatives. Although Henry contested the legality of the assembly, he also issued an invitation to League Catholics to discuss how a reconciliation could be achieved, which they accepted in Mayenne's absence in February.

On hearing details of the debates about the selection of a new monarch, Henry was worried about the discussion of the marriage of the Spanish princess, Isabella Clara Eugenia, to a French prince of the blood, in particular his ambitious young cousin, Charles, Cardinal of Vendome. However, there were strong objections in the Estates-General to the pressure exerted by the Spanish ambassador. The proposal was formally rejected. The Estates-General, however, still considered members of the Guise family, either Mayenne or Duke Charles, as possibilities, but they were regarded by some as outsiders from Lorraine. The Paris *Parlement* announced its refusal to accept a 'foreign prince'.

Henry's Catholic adviser, Francis d'O, now told him that this was the perfect time to fulfil his commitment to convert, saying that he could 'gain more in an hour at Mass than you have in twenty victories and twenty years of perilous labours.'[2] On 16 May, having gained assurances that his Catholic supporters would respect the rights of Huguenots, he announced his intention to meet leading Catholic churchmen the following month. First at Mantes and then at St. Denis, just outside Paris, he received instruction in the Catholic faith. On 25 July 1593, at the abbey of St. Denis, the burial place of French monarchs, he abjured Calvinism and was received into the Roman Catholic Church. He had invited all of Paris to witness the occasion, and ensured that those who came would see a great spectacle. He was careful, however, not to explicitly condemn his former religion. The remaining difficulty was that the pope had yet to lift the earlier excommunication, but it was hoped that Pope Clement VIII would accept the *fait accompli*. This was eventually to be the case but it took two years before he reluctantly did so, believing that Henry's conversion was less about religious conviction than political expediency. He might well have regretted his decision when Henry IV issued the Edict of Nantes in 1598, but by then Henry had secured his kingdom.

Although there was still some resistance from die-hard Leaguers, Henry IV's route to victory was now open. He was crowned on 27 February 1594, though in Chartres not Reims the traditional place of coronation as it was still controlled by his enemies. He next needed to gain control of Paris. Mayenne had left to join a Spanish army on the French border and appointed a long-standing client of his, Charles de Cosse-Brissac as governor of the city. Brissac quickly opened negotiations with Henry. Brissac was to receive a large pension and made a Marshal of France in return for arranging Henry's entry to the capital. Elements of the militia thought most hostile to Henry were sent out of Paris on various pretexts and Henry was to enter through the Porte Neuve in the west, furthest from the Spanish troops based near the Bastille in the east. On 22 March Henry entered Paris through the very gate that the previous king of France, Henry III, had fled on the Day of the Barricades, nearly six years before. His troops immediately took key buildings and bridges, while others arriving by boat entered the Latin Quarter. Crowds turned out to welcome the king whom they had held out against for years. Henry headed for Notre Dame, where he celebrated Mass and then on to the Louvre, where he had last resided in 1576 before his escape from court. The Spanish troops were offered and accepted safe conduct and an amnesty was proclaimed for all citizens, with the exception of a list of 120 individuals announced two days later, most of whom had already left with the Spanish.

This policy of payments, pensions and new appointments to officials willing to capitulate, amnesty to most of those who had fought against him, formal visits and promises of reconciliation, won over many of the towns and cities of northern France that had previously rejected him. Many of Henry's leading opponents gradually came to terms with him. By 1596 the new Duke of Guise, the former king's favourite Epernon, and Mayenne had all made peace and accepted him as king. In March 1598 the Duke of Mercoeur's submission, handing Brittany to Henry in return for substantial payments to clear his debts, effectively ended organised Catholic opposition to his accession. Henry's approach was expensive, but as the king pointed out it cost much less than a prolonged civil war.

In April 1598 Henry signed the Edict of Nantes dealing with the religious issues although the details were not published for several months. This was in order to give Henry time to win over doubters from both denominations. It confirmed Catholicism as the official religion of the state, but allowed Huguenots freedom of conscience and the right to live anywhere in the country, though they could only worship publicly in clearly defined places. Henry realised that he would never be able to meet everybody's hopes, but the compromise could be accepted by most ordinary people, thus preventing them being drawn to support the fanatics on either side. In 1595 Henry had declared war against Spain, which was still backing the residual Catholic League rebels. Although he suffered some early set-backs, Amiens was regained in 1597, and in May 1598 the peace of Vervins was signed with Philip II. This restored the borders to those of 1559, thus returning Calais to France.

Henry IV has for centuries been regarded as one of France's most successful monarchs. He brought peace to a country that had experienced civil war and foreign invasions, restoring it as a force to be reckoned with on the international stage. He increasingly pursued an active foreign policy, combining diplomacy with the readiness to use armed force if he believed it necessary. Within two generations, under his grandson Louis XIV, France came to be regarded as the pre-eminent power of Europe. The Bourbon family, through his direct descendants, ruled for nearly 200 years until the French Revolution and the execution of Louis XVI in 1793.

But despite the esteem in which he is now held, it is unlikely that any king had so many attempts made on his life. Disregarding events before the murder of his predecessor, Henry III, in 1589, there were over twenty known plots to kill Henry IV. They occurred with depressing regularity, though the majority were before 1600: 1591, 1593 (six attempts), 1594 (two), 1595 (three), 1596 (two), 1599 (two), 1600, 1601, 1603, 1605, 1608, and the final attempt in 1610. For instance, in December 1594 Jean Chatel succeeded in gaining entrance to the king's chamber and attacked him with a knife. He managed to cut the king's lip and break a tooth before being restrained. He was put on trial, condemned and executed. The Jesuits were suspected of being involved, as they had in an earlier plot, and were ordered to leave France. Henry rescinded the expulsion in 1603 and on their return even gave the order some family property in La Fleche to use as a school. In 1602 the Duke of Biron was executed, having been accused of plotting Henry's murder in a conspiracy involving Spanish agents. Other attempts to kill Henry were betrayed by informants or were poorly carried out. Does this mean that the potential murderers were particularly inept, or that he was extraordinarily fortunate, or very well guarded, or had an excellent intelligence network? Probably a combination of these factors. What these events tell us, however, is that despite all his achievements there were still many people in France who could not accept him as their rightful king and were willing to martyr themselves to end his reign.

In the early months of 1610 Henry was engaged in preparations for war in Germany concerning the succession in Julich-Cleves-Berg, an important duchy on the Rhine. He wanted to prevent a Habsburg claimant from becoming duke and intended to support a rival Protestant candidate. If the threat of his intervention did not have the desired effect, he was planning to personally lead his army into action. He therefore wished to ensure that the arrangements for the governance of the country in his absence were undisputed. He intended his wife, Marie de' Medici, to be the regent. He was aware not only of the dangers he would face on the battlefield, but also conscious of his advancing years, he was now fifty-six, and that his heir was not yet nine years old. Although married to Marie for ten years, and having produced the heir, Louis, in 1601 (as well as five other children, the youngest of whom, Henrietta Maria, was later to marry Charles I of England), Marie's coronation as Queen of France had been regularly postponed by her husband.

When Henry had married Marie in 1600, it was his second marriage. He had earlier married Margaret of Valois, the daughter of Henry II and Catherine de' Medici, in 1572, both aged nineteen, as part of Catherine's attempt to reconcile the Valois monarchy with the leading Huguenots. It was a difficult marriage, which started in challenging circumstances with the St. Bartholemew's Day massacre taking place less than a week after its celebration. Margaret was often in conflict with her brother, King Henry III, as well as ignored by her husband, who made no attempt to conceal his numerous affairs. Despite their efforts to have a child, none was forthcoming, though Henry had a number of children with his younger mistresses. They lived very separate lives, with Margaret also reputed to have taken various lovers, although her reputation has certainly been tarnished by later Bourbon propaganda. By the time Henry became king the couple were already estranged though there was a degree of reconciliation in order to try to obtain a papal annulment of their marriage, which was eventually granted in late 1599.

Henry IV had been involved in a passionate affair with Gabrielle d'Estrees since 1590. She was often with him while he was campaigning and he valued her advice. Born a Catholic, she is considered to be partly responsible for Henry converting to Catholicism in 1593 and helping to persuade Catholic nobility to make peace with Henry, taking part in negotiations with the Duke of Mayenne. Created Duchess of Beaufort, Gabrielle had three children with Henry who were legitimized and he planned to marry her when his first marriage was annulled. The idea of their son becoming the heir to the throne outraged many in France. However she died in childbirth in April 1599 before the annulment was finalised.

Henry was soon involved in other affairs, particularly with the ambitious Henriette d'Entragues, who was later created the Marquise de Verneuil. Having developed a passion for the twenty-year-old, Henry needed to gain her compliance. He arranged for a large sum to be used to purchase an estate for her, and her father received a written undertaking that should she become pregnant within six months and produced a son, Henry would marry her as soon as his annulment was obtained from the pope.[3] Although she was furious when he married Marie de' Medici in 1600, their relationship continued. They had two children and Henriette had hopes of their son, Gaston Henry, born in 1601 and legitimized in 1603, becoming Henry's heir. Although implicated along with her father in a plot against Henry in 1604 after he made it clear that Marie de Medici's son, Louis, was the heir, she was forgiven and returned to court though the affair cooled as Henry's desires moved on. Her father was required to return the incriminating document in return for his life.

In 1609 Henry developed a new infatuation – for the fifteen-year-old Charlotte-Margaret de Montmorency. In order to uphold the usual decencies she was hurried married to Henry II of Condé, who was not expected to object to the fulfilment of the king's desires. However, Condé did not co-operate.

He left Paris, taking his wife with him, pursued by Henry's guards, and managed to escape to the Netherlands where he sought refuge with the rulers, the Habsburg Archduke Albert and his wife Isabella Clara Eugenia, once the Spanish candidate for the French throne. Henry demanded their return, calling Condé a kidnapper and accusing him of planning rebellion in France. The failure of Albert and Isabella to return them resulted in this affair becoming closely linked with the dispute over Julich-Cleves-Berg, as the rulers of the Spanish Netherlands were his adversaries there as well.

Despite these extra-marital activities, in 1610 with his imminent departure on campaign, it suited Henry's plans to bolster Marie's authority with the pageant of a coronation at the abbey of Saint-Denis, to be followed three days later by a formal entry into Paris. At the coronation, on the afternoon of Thursday 13 May, princes of the blood and the elite of the nation, dressed in their fine clothes, decorated with gold and silver thread and precious jewels, took their places in the abbey. Marie was led in by the young Louis, who then sat at her side and accompanied her for the anointing and crowning, along with his eldest sister, Elizabeth. Her train was carried by the younger royal children, and Margaret of Valois, Henry's former wife and the last remaining princess of the former royal family, followed her in the procession. On leaving the abbey, the royal party was greeted by crowds whose cheering was encouraged by the throwing of gold and silver coins amongst them. Everything was designed to demonstrate the status of the queen, the harmony of the dynasty, the loyalty of the nobility and the love of the people for their monarch. Henry was enthusiastic about both the success of the ceremony and the appearance of his queen, who he embraced and complimented on her beauty, which cannot always have been the case given his devotion to long-term mistresses and a reputation for countless affairs.

They returned to the Louvre where the next morning Henry rose early. He had much to do before his planned departure on the following Wednesday – meetings with officials about internal affairs, considering the terms of an alliance with the Duke of Savoy, a walk in the Tuileries gardens with advisors, attending Mass, being informed of plans for an important river crossing when advancing into Germany and reviewing financial proposals. These were followed by a visit to the queen who tried to dissuade him from going to visit his chief minister, Sully, at the Arsenal, in order to finalise plans for the coming campaign. Although in two minds, he decided to go, and then ordered the captain of the guard to carry out an inspection of the preparations for the queen's reception on Sunday instead of accompanying him. The captain, the Marquis of Vitry, expressed his concerns about the king leaving the Louvre without his guard when there were so many visitors and outsiders in the city. Henry dismissed his worries, saying 'I have no need either of you or your guards', explaining that 'for fifty years and more I have protected myself without a captain of the guards.'[4]

There had always been the threat of assassination, some genuine and others imaginary, and there were constant predictions of danger based on bad omens. On his departure the king was not alone. Henry climbed into the rear of the covered carriage and sat on the left-hand side, with the Duke of Épernon to his right. Opposite them were Charles de Plessis-Liancourt, the head groom, and the Marquis of Mirabeau, while Lavardin, La Force, Roquelaure, and the Duke of Montbazon, took seats by the doors. A few mounted noblemen and pages on foot travelled alongside the carriage as it began its journey from the Louvre to the Arsenal shortly after three o'clock in the afternoon. The blinds in the carriage were raised at the king's request so that he could see the decorations in the streets being prepared for Sunday's celebrations. They travelled along the rue Saint-Honore until the point where the road narrowed and its name changed to the rue de Ferronnerie. This street crossed the rue Saint-Denis, which Henry wished to see because it was the main route along which Marie would travel. Having crossed the rue Saint-Denis, the rue de Ferronnerie would take them on to the Place de la Bastille, from where they would access the Arsenal. Where the road narrowed, alongside the wall of the Cemetery of the Innocents with small shops lining both sides, was well-known for serious congestion.

This day was no different. The king's carriage came to a halt, its way blocked by a hay wagon and another loaded with wine barrels. In an attempt to get moving the coachman pulled to the left only for the wheels to become struck in the gutter that ran down the centre of the street. The mounted nobles and most of the pages cut through the cemetery intending to meet the carriage further along the street once it was able to pass. One of two remaining footmen went forward to try to clear the road while the other was behind the carriage. Henry was in conversation with Épernon and Levardin, possibly talking about the river crossing that Henry had been told about earlier in the day, or listening to a letter being read by Épernon, the king having left the Louvre without his glasses[5].

Unknown to the king's party, François Ravaillac, an impoverished lawyer from Angouleme, had been following the coach on foot from the Louvre, having failed to find an opportunity to accost Henry over the previous few days. He now saw his chance. Unnoticed amongst the crowds in the busy street, with the carriage stationary and its small guard gone, he took out his knife, leapt onto the spokes of the wheel nearest to Henry. He was able to stab three times before those in the carriage could react to protect the king. The first strike wounded Henry's chest. The second penetrated deeply, piercing a lung and cutting both the aorta and the superior vena cava. A third thrust missed the king and tore the sleeve of Montbazon. But that was of no consequence. The second blow had been enough to kill the king. The autopsy, held the following afternoon, reported that the chest cavity was full of blood and concluded that this wound, between the fifth and sixth ribs, was the source of the blood that had gushed from his mouth and 'was the sole and immediate cause of death'.

Jumping down from the wheel, Ravaillac could have escaped if he had thrown away his weapon and not remained rooted to the spot, perhaps overwhelmed by the gravity of what he had just done. He was seized by one of the king's household, who might have killed him had not Épernon shouted to keep him alive. He had the awareness to realise that his dead body would be of little use to those who would be investigating the crime. A cloak was used to cover Henry, the carriage blinds were drawn down and onlookers were told that the king was not seriously wounded in order to prevent the spread of panic and the likely lynching of the assailant. The carriage returned as quickly as possible to the Louvre, where it was confirmed that Henry was already dead, and the queen informed.

News of the attack spread quickly. Within minutes a message was sent to the presiding officer of the Paris *Parlement* that the king had been wounded, and he informed the assembly. This was soon corrected when representatives, who had been dispatched to find out more details of what had happened, returned from the Louvre. They left no doubt that Henry IV had not survived the attack. The *Parlement* sent messages of support to the queen, who they immediately recognised as the regent for the new king, Louis XIII. Soon Henry's death was being spoken about throughout the city. There were reports of widespread distress. 'Shops were shut, everyone, young and old rich and poor, was caught up in an orgy of weeping and wailing.'[6] The king lay in state for six weeks and his body was then entombed at Saint-Denis on 1 July, though his heart was buried at the Jesuit school in La Fleche as he had requested. During the French Revolution his remains, along with those of his royal descendants, were taken from the crypt and thrown in a ditch, to be recovered and reburied in a communal grave after the restoration of the monarchy in 1815. His heart was burned, though the ashes were retained and buried in the chateau of Pau in 1953.[7]

Ravaillac was questioned on a number of occasions over the following ten days, at first in the hotel de Retz, where he was initially held, and then in the Conciergerie, the prison in the old royal palace in Paris. These interrogations, by lawyers from the *Parlement*, involved questions about his background, his acquaintances, where he had travelled to, why he was in Paris, and most of all, about his motives and his supposed accomplices. They also involved the use of torture, including a version of the boot, designed to crush the foot and leg. Despite this, Ravaillac consistently claimed that he alone was responsible for the attack and that he was not part of a wider conspiracy, something which he repeated during his final questioning and torture on 25 May before judgement was passed on him. He was declared 'guilty in fact and in law of the crime of high treason to God and man, principally on account of the most wicked, abominable and detestable parricide committed on the person of our late King Henry the fourth'.[8]

His punishment was to be exemplary. He was to be executed, his property confiscated, the house of his birth torn down, and his parents were to leave the country under threat of hanging if they ever returned. His siblings and all other relatives were forbidden to use the name Ravaillac. On 27 May he was taken in a cart to the main door of Notre-Dame, accompanied by shouts of hatred and the throwing of stones by the large crowd that had turned out to watch his end. Outside the cathedral he stood in a long shirt holding a lighted candle and publicly confessed his crime, repented and asked God, the King and the Law for forgiveness. He was then taken to the Place de Grève (now the Place de l'Hôtel de Ville) where he mounted the scaffold and was once again tortured and told to name his accomplices. The arm with which he had committed the murder was plunged into burning sulphur. Much of the rest of his flesh was torn by red-hot pincers and molten lead and sulphur, boiling oil and resin were poured into the wounds. He still maintained that he had nothing else to say except to beg forgiveness and that no-one else was involved. As the clerics began to say the prayers traditional at an execution the crowd shouted them down saying that he did not deserve them and calling for the executioner to prolong his pain. After at least an hour his limbs were attached to four horses which then pulled in different directions. Slowly his joints were pulled apart and after another hour or more he died. His body was dismembered and his limbs grabbed from the scaffold by the mob who chopped them up. The remains were eventually burned and the ashes disposed of.

His interrogators had found it difficult to believe that someone of his lowly social status could have planned it alone. They looked for evidence of the supernatural and diabolical in his thinking, but Ravaillac regarded himself as a devout Christian and considered such beliefs sinful. The records of the questioning show that he had been brought up by his mother, in considerable poverty, as a pious Catholic. He had some legal training in Paris but had returned to Angouleme, where he spent time in prison for debt, and on his release made a living by instructing young people in religion. It was discovered that he had been rejected by two religious orders. He had joined the Congregation of the Feuillants, many of whom were closely linked to the Catholic League, but had been told to leave after six weeks because he claimed to have had visions while at prayer. After one of these visions he believed that God had given him the special task of converting King Henry IV to true Catholicism, presumably believing, like many others, that Henry's formal conversion in 1593 had not been sincere. He later applied to the Jesuits but they rejected him because he had already been a member of a different religious order. During visits to Paris in 1609, at Whitsun and Christmas, he found that it was impossible for him to gain access to the king to be able to carry out his self-appointed task of conversion and so he decided to kill him. Immediately after Easter in 1610 he walked to Paris and looked for an opportunity to attack Henry. Having been thwarted on a number of occasions his chance came in the rue de Ferronnerie.

As a committed Christian Ravaillac believed that murder was a sin, but he had managed to convince himself that it was his duty to kill Henry IV. During interrogation he had said that Henry IV had failed in his duty to God to remove all Huguenots from office, and drive heresy out of France. He had, in fact, permitted and encouraged them by issuing the Edict of Nantes. He believed that the Huguenots were plotting to carry out a slaughter of Catholics in revenge for the Massacre of St. Bartholomew's Day and that the king had done nothing to punish those involved. To Ravaillac, Henry IV remained a heretic at heart and therefore could not be the legal king of France. The king was just about to lead a campaign into Germany to prevent a Catholic succeeding to a dukedom. This, Ravaillac apparently believed, was just a prelude to the king making war on the pope, God's representative on earth. In such circumstances it was beholden upon him to serve God and end such blasphemy.

It is clear that Jacques Ravaillac was not the only person in France to hold these views. Such had been the beliefs of many who had belonged to the Catholic League and although the vast majority had publicly accepted Henry IV's conversion, in private many had not altered their opinion. However, did this meant that there was a wider conspiracy to kill the king of which Ravaillac was merely the figurehead? Several groups were accused of encouraging and assisting him. Initially those who were opposed to Henry's imminent military intervention in Germany were suspected. The Jesuits also came under suspicion as many of them held views similar to Ravaillac. Others believed that the Spanish might have been involved, given their record of interference in French politics over the previous fifty years.

Finally, there were persistent rumours that Henry's failure to keep his promises to Henriette d'Entragues might have motivated the murder. Claims of treasonous conversations between her, the Duke of Épernon and others were made. Although there was an investigation, the evidence, as in the case of all the other theories, was insufficient. Many of these ideas had been put forward by those who wished to blacken the name of others. Although it is possible that any convincing evidence was covered up by powerful figures at court, it seems most likely that Henry IV was killed, like Henry III, by an individual attacker who had been influenced by the heightened religious tensions and increasingly violent polemics of the time.

What had these two murders achieved? Clément's killing of Henry III certainly did not prevent the accession of the Huguenot, Henry of Navarre, who became Henry IV. The Catholic League's hostility towards Henry III had weakened the almost sacred authority of the monarchy opening the way for his murder. Henry IV accepted that he could only truly become king of France if he converted to Catholicism. This would never be accepted as genuine by some and so he became the target of numerous assassinations attempts. The man who had managed to establish peace within France was one of the last victims of the many sectarian assassinations that had taken place since 1560. Ravaillac's success in killing him did not end the Bourbon dynasty. The regency of Marie de' Medici successfully passed power to Louis XIII, who with his chief minister, Cardinal Richelieu, greatly strengthened the power of the monarchy and the Catholic Church, defeating Huguenot rebels and their English allies at the siege of La Rochelle in 1627-8. When his son, Louis XIV, came of age, France entered a period of absolute monarchy and unprecedented influence in Europe. The Huguenot's freedom of worship had always depended upon royal favour. In 1685 Louis XIV revoked the Edict of Nantes, removing this freedom, forcing many Huguenots to flee the country, many of them to England. Those who had supported the actions of Clément and Ravaillac would have approved, though it seems unlikely that the murders of Henry III and Henry IV made any direct contribution to this outcome.

RUSSIA'S 'TIME OF TROUBLES'

From Rurikids to Romanovs

'Our sun is rising; it has long been set; Dmitry Ivanovich is restored to us.'

False Dmitry I being greeted in a Russian town as the true son and heir of Ivan IV, quoted by Maureen Perrie from the unpublished diary of a Polish Jesuit priest who accompanied False Dmitry I on his march to Moscow

---

'Andrei Sherefidinov seized the tsarina and her son [Tsar Feodor II], a handsome and well-built young prince, who had promised to become an excellent sovereign, suffocated them between two pillows ... and told the townspeople that mother and son had just poisoned themselves.'

The killing of Tsar Feodor II from the account of Issac Massa based on his contemporary notes

---

'The boyars and princes drew their swords and daggers. One thrust at him through the head in front, another struck in the same place from behind... a third struck him in the arm, a fourth just above the legs and a fifth stabbed right through his body.'

The murder of False Dmitry I in 1606 as described by Conrad Bussow, a German mercenary soldier

CHAPTER 10

DESCENT INTO CHAOS AND REGICIDE

T he early seventeenth century was a time of political and social instability in Russia, with civil wars, foreign invasion, and the murder of Tsars, their families, and several pretenders to the throne. The lives of millions of inhabitants were blighted, as they became directly caught up in the chaos or suffered the consequences of military campaigns and sieges. This 'Time of Troubles' is usually regarded as beginning in 1598, with the death of Tsar Feodor I, and ending in 1613 with the choice of Michael Romanov as a new Tsar. However, the term has been used to describe a period starting as early as 1584, when Ivan IV died, or as late as 1604, when open civil war broke out.

Russia's problems during this time were both dynastic and social. The ruling Rurik family died out with Feodor I and over the next fifteen years successive tsars failed to be accepted as the rightful ruler. Also, many sectors of the population had grievances which they were more likely to act upon if they did not recognise their ruler as being legitimate. The country became embroiled in widespread social unrest and civil war, with a struggle for supremacy amongst the nobility and attempts by the dispossessed and oppressed to improve their situation. Foreign powers, particularly Poland and Sweden, saw the opportunity to take advantage of their neighbour's weakness. It was only when a national movement to bring an end to foreign intervention was able to achieve a degree of cohesion that there was any hope of ending the turmoil.[1]

Ivan IV, usually known as 'the Terrible', though more accurately 'the Fearsome' or 'the Formidable', died after a reign of 51 years in 1584. He had become the Grand Prince of Muscovy at the age of 3 in 1533 on the death of his father, and was the first ruler to be crowned as Tsar of All Russia, in 1547. Though he greatly expanded Russian territory in the south, with the conquest of Kazan and Astrakhan in the 1550s, the Livonian Wars later in his reign were largely unsuccessful and extremely costly. This attempt to gain a significant coastline on the Baltic Sea brought Russia into conflict with both Poland and Sweden. Ivan's rule became increasingly oppressive when he created the *oprichnina*, a large area of the country ruled directly by Ivan himself, backed by the *oprichniki,* a corps used to crush any opposition and to weaken the traditional influence of many princely and noble families. The *oprichniki* were granted extensive land holdings, often at the expense of the old aristocracy, and given complete power over the peasants that lived on that land. Even though Ivan ended this experiment in the 1570s, many sections of society were damaged by his increasingly paranoid search for security.[2] On his death Ivan left a society that was in serious trouble.

His family life also contributed to Russia's future problems. Ivan married seven times in all.[3] His first three wives died, as did his sixth, while his fourth and fifth wives were divorced and sent to a convent. By 1580 he had two surviving sons, both born to his first wife, Anastasia Romanovna. She had also given birth to four other children who had died in infancy. The eldest surviving son, Ivan Ivanovich, born in 1554, had been the heir since his birth. He was well educated and regarded as a capable successor. However, his first two marriages had ended in divorce, with the wives being sent to a convent, probably on the insistence of his father because they had not produced an heir. Early in 1581 he married Yelena Sheremeteva and she soon became pregnant. What then happened was to have a disastrous impact on the dynasty and the country. In November 1581 Tsar Ivan, angered by the 'inappropriate' clothes that the pregnant Yelena was wearing, berated and physically assaulted her. His son, with whom his relationship had been deteriorating for several years over both personal and political issues, was furious and confronted the Tsar. During this altercation Ivan accused his son of inciting rebellion and struck him on the head with the sceptre. Ivan Ivanovich died four days later and his wife miscarried shortly afterwards.

This left Ivan's other son, Feodor, three years younger than his brother, as the heir apparent. He had never been expected to inherit the throne and was generally considered unsuitable. From the age of three, on death of his mother in 1560, he grew up in the shadow of his older brother and a distant father who was greatly affected by the death of his first wife and became increasingly violent. Feodor was good natured, quiet and pious, with little interest in politics. He was also sickly and it was generally believed that he was simple-minded. Less than 2 years before Ivan IV's death his last wife, Maria Nagaya, who he had married in 1581, gave birth to a son, Dmitry. On the Tsar's death, Dmitry and his mother went to live on Dmitry's appanage (land granted to the younger son of a monarch who would otherwise have no inheritance) at Uglich, some 100 miles north of Moscow. Dmitry died in 1591. His role in Russian history was to be far more significant after his death than during his short lifetime.

By 1584, when Feodor I inherited the throne, it had already been recognised that others would have to take the lead in ruling the country. Ivan had appointed a regency council, of whom the leading members were from the Shuisky and Mstislavsky families of the old aristocracy, together with Nikita Romanov and Boris Godunov,[4] who had risen to prominence during Ivan's reign and had close family links to the new Tsar – Romanov was his uncle and Godunov his brother-in-law. In the inevitable struggle for power it was Boris Godunov who was best placed to take advantage of the situation. Although not from a particularly distinguished lineage, he had risen through the ranks of the *oprichniki* to become one of Ivan's closest advisers, and his sister, Irina, had married Feodor in 1580. Initially with Romanov support, Godunov secured a dominant position, removing some of Ivan's more unpopular ministers. Nikita Romanov died in 1586 and by 1588 Godunov had overcome plots to replace him and for the time being ended the influence of the Shuiskys, the Nagois (the family of his young brother Dmitry's mother), other princely families and former *oprichniki*.

The problems that Godunov faced were considerable and not of his making. By the late sixteenth century Russia was in turmoil, with the threat of unrest existing in all sections of society. The *boyars* or aristocracy were growing in number, with the old elite being added to by those who were rewarded for more recent service to the Tsar. There were considerable rivalries and a complex system of precedence developed, based on family genealogy and royal service. This resulted in there being many who considered themselves to be under-valued. As *boyar* family size grew and estates were sub-divided between sons, it became harder for them to maintain the life-style expected of their rank. They spent more time in Moscow seeking further advancement[5] and lost touch with their home area, coming to regard their estates as simply a source of revenue.

More was therefore demanded of the already hard-pressed peasants, from both their landlords and the government. They owned no land and by the 1570s large numbers were leaving the estates to which they belonged, in order to avoid the tax collector, to find a new master or, increasingly, to abandon their home region altogether.[6] They were joined by slaves, sometimes former peasants but also impoverished gentry who had sold themselves into time limited slavery because of indebtedness and served as soldiers for their masters. Law and order broke down and in some areas banditry became common, especially in times of particular hardship.

Many moved to the steppes in the south, to the area known as the 'Field', where there was fertile land and where they would be further removed from the control of central government. Some were tempted to join the Cossacks, semi-nomadic, semi-militarised groups, who lived in the area further south, the 'Wild Field'. Although these groups often worked as mercenaries for neighbouring governments, they fiercely defended their independence from Moscow, Poland and the Crimean Tatars. The two most significant Cossack groups or 'hordes' were the Don Cossacks and the Zaporozhian Cossacks. This migration continued into the seventeenth century, as the situation deteriorated further. The consequence in their original homeland was that lesser land owners, the gentry, many of whom held land in return for military service for the tsar, found it increasingly difficult to maintain their status and standard of living, and were unable to continue in their traditional role. Only the far north, with its vast areas, sparsely populated by free peasants with few aristocratic estates and its position on the White Sea trade routes with England, was the exception to this picture of economic and social discontent.

Godunov proved to be a capable ruler. He dealt successfully with the on-going threat of raids by the Crimean Tatars, maintained an uneasy peace with Poland, and after years of war negotiated a peace settlement with Sweden in 1595. Internally, he reduced the tax burden on the estates of the lesser nobility and gentry, and attempted to recruit more of them into military service. In an effort to control the movement of peasants he decreed that peasants who had left their estates could be reclaimed. The problems, however, were too deep-seated to be solved quickly and the death of Tsar Feodor I in January 1598, without an heir, moved Russia a step closer to chaos.

With Feodor's death the ancient Rurikid dynasty came to an end. The crown of Muscovy had passed from father to son with little dispute for almost three hundred years. By the sixteenth century they were accepted as almost sacred God-chosen tsars and there were no rules for selecting a successor. Irina, Feodor's wife, had been made co-ruler in the 1590s, but within days of her husband's death she entered a convent. There was the inevitable political manoeuvring, with several *boyars*, particularly Feodor Romanov, the son of Nikita Romanov and Tsar Feodor's cousin, having a good claim to the throne. Godunov, however, was in the strongest position. With the backing of many *boyars* and Patriarch Job of Moscow and All Russia (Russian Orthodox Church), some carefully managed popular demonstrations, and an army raised to see off a Tatar threat from Crimea, he won widespread support. He was crowned Tsar Boris I on 3 September.[7] However, lingering doubts about his legitimate right to be tsar made it difficult for him to secure the loyalty of his subjects and provided a ready-made cause for those with jealousies and grievances, of whom there were many. To secure his position he moved against his rivals at court. In 1600 Romanov and his brothers were arrested, accused of an assassination plot. Feodor Romanov and his wife were forced to take monastic vows, taking the names Filaret and Martha, and held in strict confinement, thus preventing further involvement in politics. His brothers were sent into internal exile where some died.

One event that was to plague the reign of Tsar Boris and his immediate successors was the death, years before in May 1591, of Ivan IV's youngest son, Tsarevich Dmitry of Uglich. The nine-year-old died of knife wounds to the throat. His mother and others accused the then regent, Boris Godunov, of arranging his murder in order to ease his own way to the throne in the future. They claimed that there had already been attempts upon his life and that the purpose of Michael Bityagovsky and others, who had been sent to Uglich by Godunov as royal representatives the previous year, had been to kill Dmitry. Most local people believed this. There were riots in Uglich and the three youths who had been with Dmitry at the time of his death, including Bityagovsky's son, Bityagovsky himself and other royal officials, were killed. An independent enquiry led by Prince Vasily Shuisky was set up by Godunov. Having interviewed several eye-witnesses, whose stories did not always match, their conclusion was that Dmitry had suffered an epileptic seizure while playing with a knife and accidently cut his own throat. The Nagoi family of his mother were accused of provoking the riots and interfering with evidence in order to implicate Godunov. They were arrested and exiled.

Whether Godunov was actually responsible for Dmitry's death depends largely on whether he was already planning to become Tsar himself as early as 1591. This is highly questionable. While Tsar Feodor was still alive, Godunov was unlikely to be replaced as his chief minister. Feodor and his wife shared a warm relationship. Despite concerns about their ability to have children, Irina gave birth to a daughter in 1592. Although the girl died two years later there might still have been another child, which would have made Dmitry irrelevant to the succession. In any case it might well have been argued that the young prince was not eligible because the Orthodox Church usually only recognised three marriages for an individual and Dmitry was the result of Tsar Ivan's seventh (or even eighth). Such arguments lay in the future. At the time Dmitry was quickly buried without ceremony in Uglich and largely forgotten until, that is, Godunov became Tsar. The accusations against him were then resurrected and his reputation seriously damaged, both at the time and later when subsequent rulers wished to blacken his name.[8] Despite his successes when ruling for Tsar Feodor, Russia's ills, including the famines of 1601-03 and subsequent problems, were soon being blamed on Godunov for his ending of the Rurik dynasty, or even seen as God's punishment for his murder of the young prince.

Matters got even worse for Tsar Boris when there appeared in Poland a figure who claimed to be Tsarevich Dmitry. Usually referred to as the First False Dmitry, he said that his mother had helped him to avoid the assassins sent by Godunov in 1591 and that they had killed somebody else instead. He had hidden first in a monastery in Russia and then, when his whereabouts became known to Godunov, he had fled to Poland (part of the Polish-Lithuanian Commonwealth). He kept such details vague but emphasised that it was clearly God's will that he had been saved so that he could now become the saviour of Russia from the cruel rule of Boris Godunov. Vague rumours about the survival of Dmitry first circulated at the time of Tsar Feodor's death and again in 1600 when Tsar Boris moved against the Romanovs,[9] but the pretender chose his moment to make his move.

Cold, wet summers and severe early frosts destroyed much of the Russian harvests of 1601 and 1602. Millions faced starvation and despite government famine-relief efforts hundreds of thousands died of hunger and disease. A contemporary account, written by Issac Massa, a Dutch trader who lived in Russia through these times, recorded the distress. 'The peasants ... having consumed all their resources, cows, horses, sheep, fowls ... began to look for vegetables such as mushrooms and other fungi in the forests. They ate them hungrily along with husks and the winnowings of wheat, cats and dogs. Then their bellies swelled; they became distended like cows, and died swiftly in great agony.' In the villages bodies lay where they fell to be eaten by wild animals, and in Moscow 'teams of men went every day with carts and sleds to gather bodies and take them outside to large ditches ... where they were thrown in heaps' until they were full.[10] Another observer, Conrad Bussow, a German mercenary soldier, described the eating of grass, hay and even human flesh.[11] He also testified to Tsar Boris' efforts to alleviate the suffering by feeding the hungry and burying the dead, as a result of which 'the treasury was somewhat exhausted'[12]. In such circumstances localised uprisings took place in 1603. These Tsar Boris's army could deal with. However, he faced a much greater threat when 'False Dmitry' announced to Prince Adam Vishnevetsky, at Brahin in Poland-Lithuania, that he was really Ivan IV's son[13] and set about building up support for his claim to the Russian throne.

Once he had declared himself, efforts were immediately made to expose this Dmitry as a 'pretender'. In 1603 Tsar Boris announced that the impostor was in fact a former monk, Grishka Otrepev, a Muscovite who had been groomed for the role by hostile boyars, implying the Romanovs.[14] He brought forward witnesses to prove it, although these were generally regarded as unreliable – Otrepev's uncle who had been well rewarded through service to the Tsar, and two monks who claimed that they travelled to Poland with Otrepev and knew of his transformation into Dmitry.[15] Whoever he was, he was able to play the part of Dmitry so convincingly that it seemed as though he himself believed that he was who he claimed to be. He certainly convinced King Sigismund III of Poland, who he met in March 1604[16], and the Jesuits when he indicated that he might convert to Catholicism. This was probably a political ploy to gain the support of the Polish king who, like the Jesuits in Poland, wished to convert Russians from their Orthodox faith. Sigismund was not yet able to openly provide direct military support for False Dmitry because of opposition from much of the Polish nobility, but he secretly encouraged those who did wish to support him. These were mainly Polish landowners, often in financial difficulties, notably Jerzy Mniszech, who backed False Dmitry in the hope of rich pickings in the event of his success.

If not Otrepev who was this 'pretender'? Much effort has since gone into attempting to find the true identity of False Dmitry and it has been generally accepted that he was Otrepev,[17] perhaps because of the propaganda against him and partly because it has been impossible to prove that he was anyone else. There is still the remote possibility, though generally disregarded, that he was indeed the Tsarevich and not a pretender at all. It has also been put forward that he might have been a child raised in secret as Dmitry by the Nagoi family of Tsarevich Dmitry's mother, in the hope that he could one day take revenge on Godunov and claim the throne.[18] Despite the negative propaganda against him by Tsar Boris's regime and later, all of which portrayed him as a charlatan and the tool of others, it is clear that False Dmitry was intelligent, well educated, of imposing manner, brave in conflict, well-versed in statecraft, and able to inspire confidence in his backers.[19]

He mobilised a small body of 2,500 Polish and Cossack irregulars and entered Moscow's territory from the south-west in the autumn of 1604. His supporters had already issued propaganda leaflets in the towns and villages of the area declaring that the rightful Tsar was returning to claim his crown. Whether they believed this or not, and many did, he provided a focus for discontents of all social classes who blamed Boris for their troubles. It was not just the peasants of the south, but also some of those who were expected to provide military service for the Tsar, garrisons and the people of towns in the area, as well as many Cossacks, initially the Don Cossacks, who rapidly joined his forces. In October he captured border forts and towns. He then besieged the well defended Novogorod Seversk. Even though his attempts to storm the fortress failed, in other towns, such as Putivl, both garrison and townspeople declared their support for False Dmitry. He then moved further north-east to occupy Sevsk. Tsar Boris sent an army under Prince Mstislavsky to deal with the invasion. Although in December Mstislavsky failed to lift the siege of Novogorod Seversk, on 21 January he inflicted a major defeat on False Dmitry's forces. However, he was unable to retake those towns that had already sided with the pretender. According to Issac Massa, the harsh treatment of those who supported False Dmitry by Tsar Boris's troops, including destroying their crops, torture, rape, selling them into slavery, and executions, only harmed Boris's cause. They said that 'If our own army and our own sovereign of Moscow begin treating us in this manner, we have no recourse but to throw ourselves with all speed into the arms of Dmitry'.[20] The pretender escaped to Putivl where he set up his headquarters.

Both sides continued their propaganda efforts with claim and counter-claim, stories of his recognition as Prince Dmitry by those who knew him well and accounts of those prepared to deny this. It was while in Putivl that False Dmitry began calling himself 'Tsar', but most of the *boyars* in Moscow remained loyal to Boris. However, on 13 April 1605, Tsar Boris died. He had been in ill health for some time after a stroke and the threat of False Dmitry must have increased the pressure on him. Some contemporaries, such as Massa and Bussow, believed that he poisoned himself, but his death was almost certainly from natural causes. Boris's heir was his sixteen-year-old son who was immediately proclaimed Tsar Feodor II. He was physically robust, had a fine education, and was familiar with state affairs, having regularly sat in on council meetings with his father. Massa described him as 'a handsome and well-built young prince' who 'promised to become an excellent sovereign'[21]. He never had the chance to prove himself. Many doubted his right to be tsar, just as they had his father, the country was in chaos and a ready-made alternative had established himself in the south-west. There were even rumours that Feodor II planned to travel to England with the ambassador, Sir Thomas Smith, and seek asylum there. To make matters worse, much of the government's army in the south rebelled and its new commander, Basmanov, and other generals, such as Vasily Golitsyn, joined the troops in declaring their loyalty to False Dmitry.

The pretender managed the situation extremely well. He sent word that he thanked the soldiers and would permit them to return home if they wished. Within a month of Boris' death Dmitry began his advance on Moscow, still nearly 400 miles away. His progress was rapid. More and more towns welcomed him as the 'true tsar'. Although Tsar Feodor II dispatched loyal troops to attempt to block the advance, they could only delay it. On 1 June two of False Dmitry's representatives arrived in Moscow, protected by a large crowd, to deliver a proclamation which called upon its inhabitants to recognise him as the rightful tsar and swear allegiance to him. He also recounted the story of his being saved from Godunov's murderers by God's will, listed all that they and country had suffered while under the control of the Godunovs, and assured them that he did not hold the *boyars* or the general population responsible because they had followed Boris through ignorance and fear. They would be forgiven, and 'all Orthodox Christians would be able to live in peace and tranquillity and prosperity'.[22]

Although Prince Vasily Shuisky, who had led the enquiry into Tsarevich Dmitry's death in 1591, publicly declared in Moscow that the true Dmitry really was dead, many of the aristocracy did little, if anything, to support Tsar Feodor II. Some, such as Bogdan Belsky, once powerful under Ivan IV but increasingly sided-lined by the Godunovs, wished to take advantage of the situation and further their own ambitions. They recognised that the momentum was with False Dmitry, a fact proved by the popular reaction to his proclamation. In a clearly planned move, the Moscow jails were opened, allowing the political prisoners to escape. They then gave accounts of their brutal treatment at the hands of their jailers, provoking the crowd into action. A large group attacked the Kremlin, the fortified complex in Moscow which housed the royal palace. As the guards fled they broke in. The palace was ransacked. 'Nothing remained intact; everything was pillaged and sacked. From there the crowd spread through the city.'[23] Tsar Feodor, his mother and the whole Godunov family were seized. The rest of the mob took to man-handling the wealthy, pillaging their houses and drinking large quantities of stolen liquor until, with some difficulty, the *boyars* managed to quell their enthusiasm. Remarkably the only deaths were among the rioters, some of whom died of excessive drinking or fighting over the spoils.[24] Tsar Boris's body was disinterred from Archangel Cathedral, hacked about and then reburied in the grounds of a minor convent.

Belsky was able to take charge and the boyar council declared Tsar Feodor deposed. They announced support for the new monarch, Tsar Dmitry, and sent a delegation to surrender the city to him. Having been informed of these events, Dmitry took steps to secure his position. The first *boyar* delegation sent to greet him as he approached Moscow consisted of 'second-rank figures'[25] and Dmitry made clear his dissatisfaction, having some of them temporarily imprisoned. The lesson was learnt. The next *boyar* group sent to him included those of the highest distinction, including Prince Mstislavsky. They swore an oath of obedience and provide a fine banquet for their new tsar. They also brought with them the tsar's carriage for his entry into Moscow. Dmitry let them know that before he entered the capital he expected that all 'those who had betrayed him were so utterly exterminated that not one of them could any longer be found'[26].

He sent a group led by Basmanov and Vasily Golitsyn, now his senior commanders, ahead of him into Moscow to make the final arrangements. The next day it was announced that Tsar Feodor and his mother had poisoned themselves, but all the evidence suggests that they had been murdered, strangled or suffocated in front of Golitsyn. The first regicide of the 'Time of Troubles' had occurred. Tsar Feodor II had reigned for less than two months. There was no popular outcry when the news of his death spread. The Godunov name had been successfully defamed. Feodor's sister, Xenia, was taken captive and later allegedly raped by the pretender before being dispatched to a convent. Bussow commented on the end of Godunov and his family that Tsar Boris: 'Came like a wolf, reigned like a lion and died like a dog'.[27]

Patriarch Job of the Orthodox Church, who had remained loyal to the Godunovs, was denounced by Basmanov, dragged out of the cathedral and abused by the angry crowd before being banished from the capital. Dmitry nominated one of his own supporters, Ignaty, the first bishop to have recognised him as tsar, as the new Patriarch, an appointment later confirmed by the Holy Synod. All was now ready for False Dmitry's triumphal entry to Moscow. On 20 June he was accompanied to the Kremlin by Russia's leading aristocracy, along with thousands of troops. He was greeted by cheering crowds and the ringing of church bells. Once inside the Kremlin his first act was to visit Archangel Cathedral and weep over the tombs of his 'father', Ivan the Terrible and his 'brother' Tsar Feodor I. When taken to the palace the *boyars* seated him on the throne. He was officially crowned by the new Patriarch a month later. His assumption of power was remarkably straightforward. For the first and only time a Russian Tsar attained the throne as a result of a popular uprising.

CHAPTER 11

PRETENDER AND USURPER – TSAR DMITRY AND TSAR VASILY

Tsar Dmitry's (or False Dmitry I's) reign was to last less than a year. In the early months he made every effort to prove that he was indeed Dmitry of Uglich, the son of Ivan IV and the legitimate tsar of Russia. He had Maria Nagaya, the dowager tsaritsa, the last wife of Ivan IV and Dmitry's mother, returned to Moscow from her convent. She was prepared to publicly confirm that this was indeed her son. Her family members were restored to positions of influence and given large estates. Prince Vasily Shuisky, who had produced the report into Tsarevich Dmitry's death in 1591 and had reiterated his findings in 1605 at Tsar Boris's bidding, now declared that Dmitry had indeed survived! The *boyars* who had assisted False Dmitry from the start, those who had recently gone over to his side, or had been out of favour with the Godunovs and now returned to court, were richly rewarded and became his most influential advisers. Both his 'mother' and these nobles had every reason to give him their support. Marriages were arranged between members of his mother's family and those who now worked closely with the new tsar.

Nevertheless, there were those who resented his seizure of the throne and their exclusion from power. Vasily Shuisky could trace his heritage back to the early Rurikid dynasty and believed that he should have been the one to replace the Godunovs. Despite his most recent statement about the events of 1591, he and his brothers put together an ill-considered and poorly supported plan to have the new tsar assassinated. A fire would be started in the Kremlin which would distract the guards, thus allowing the killers to dispatch the tsar. It was soon betrayed. Rather than have the Shuiskys quietly done away with, False Dmitry wished to show that he was a just and honourable ruler. In a public trial he brought a convincing case against them, and when it became obvious that they would be found guilty, Shuisky made a full confession and begged for mercy. Sentenced to death he was taken to the place of execution, the large square immediately outside the Kremlin, now known as Red Square[1], where the axeman awaited, before being given a last-minute reprieve. Only two lesser conspirators were executed while Shuisky and his brothers were banished to distant Viatka, over 500 miles to the east, though they were allowed to return to Moscow by the end of the year. It has been suggested that this act of clemency showed his weakness in the face of *boyar* pressure, but it can just as easily be seen as a show of strength, his wish to demonstrate to everyone that he had nothing to fear from those who might plot against him.

Tsar Dmitry was somewhat unconventional. He did not always follow the expected behaviour of a tsar. He discontinued 'many awkward Muscovite customs and ceremonies at table, namely that the tsar must incessantly make the sign of the cross and have himself sprinkled with holy water.'[2] He would ride or walk out unaccompanied by boyars, he sometimes wore western dress, and expressed the belief that a foreign education for the youth of wealthy families would be beneficial. He announced that he wished to deal with complaints about corrupt local officials and made efforts to clarify the laws relating to the relationship between bondsmen and their masters, particularly those who had deserted their original masters during the famine of 1601-3.[3] But he also gained a reputation for behaving indecently towards women, as witnessed by his alleged rape of Boris Godunov's daughter and others, and it was said that he did not always attend church services nor strictly adhere to religious fasts.

These issues were matters of concern to many in Russia and were an indication of greater problems for Tsar Dmitry. When first arriving in Russia he had brought with him numerous Polish supporters. Their growing influence in Moscow came to be strongly resented. In November 1605, he was married by proxy to Marina Mniszech, the daughter of one of his main Polish backers. She insisted on remaining a Catholic but Dmitry still went through with the marriage despite efforts to dissuade him. It was increasingly being said that he had secretly converted to Catholicism while in Poland. Although he denied this and attended Orthodox services, even the rumour of such heresy angered the Russian Orthodox clergy and could be used to whip up opposition to him.

Since their return to Moscow the Shuiskys had continued to encourage conspiracies against the tsar, even though these gained little support. They merely provoked Dmitry to establish an elite bodyguard, including many foreign mercenaries, which made it more difficult for any potential assassin to gain access to him in the Kremlin. The Shuiskys looked for opportunities to strike when Dmitry was out on manoeuvres with the army. When this failed they attempted to infiltrate the bodyguard. In March 1606 Dmitry, accompanied by Basmanov and other notables, assembled the whole guard, made an impassioned speech explaining once again how divine providence had saved him in 1591 and declared that any guard who identified a traitor would be considered innocent of any offence. The guards 'set upon the guilty like dogs ... and they tore them apart'.[4] Opposition to Dmitry had been successfully suppressed, but it had not gone away. In the south a group of Cossacks, perhaps inspired by the success of False Dmitry, championed the cause of 'Tsarevich Peter', who claimed to be the son of Tsar Feodor I and Irina Godunov, and therefore the rightful tsar. Supposedly born around 1588, no such son existed. Tsar Dmitry wrote to him in April 1606 inviting him to Moscow so that he could be honoured if he were the true son of Tsar Feodor. The new pretender wisely did not accept the offer, knowing that if he did go to the capital he would almost certainly have been executed.

What brought matters in Moscow to a head was the arrival of Tsar Dmitry's bride, Marina Mniszech. Not only did this marriage go against the tradition of tsars marrying members of leading *boyar* families, but it led to a great increase in the number of armed Poles in Moscow. After elaborate preparations, Marina entered the capital on 2 May 1606 in grand style, accompanied by her family and an entourage of many thousands. These included 2,000 troops, who were actually coming to Moscow to join Tsar Dmitry's campaign against the Crimean Tatars planned for the summer. When Muscovites asked the guests whether the carrying of weapons was usual for weddings they were either ignored or insulted.

On 8 May the marriage ceremony was preceded by Marina's coronation as tsaritsa. The actual rituals had been planned so as to give the impression that everything had been done according to Orthodox traditions but without offending Marina's Catholic faith. Nevertheless charges were still made that Dmitry had broken Orthodox customs, especially as the wedding was held on a Thursday and the feasting went on well into the Friday, a fast-day for pious Russians.[5] The public drunkenness, street-fighting between Poles and Russians, and the deteriorating atmosphere in Moscow as the festivities continued, convinced those boyars, led by the Shuiksys, who wished to remove Tsar Dmitry that this was the time to act. They stirred up popular discontent about the behaviour of the Poles and the supposed offences against the Orthodox religion. On 14 May there was a confrontation between perhaps 4,000 Muscovites and Poles who had to defend themselves. Tsar Dmitry sent troops to restore order, but seems not to have taken seriously reports of threats against his own life, believing, probably correctly, that he was still popular. He stood down half of his personal bodyguard, saying that they needed a rest – a fatal error.

This time the conspirators' plan was well thought out, though undoubtedly of high risk. On the night of 16-17 May soldiers loyal to Shuisky were brought into Moscow. Just before dawn, a small group of *boyars*, led by Shuisky and Golitsyn, rode up to one of the Kremlin gates. The guards, who knew them and suspected nothing, opened the gates and were quickly overcome. The way was now clear for Shuisky's men and some merchants who were in on the plot to advance to Dmitry's palace, intent on murder. Timing was important. As the gates were closed behind the plotters, the people of Moscow were awoken by the ringing of church bells and news was sent around the city that 'the Poles want to assassinate the tsar! Do not let them into the Kremlin'.[6] It was claimed that they were going to kill Dmitry and then impose foreign rule on Russia. Crowds rushed to Red Square where Shuisky confirmed the rumour and encouraged them to take action. The cry went up: 'Death to the Poles! Let us take all they have!' In the riots that followed Poles and other foreigner merchants were set upon, their houses ransacked and many hundreds killed. The mob carried off 'what they had pillaged from the Poles – beds, mattresses, clothing, horses, harness, saddles, and furniture. It looked like the salvage from a conflagration'.[7] The chaos in the streets prevented those of the tsar's guards who were outside the Kremlin from reaching their posts.

Meanwhile inside the Kremlin the infiltrators hunted down Tsar Dmitry. Those who opposed them were either killed or taken prisoner, disarmed, and locked into a small room. Dmitry sent Basmanov to find out the cause of the commotion. When the general remonstrated with the intruders he was seized, stabbed and thrown from the balcony. The tsar seized a halberd and together with a few guards, barricaded himself inside his apartments. When his assailants began to take axes to the door he fled along a passageway and then jumped from a window. His leg was broken in the fall. Although defended by some surviving guards he was unable to escape and was apprehended by his pursuers. He pleaded with them to take him to Red Square and allow him to speak to the crowds, or to find his mother who would confirm that he really was the legitimate tsar. They would not allow either, as they knew as well as he did that the crowds would fully support him. As Massa wrote 'the townspeople would have massacred the lords and conspirators; but knowing nothing of the affair, the people believed that the tsar was being attacked by the Poles and that the conspirators were trying to save him'.[8] Not wishing to risk the crowds learning the truth about what was happening, he was immediately killed. He was shot and then hacked to death, with many of those present striking a blow. A second regicide within a year had taken place.

Although Dmitry was dead, Shuisky and the other the conspirators now faced what was their most difficult task – to persuade the Muscovite population that their actions had been justified. The *boyars* and their men immediately began to spread the word that before his death Dmitry had admitted that he was merely the priest, Otrepev. They also ensured that it became known that Dmitry's mother had also declared him to be an impostor even though at the time she had done nothing of the sort, though she later recognised that in the circumstances she had no choice but to agree. Shuisky also wished to expose Dmitry as a sorcerer in league with the devil who, unless killed, would have brought untold harm to the Orthodox Church and the Russian people. The disfigured bodies of Dmitry and Basmanov were stripped, tied by the genitals and the feet, and dragged into Red Square along with masks worn by minstrels who, in the minds of many Russians, were associated with the devil. Dmitry was referred to as a 'pagan' and a 'Polish minstrel', while a list of his supposed crimes against religion were read out, including the charge that he and his wife would rather go to the bathhouse than church.[9] Tsaritsa Marina was captured, but her life was spared. She was imprisoned and then sent back to Poland in 1608, though this was not to be the end of her or her father's involvement in Russia's 'Time of Troubles'.

Prince Vasily Skuisky knew that after Dmitry's death his own ambition to become tsar would not go unchallenged. Some on the *boyar* council had been supporters of Dmitry and were horrified by his murder, but the dead tsar had no heir or powerful family member around whom they could coalesce. The council was therefore divided between Skuisky's supporters, who needed him to take power in order to avoid the possibility of being charged with the murder of the former tsar, and those who opposed his selection, either because they distrusted him or because they believed that other families had a better claim. The obvious alternative candidate was Prince Feodor Mstislavsky, the chairman of the council. He had the backing of the Romanovs and the Nagoi families but had no real interest in being involved in a power struggle. As a result, even though perhaps most *boyars* still opposed Shuisky, the efforts of his supporters enabled him to seize the throne and then give the impression that he had been the popular choice of *boyars*, churchmen, merchants and the people. On 19 May, at a meeting attended by his brothers and close supporters, Shuisky's royal ancestry was emphasised, descended as he was from the medieval hero and saint of the Orthodox Church, Alexander Nevsky. He then signed documents intended to reassure the *boyars* that they and their property would be secure once he was on the throne. The group then went to Red Square where he was proclaimed Tsar Vasily IV in front of a selected crowd, who cheered obediently, only two days after the murder of Tsar Dmitry.

Had the *boyar* council immediately challenged the controversial way in which Vasily had become tsar the civil wars and foreign invasion that Russia

IANA GRAYA

Regis sobiņs trifti cinci diademate trines
Regna sed omnipotens hinc meliora dedit

Above left: **Plate 1.** Lady Jane Grey. An engraving by Willem and Magdalena de Passe, published in 1620, nearly seventy years after her execution. Although not responsible for the plan to prevent the Catholic Mary from becoming queen, Jane was an ever-present threat to her.

Above right: **Plate 2.** The future Edward VI (1537–53), a portrait from the workshop of Hans Holbein, reworked after he became king in 1547. He was keen to introduce further evangelical reforms in the Church and wished to prevent his Catholic sister Mary succeeding him. He therefore named Lady Jane Grey as his successor if he were to die childless.

Plate 3. An extract from Edward VI's 'Devise for the Succession'. On the third line (after the title) it is clear that Edward has changed 'L Janes heires masles' (Lady Jane's male heirs) to 'L Jane and her heires masles' (Lady Jane and her male heirs), thus naming Jane Grey as his heir, despite his original wish to avoid a female successor.

Plate 4. Queen Mary I of England, 1555. The image is very similar to the well-known portrait by Anthonis Mor. The inscription reads: Mary I Queen of England, France and Ireland, Defender of the Faith. She restored England to the Roman Catholic Church and intended to reverse the changes brought about by the Reformation.

Above left: **Plate 5.** Mary, Queen of Scots in an engraving by Frans Huys (1522–66), made in 1558–9 when Mary was still in France. She had just married Francis, soon to be King Francis II. After he died in 1560 Mary returned to Scotland.

Above right: **Plate 6.** Henry Stuart, Lord Darnley, the second husband of Mary, Queen of Scots. This etching was produced after the accession of Mary and Darnley's son, James, to the English throne in 1603. Although Darnley was killed in February 1567, the image says 'Obiit 1566' (died 1566), because at the time the new year began on 25 March in England (until 1752) and Scotland (until 1600).

Above left: **Plate 7.** Queen Elizabeth I in 1592, by which time she had already been queen for thirty-four years. Five years earlier, after much hesitation, she had signed the death warrant of Mary, Queen of Scots.

Above right: **Plate 8.** William Cecil, Lord Burghley (1520–98) in an engraving published in 1620. Cecil was Elizabeth's chief adviser for forty years. He considered Mary, Queen of Scots to be a major threat to Elizabeth and Protestant England.

Plate 9. Sir Francis Walsingham organised an efficient, Europe-wide, intelligence network that uncovered several plots against the queen. He facilitated the smuggling in and out of letters between Mary and Anthony Babington which implicated Mary in plans to kill Elizabeth and support an invasion of England.

EUROPEAN MAGAZINE.

The Death of Mary Queen of Scots.

W. Walker sculp.

Published June 1,1782, by I.Fielding, Pater noster Row, I.Sewell, Cornhill, & I.Debrett, Piccadilly.

KATHARINA REGINA·HENRICI + II·
VXOR, FRANCISCI · CAROLI · ET
HENRICI REGVM MATER

Above: **Plate 10.** The Death of Mary, Queen of Scots, an illustration from the late eighteenth century. It portrays Mary being prepared for her execution by her attendants, Jane Kennedy and Elizabeth Curle, in the Great Hall of Fotheringhay Castle. She is ignoring the words of the Protestant Dean of Peterborough, Richard Fletcher. The axeman, 'Mr Bull', looks on.

Left: **Plate 11.** Catherine de'Medici, the mother of three kings of France and a major force in French politics between 1559 and her death in 1589. She struggled hard to maintain royal power during the French Wars of Religion.

SECOND ROY DE FRANCE FRANCOIS

Lors que cest arbrßeau plein de si belle fleurs,
Promettoit plus de fruit pour le bien de sa france
La mort le luy osta, pour lemplir de malheurs
Et mourut auec luy de son heur l'esperance

Plate 12. Francis II, the first husband of Mary, Queen of Scots. He married Mary when he was fourteen years old (she was fifteen), became king fourteen months later, and died when still only sixteen. During his reign the Guise family of Mary's mother held great power and they played a major role in the French Wars of Religion.

Plate 13. Henry III, king of France between 1574 and 1589. During his reign the Wars of Religion continued despite his attempts to find a solution, whether by compromise or military victory. He became the first French monarch to be assassinated when killed by a supporter of the Catholic League, Jacques Clément.

IANA ELEBRETA NAVARRORVM REGINA
HENRICI BORBONII EORVMDAM NVNC
REGIS MATER.

Plate 14. Jeanne d'Albret (1528–72), the Queen of Navarre and mother of Henry IV of France. She became a leading Huguenot, arguing the case for their right to worship and opposing the attempts of some Catholics to drive them from France.

Plate 15. Henry IV (1553–1610), known as Henry of Navarre until he acceded to the throne. He was the leader of the Huguenots from the mid-1570s. The Catholic League was determined to prevent him from becoming king, but after the murder of Henry III he eventually defeated their forces and then publically converted to Catholicism.

Plate 16. Marie de' Medici was the second wife of Henry IV of France, whom she married in 1600 after the annulment of his marriage to Margaret of Valois after twenty-seven years. She gave birth to six children, five of whom reached adulthood. These included Louis XIII, for whom she was regent for several years after Henry IV's death, and Henrietta Maria, the wife of Charles I.

Plate 17. Tsar Ivan IV (1533–84), often referred to as 'the Terrible', but more accurately 'the Fearsome'. Russia was a weakened state at the end of his reign. His accidental killing of his oldest son in a fight resulted in the reign of his ill-prepared younger son, Feodor I, the last Rurikid monarch.

Above left: **Plate 18.** Feodor II (1589–1605) was the son of Boris Godunov. Boris had made himself Tsar in 1598 and his right to rule was never accepted by many Russians. Feodor became Tsar on his father's death at the age of sixteen but less than two months later was deposed and murdered in an uprising that had the support of both the nobility and the people of Moscow.

Above right: **Plate 19.** False Dmitry I became Tsar in 1605 after he called for the removal of the Godunov family while his army was camped outside Moscow. His marriage to Marina Mniszech, a Pole and a Catholic, and the resultant influx of Poles into the capital, united his opponents. He was murdered in the Kremlin in a plot led by Vasily Shuisky, who went on to became Vasily IV.

Plate 20. Tsar Vasily IV, another tsar whose rule (1606–10) many Russians believed had no legitimacy. During his reign rebellions, civil wars and an invasion by King Sigismund III of Poland engulfed the country. Vasily was overthrown by a group of *boyars* cooperating with the Poles, who occupied Moscow for over two years.

Plate 21. Sultan Ahmed I. Ahmed was sultan between 1603 and 1617 and was responsible for the construction of the Blue Mosque, shown below his portrait. He was the father of both Osman II and Ibrahim I, the two sultans assassinated in the seventeenth century.

Plate 22. Kosem Sultan. She was the *Haseki Sultan* (chief consort) of Ahmed I and became an influential figure in the Ottoman court for nearly half a century. She was *Valide Sultan* (mother of the sultan) of Murad IV and agreed to the execution of another son, Sultan Ibrahim I, in 1648. She was herself executed in 1651.

Above left: **Plate 23.** Sultan Mustafa I was sultan twice, from November 1617 until February 1618 and then from May 1622 until September 1623. He was deposed on both occasions by court factions who concluded that he was incapable of ruling. His life was spared and he spent the remainder of his life in the *kafes*.

Above right: **Plate 24.** Sultan Osman II was the first reigning Ottoman sultan to be murdered. Having become sultan at the age of fourteen, he was brutally removed by the janissaries (a key element of the Ottoman army), with the support of a court faction, after only four years.

Plate 25. Sultan Ibrahim I ruled from 1640 until his deposition and strangulation in 1648. He has generally been regarded as being mentally unstable and many of his actions support this. Those responsible for replacing him with his young son Mehmet IV wished people to believe in his inability to rule.

Plate 26. King Charles I (1600–49) as painted by Daniel Mijtens in 1629. Mijtens (1590–1648) was the court painter for James I and then Charles I, until Anthony van Dyke became established in England in the early 1630s. Charles was short, just under five feet, and presented challenges to the portrait artist.

Plate 27. Queen Henrietta Maria, with Sir Jeffrey Hudson and Pug the monkey, by Anthony van Dyke, 1633. Charles I and his queen were keen patrons of art and fully appreciated the skills of van Dyke. She is portrayed in a satin riding costume with a fashionable hat, an image of grace and vitality. The young Sir Jeffrey and Pug were both favourites of hers.

Plate 28. Oliver Cromwell in an engraving by Francesco Bartolozzi (1802) after Robert Walker (1607–60). Cromwell's stern, determined look, dressed in armour, is intended to remind viewers of his career as a military commander during and after the civil wars and as Lord Protector from 1653 until his death in 1658.

c **Engelandts Memoriael/**
Tot Eeuwige gedachtenis.

Verhalende de Proceduren, Declaratien, Befchuldigingen, Defencien, Vonniffen, Laetfte
woorden en Executien, van

De Vice-Roy van Yrlandt, *Onthalft den* 22 *Maey*, 1641.
De Biffchop van Cantelbury, *Onthalft den* 10 *Ianua.* 1645.
Den Koningh van Engelandt, Schotlandt, en Yrlandt, *Karolus Stuart*, d'eerfte van dien
Name, *Onthalft den* 30 *Ianuarij*, 1 6 4 9. *Ouden-Stijl.* Alle binnen Londen ge-executeert.

In defen leften druck-vermeerdert en verbetert/ als op de volgende zijde te fien is.

WHITE HALL

Charles I Alles naer de Copyen van L O N D E N.

't Amfterdam, By Jooft Hartgerts, Boeck-verkoper bezijden het Stadhups/ 1649.

Above: **Plate 29.** The Execution of King Charles I, from *Engelandts Memoriael* (England's Memorial) published by Joost Hartgerts in Amsterdam in 1649. It shows the raised scaffold, the armed soldiers surrounding it and the large crowds in attendance at the execution outside the Banqueting Hall of Whitehall Palace on 30 January 1649.

Left: **Plate 30.** Charles I: The Juxon Medal (obverse). Charles I gave one of the gold medals, produced by Nicholas Briot in 1639, to Bishop Juxon as a token of his gratitude for the spiritual guidance that the bishop had provided during the final weeks before the king's execution.

Plate 31. The Frontispiece of *Eikon Basilike – The Portrait of His Sacred Majesty in his Solitudes and Suffering,* one of the most effective propaganda publications of the age, which began the cult of Charles the Martyr.

Plate 32. The Second Great Seal of England, Under the Commonwealth, produced by Thomas Simon *c.*1656. The image is of a mounted Oliver Cromwell with the inscription reading: *OLIVARIVS.DEI.GRA.REIP.ANGLIAE. SCOTIAE.ET.HIBERNIAE.*&c. PROTECTOR 'Oliver, by the grace of God, Protector of the Republic of England, Scotland and Ireland'. Although Cromwell rejected the offer of the crown, his position as Head of State was such that many of his former colleagues and fellow regicides opposed the whole idea of the Protectorate.

Plate 33. This engraving by George Bickham Sr. (1684–1769) 'Oliver Cromwell – A Genealogy of Anti-Christ' presents a satirical genealogy portraying Cromwell 'Triumphant as the Head of Fanatics and their Vices, supported by Devils'. Anti-Christ, Pontiff of Hell and Pride produce Independents, Puritans and others, which result in Rebellion, Civil War, Murders and Regicides. It is based on a broadside (a single sheet printed on one side intended to be used as a poster) 'The True Emblem of Antichrist', first printed in 1657.

Plate 34. King Charles II enthroned, being crowned by Peace, 1661. The inscription on the medal by Thomas Simon translates as: 'Sent to support a fallen age, 23 April 1661'. The emphasis is on Charles's divine right to rule.

was subjected to over the following seven years might have been avoided. Although he had seized power he was never recognised as the legitimate tsar by many *boyars* or by a large section of the population. This caused him difficulties throughout his reign, even though his *boyar* opponents, without an alternative to him, preferred the safer route of seeking power through court intrigue rather than that of open rebellion. This had not prevented them from undermining Vasily even before his coronation when they refused to accept his chosen candidate as the new patriarch of the Orthodox Church. Instead they insisted on the appointment of Filaret Romanov, his long-time opponent. Nor was it a difficult matter for the Muscovite crowd to be provoked into violent demonstrations against him, as happened within a week of the death of Dmitry. Although these were quelled without the need to use force, the danger was always there.

Nothing showed Vasily's problem more clearly than the extraordinary events surrounding the fate of Tsar Dmitry's body and the macabre claims made about it by both Tsar Vasily and his opponents. The week after his murder there was unseasonably cold weather which was said by Dmitry's supporters to be God's punishment for his murder and by Vasily's supporters to be proof that Dmitry was a sorcerer. In addition, the extent of the disfiguration of his body and face as he lay for two days in Red Square resulted in claims that this was not Dmitry at all and that he had once again managed to escape his would be assassins. Vasily rightly recognised the danger of such rumours and they were to be a constant threat to him throughout his reign. In an initial attempt to end them he first had the body removed from the square to a paupers' graveyard on the edge of the city. Although locked in, it was said to have been found outside the gates the next morning. This, it was claimed, was further proof of the devil at work. The body was next cast into a ditch and covered with earth. A week later it reappeared in a distant churchyard and Vasily announced that this was because the earth had refused to accept such an evil corpse. Then it was burned and the ashes scattered, allegedly fired from a cannon in the direction from which he had arrived in Moscow.[10] Of course others claimed that the burning of his body was to prevent any formal identification taking place which would show that the body was not Dmitry's.

Towards the end of May it was announced that the remarkably preserved body of the true Tsarevich Dmitry had been dug up at Uglich and recognised by his mother. Vasily decided that the body should be brought to Moscow for burial in the Cathedral of the Assumption, where coronations and the laying to rest of Russian Orthodox Patriarchs traditionally took place. Patriarch Filaret was appointed to lead a delegation sent to escort the body back to Moscow. Regarded by Vasily as untrustworthy, Filaret was accompanied by members of Vasily's family to ensure that all went according to plan. In the Patriarch's absence, breaking all tradition, Vasily's coronation was hurriedly performed on 1 June[11] in a bid to consolidate his position. Meanwhile both at Uglich and on the body's route to Moscow various miracles were said to have taken place. By the time the body had reached the capital Tsar Vasily had decided that the tsarevich should be canonised. He once again altered his view as to how Dmitry died, now accepting that he had been murdered. Large crowds assembled for the arrival of the body but it was already in a sealed casket and no-one could view it. A small number of the sick and crippled were allowed into the cathedral and more miracles were reported, each signalled by the ringing of bells. However the stench of the body, despite the burning of much incense, meant that it had to be rapidly interred.

Not surprisingly this performance did not satisfy the doubters. No-one had seen the body and word was soon spreading that Vasily had ordered the killing of a young boy to be put in the casket. Also, the bodies of saints were supposed to smell sweetly and this body certainly did not. A plot to stir up the people against Vasily resulted in the removal of Patriarch Filaret who, along with other known opponents of the new tsar, were exiled from Moscow. Filaret was replaced as patriarch by Vasily's preferred choice, and great supporter, Hermogen, and the influence of the church was used to back Vasily. By these means the tsar gained control in Moscow. However, in the rest of the country, the idea that Tsar Dmitry had escaped death spread rapidly, with accounts of mysterious horsemen leaving the capital on the night before the murder. The belief in Dmitry's survival provided a focus for opposition to the new tsar.

Within a month of Tsar Vasily's coronation civil war had broken out. The rebellion, in Dmitry's name, was led by men of very different backgrounds. At Putivl, in the far south-west, the new military commander, Prince Gregory Shakhovskoi, signalled his opposition to Vasily. He was joined by Ivan Bolotnikov, who proved to be a very competent military leader, having had a remarkable career. Initially an indentured military slave, he had escaped to join the Cossacks, was then captured by Crimean Tatars and sold to be a galley slave for the Turks. Freed after a sea battle, he was taken to Venice and from there made his way to Poland-Lithuania. There he met Mikhail Molchanov, who had been a close associate of Tsar Dmitry and was keeping alive the belief that Dmitry had escaped death in Moscow. Bolotnikov was sent to Putivl as Dmitry's commander-in-chief. The other major commander was Istoma Pashkov, who led a substantial force of men, many of whom held small plots of land in return for military service and were experiencing relative poverty. Between them these leaders were able to attract many of the same people that had already fought for False

Dmitry, a cross section of society including Cossacks, the dispossessed, impoverished petty nobles and all those who resented central government interference with their freedom.

By July 1606 towns in the south were declaring their allegiance to the rebels and men were joining their forces in large numbers. Tsar Vasily sent troops, under the overall command of Prince Mstislavsky, to deal with the uprising. They besieged the major military stronghold of Elets and the town of Kromy, but by September both sieges had failed and the Tsar's armies were withdrawing north, pursued separately by Bolotnikov and Pashkov. Success brought even more recruits to the rebels' cause. The relatively prosperous areas around Tula and Riazan, nearer Moscow, abandoned Vasily. The Riazan nobles, who often felt slighted by the Muscovite *boyars*, backed their leading figure, Liapunov, when he announced his support for Dmitry. As the rebels advanced on Moscow, Tsar Vasily appointed his able and popular nephew Prince Skopin-Shuisky as his commander. Although not able to stop the advance, he managed to organise and improve the defences of the capital. By mid-October Pashkov and Bolotnikov had reached Kolomenskoe, ten miles from Moscow. There they made their headquarters in the royal summer residence and planned to blockade the city, and, if possible, overcome its defences.

Tsar Vasily's position looked precarious. To stiffen the resolve of Moscow's inhabitants, estimated to be around 70,000, he spread rumours that the rebels intended to massacre the whole population for their treatment of Tsar Dmitry, and had them take an oath of loyalty to him. Patriarch Hermogen ordered special church services to be held where the threat to the Orthodox Church was emphasised. Vasily also made effective use of the very real tensions within the rebel camp. Divisions existed between those who had social and economic grievances against the *boyars* and the land-owners, and the wealthier elements, such as the Raizan nobility, whose main object was the removal of Vasily. The tsar's propaganda spread the word that Bolotnikov's aim was to completely overthrow the established social order. There was also personal animosity between Pashkov and the overall commander, Bolotnikov. Pashkov had achieved early victories and was the first to reach Kolomenskoe, but considered himself dishonoured when Bolotnikov arrived and insensitively demanded that he took over the royal residence as his headquarters. The other problem for the rebel leaders was that the morale of their troops was weakened by the continued failure of their supposed leader, Tsar Dmitry, to make an appearance, despite Bolotnikov's appeals to Prince Shakhovskoi in Putivl that someone should be sent.

There were daily skirmishes between the two sides as the rebel forces attempted to encircle the city. During November Skopin-Shuisky was unable to defeat them, but he did prevent them from storming the city or taking control of strategically important villages to the north. The capture of these villages would have enabled the rebels to cut another of Moscow's main supply routes and provided them with a dominating position over-looking the city. However, on 15 November, during an attack on one of the city gates, Liapunov and the Riazan nobles defected to Tsar Vasily. Further inconclusive hostilities took place but at the end of the month, in secret negotiations, Vasily's representatives also persuaded Pashkov to switch sides. In a carefully planned move, Skopin-Shuisky launched a major attack on 2 December, and Pashkov's troops turned on their former allies. Bolotnikov's army was defeated and forced to retreat, with considerable loss of life and many thousands of his troops captured. The siege of Moscow ended and Pashkov was rewarded with a senior military rank and large estates. The fate of the prisoners was grim. Vasily claimed that they were all dangerous revolutionaries, bandits, slaves and serfs who had deserted their masters. He wished to use them as an example to others who might rebel. Thousands were executed, 'brought out by the hundreds at night and led off to their deaths like lambs to the slaughter. They were lined up and butchered like cattle with cudgel blows to the forehead, then thrust under the ice of the river Yauza'.[12] Others were impaled in public. Those who survived were given as slaves to those loyal to Tsar Vasily or remained in overcrowded prisons until offered release on the condition that they fought for Vasily.

This defeat and the subsequent brutality did not end the rebellion against Tsar Vasily. His opponents still controlled large areas of the country and it seems likely that the reported executions provoked both a greater hatred of the Tsar and the use of similar tactics by his enemies.[13] Bolotnikov's remaining army retreated to Kaluga, 120 miles south-west of Moscow, a strongly fortified town where they prepared for a siege. In an effort to take the town, Skopin-Shuisky ordered the construction of a huge wooden siege tower but Bolotnikov's soldiers managed to tunnel out under the defences and place mines beneath it just as it was being completed. The resulting explosion, timed to coincide with an attack from the town, destroyed the tower, killed many of the besieging troops and demoralised the rest. Skopin-Shuisky settled in for a lengthy siege.

During late 1606 Prince Shakhovskoi in Putivl, having been unable to 'find' Tsar Dmitry, made contact with the pretender, Tsarevich Peter. He still had a Cossack army and was persuaded to declare his support for Dmitry, expecting that if Dmitry failed to materialise then he could become the tsar, as the supposed son of Feodor I. Peter and his troops arrived in Putivl and began to use his authority to order the public execution of Vasily's supporters who had been captured. Having visited Poland in December 1606 – January 1607, he moved his army and court north to Tula, planning to relieve Bolotnikov in Kaluga. His first attempt, in late February 1607, failed, and Kaluga came under increasing pressure. After regrouping, however, his army commanded by Prince Teliatevsky crushed the tsar's forces on 3 May 1607 and the besiegers of Kaluga were then put to flight. Tsarevich Peter, however, failed to follow up his victory preferring to return to Tula where he was joined by Bolotnikov and Shakhovskoi.

This delay enabled Tsar Vasily and Skopin-Shuisky to prepare for another offensive. Orders were given for a full mobilisation. Landowners had to present themselves for military service, along with all the able-bodied men on their land. Those who failed do so were threatened with compulsory recruitment and loss of their estates. Within weeks a powerful force had been assembled and the tsar himself led his army south from Moscow. In early June 1607 a rebel force that had been sent north from Tula was routed, with prisoners once again executed in large numbers. This victory ended any immediate threat to Moscow and demoralised the rebels, many of whom were now doubting that Dmitry would ever appear. Some were also concerned by the increasingly violent and sadistic actions of Peter, who they all knew to be a pretender. By the end of the month his army was besieged in Tula.

Tsar Vasily knew that it would be well-nigh impossible to force his way into the city and that a long siege would be needed to force its surrender. As the summer progressed, a new threat appeared which put additional pressure on the tsar to conclude the siege as quickly as possible. In early 1607 a new false Dmitry (usually referred to as False Dmitry II or sometimes as 'the Brigand') had announced his existence in Poland and, as the siege of Tula began, he quietly crossed into Russian territory. Vasily received reports about him from July, as False Dmitry II started to gather soldiers, move north-east and send envoys to Tula. He reached Briansk by late September and on 11th October took Kozelsk, less than 100 miles from Tula. Meanwhile, in August, the tsar's soldiers had started the construction of a large dam across the river Upa near Tula. When completed it would block the river and flood the town. In a race against time the dam was finished by the end of September. Within days flood water ruined much of the stored food in Tula and much of the population were having to take to the roofs of their houses. Hundreds were leaving each day and it soon became obvious to the defenders that the town could not hold out much longer. Vasily, concerned about the arrival of False Dmitry II, also wanted a swift conclusion.

Negotiations took place and on 10 October Tula surrendered to the tsar. It is not clear who was directly involved in the negotiations. Was it the townspeople who betrayed the rebel soldiers, or did some of the commanders decide to come to terms in order to save their own lives and those of their soldiers, or was it the soldiers themselves who were the driving force behind the decision? What we do know is that officers from Vasily's army entered the town and Tsarevich Peter, Bolotnikov, Shakhovskoi, Teliatevsky and other commanders of the rebel army surrendered and were taken prisoner. As part of the deal most of the rank-and-file soldiers were allowed to leave Tula. Despite Vasily's promise of clemency, the fate of the captive leaders depended on their social standing. The pretender, Peter, who had never wished to give himself up, was tortured, forced to admit his humble origins and then publicly hanged. Vasily did not dare treat the popular and respected Bolotnikov in the same way. He was held prisoner and later secretly killed while journeying into exile. Shakhovskoi and others of noble birth were merely dismissed from court. Although claimed as a major success for Tsar Vasily, the capture of Tula turned out to be a pyrrhic victory. Although he had prevented the two armies of his enemies joining forces, many of the soldiers released in the deal renewed their fight against the tsar by joining False Dmitry II's army, as did Shakhovskoi when he escaped from the monastery to which he had been sent.

Initially the surrender of Tula disheartened False Dmitry II and he withdrew to Orel in the south-west. Vasily, believing that his troubles were largely over, returned to Moscow, paraded his prisoners through the streets, and made no major effort to redirect the military campaign against False Dmitry II. The new pretender's army grew rapidly, attracting not only those who had escaped from Tula, but also more Cossacks, including a force of 8,000 commanded by Ivan Zarutsky, Polish lords with mercenary soldiers, and many runaway peasants and slaves who were promised their freedom. In spring 1608 he advanced north, defeated an army sent by Tsar Vasily at Bolkhov in late April, and by June approached Moscow. Once again Skopin-Shuisky's troops managed to prevent the capture of the capital but False Dmitry II made his base at Tuchino, ten miles north-west of Moscow. The lengthy siege that followed lasted until December 1609.

In Tuchino False Dmitry II set up a rival court to that of Vasily and attempted to attract more lords and nobles to his cause. Many Muscovites had to choose between the two sides. Some families opposed to Tsar Vasily, such as the Romanovs, were happy to accept invitations to Tuchino. Filaret (formerly Feodor Romanov) arrived and was soon given his old title as Patriarch of the Orthodox Church. In September, Marina Mniszech, the wife of Tsar Dmitry I, and her father (both having been released by Vasily in agreement with King Sigismund of Poland in July 1608) arrived. Once in

Tuchino, after secret negotiations, she announced that the new pretender was indeed her husband, Tsar Dmitry. Throughout the rest of 1608 and into 1609 they attempted to storm Moscow or, failing that, blockade the city. Although unable to complete the blockade as road to Riazan remained open, False Dmitry II's army did succeed in capturing much land in the north. By the end of 1608 over half country was controlled by the Tuchino government.

However, not everything went his way. False Dmitry II was short of money to pay his mercenary soldiers and to reward other backers. Many of the local commanders appointed by him proved to be greedy, violent, corrupt and arrogant.[14] Taxation levels rose and raids on villages and towns, especially in the more prosperous north, for food, horses and other valuables alienated the population. Such behaviour, more reminiscent of an invading army than liberators from Tsar Vasily, turned many people against False Dmitry II, whose violent punishment of any opposition only made matters worse. By the beginning of 1609 a popular rebellion in the north against their new ruler had started.

Meanwhile, in Moscow, Vasily was clinging to power. He had to deal with a serious attempt to remove him in February 1609 and further plots were unmasked during the spring and summer. Vasily looked for foreign assistance. A treaty with King Sigismund of Poland, in which Sigismund agreed to prevent Polish soldiers joining False Dmitry II, proved to be worthless when Jan-Piotr Sapieha arrived in Tuchino with 7,000 Polish-Lithuanian cavalrymen. Vasily's talks with King Charles IX of Sweden proved to be more successful. In return for land and towns on the Baltic, Sweden sent 3,000 troops to join Skopin-Shuisky's army. In May 1609 he began an offensive from the north-west against False Dmitry II which he coordinated with the northern rebels. The advance was slow but steady, defeating all attempts to hold them back. To make matters worse for Russia, King Sigismund, provoked by Sweden's involvement, invaded from the west. Sigismund, a devout Catholic, had been elected as king of Poland in 1587. On the death of his father in 1592 he also became king of largely Protestant Sweden. However, he had been deposed by his uncle, Charles IX, and therefore wished to foil any plans that Charles might have for territorial gains. Sigismund besieged Smolensk and was joined there by some of False Dmitry II's Polish troops. The court at Tuchino, lacking funds, suffered divisions and desertions. In December 1609, as Skopin-Shuisky's army approached Moscow, the siege came to an end and False Dmitry II fled to Kaluga in disguise. However, although it looked as though Tsar Vasily had been saved once again, his victory was to be short-lived, as foreign invasion was added to the horrors of civil war.

CHAPTER 12

FOREIGN OCCUPATION AND THE RISE OF THE ROMANOV DYNASTY

With False Dmitry II's flight from Tuchino many of the Muscovite nobles who had been with him, such as the Romanovs, were in a difficult position. Unable to make peace with Vasily, they opened talks with King Sigismund. On 4 February 1610, after difficult negotiations, they agreed that once Vasily was removed, Sigismund's son, Wladyslaw, would become tsar, so long as he converted to the Orthodox faith and respected the *boyars'* traditional powers. Sigismund saw this as an opportunity to control Russia and then go on to defeat Charles IX and regain the Swedish throne. Meanwhile in Moscow, Skopin-Shuisky was greeted as a hero for breaking the siege and was already being talked about as the successor to his unpopular uncle, who was being urged to abdicate. However, on 3 May he unexpectedly died. The widespread belief was that he had been poisoned by either Tsar Vasily or by the tsar's brother, Dmitry, who himself hoped to succeed his childless brother. Vasily's reputation never recovered. Calls for his removal increased and were joined by the influential *boyar* Liapunov, who openly named him as the murderer.

The tsar's best commander was dead and on 4 July 1610 Vasily's army suffered a major defeat by the invading Polish army under Hetman (Field-Marshal) Zolkiewski near Klushino, between Smolensk and Moscow. To make matters worse False Dmitry II had been welcomed in Kaluga, where he was able to establish a power-base with the support of Cossack soldiers and was joined by his 'wife', Marina Mniszech. From there he once again advanced and reached the outskirts of Moscow in July. With Moscow endangered, large crowds organised by Liapunov and Golitsyn assembled in Red Square on 17 July to demand Vasily's overthrow. He was arrested by the leading *boyars* and when he refused to abdicate he was beaten, forcibly tonsured as a monk and held under close guard in the Kremlin. Having already escaped the death sentence twice, he was fortunate not to be the third tsar to be killed within four years.

The *boyars* could not agree on who should replace him. Both Vasily Golitsyn and the young Mikhail Romanov, Filaret's son, were put forward but failed to gain the support of the majority. Instead a council of seven senior *boyars* was appointed to take charge. With the Polish army rapidly advancing, their first task was to continue the negotiations about Prince Wladyslaw becoming the new tsar. This was certainly not universally popular. Patriarch Hermogen and some *boyars* refused to consider the possibility of a foreign tsar, while many towns opened talks with False Dmitry II. Meanwhile, the Polish commander offered the *boyar* council of seven help against False Dmitry II. When Dmitry rejected the offer of lands in Poland-Lithuania, Zolkiewski surrounded the pretender's camp and over the summer gradually cleared the area around the capital of his supporters. Dmitry retreated again to Kuluga, though Zarutsky's Cossacks defeated an army that pursued him.

Soon after, members of False Dmitry II's bodyguard were denounced as traitors, possibly in a plot to destabilise the situation in Kaluga. If so, it worked. Dmitry reacted by having them beaten and tortured before they were released. In revenge, on 11 December 1610, a Tatar prince, Peter Urusov, with members of the bodyguard, attacked Dmitry while he was out on his sleigh having been drinking with local landowners. Urusov 'galloping up to the sleigh first shot him with the pistol, then cut off his head and hand with his sabre.[1] Dmitry's furious supporters massacred the Tatars who were still in Kaluga, recovered his body and buried it at the local cathedral. This was not quite the end of False Dmitry II's place in Russian history, or the end of pretenders to the throne. Shortly after his death, his wife gave birth to a son, Ivan Dmitrievich. Marina Mniszech claimed that the boy was Dmitry's son, though even that is sometimes disputed. However, the infant, often referred to as 'Baby Brigand', was for a time presented as the 'rightful' tsar by his mother and those who later wished to take advantage of Russia's difficulties, including the Cossack commander, Zarutsky.

In Moscow, by August 1610, power had effectively passed to Hetman Zolkiewski. He organised a delegation of leading Russian *boyars* to meet King Sigismund in his camp outside the besieged Smolensk. These included Vasily Golitsyn, Filaret Romanov and even the former tsar, Vasily Shuisky and his brothers. Thus powerful figures who might have led the opposition to foreign intervention in Russia were removed from Moscow.[2] On their arrival they were eventually told by Sigismund that he had no intention of allowing his son, the fifteen-year-old Wladyslaw, to become tsar and that he would rule Russia himself. He also insisted on the surrender of Smolensk. Even Sigismund's commander, Zolkiewski, realised that his king's plan would provoke widespread hostility. He wrote that he had 'sufficiently explored the wishes of the men of the Muscovy nation' to know 'that if His Majesty wanted to obtain power for Crown Prince Wladyslaw it would come with no great difficulty, but if for himself, not without great bloodshed'.[3] The king insisted and Zolkiewski was replaced as military governor of Moscow. After their immediate rejection of these terms, the Russian delegates were arrested and taken to Poland as prisoners, where many remained for almost ten years. Vasily Shuisky (formerly Tsar Vasily) and his brother, Dmitry, died in sinister circumstances in September 1612[4], Golitsyn died while still a prisoner in January 1619 and Fliaret Romanov was only released in February 1619.

Sigismund's actions had precisely the effect that Zolkiewski had predicted. In late 1610 Patriarch Hermogen began to speak out against the idea of a Roman Catholic ruler. Although he was soon arrested, many in Moscow and across Russia responded to his call. After the murder of False Dmitry II it was possible for Russians to unite, albeit temporarily, against the foreign occupation.[5] They began to regard the council of seven and all those who cooperated with the Poles as traitors. The Riazan nobility, led by Liapunov, raised troops and were joined by those of other provinces and Cossack groups that had previously fought for the pretenders, such as those commanded by Zarutsky. In Moscow looting by the Polish soldiers provoked attacks on them, and they retaliated with considerable violence. In March 1611, as Liapunov's forces moved towards the capital, the clashes there turned into a battle. The Polish occupiers were hard pressed and in the fighting a massive fire was started which burned for days and destroyed much of the city outside the centre. By the summer, as Russian soldiers of what became known as the 'national militia' moved into the burnt suburbs, the Polish garrison controlled only the inner area. Elsewhere things were not so going well for Russia. In June Smolensk was finally captured by Sigismund's army and in July, after a brief siege, Novgorod was taken by the Swedish forces with the secret agreement of Liapunov, who hoped to gain Swedish support against the Poles.

However, it was the diverse nature of the Russian forces that caused the failure of this first attempt to drive out the foreign occupiers. Believing the promises of freedom and land that Liapunov had made in order to raise more troops, thousands of fugitive slaves and peasants had joined Cossack detachments in his army. Liapunov and other nobles and landowners now wished to ensure that the established order was not entirely overthrown. Although their published programme punished the *boyars* who had supported the Polish occupation by giving their land to impoverished gentry from the areas seized by Poland, it also included a plan to return recent fugitive serfs to their estates. Also, Cossack units had become used to being given the right to collect rent and food supplies from certain lands and this brought them into conflict with the gentry. When short of supplies they often foraged for food and booty in nearby villages which damaged support for their 'national' cause. Liapunov ordered this to stop and when it didn't he resorted to executions. Many Cossacks already hated him for what they regarded as his betrayal of Bolotnikov during the siege of Moscow in November 1606 and their reaction was swift and violent. Liapunov was murdered on 22 July. His death was a blow, but it was also the defeat of two major efforts to capture Moscow and the lack of provisions as the winter weather closed in, that resulted in first the gentry and then Zarutsky's Cossacks abandoning the siege of the capital.

Another issue that divided the national cause was Zarutsky's backing of Ivan Dmitrievich, 'Baby Brigand', the son of False Dmitry II. Patriarch Hermogen issued a statement from prison condemning the effort to promote a new false tsar, urging people to have nothing to do with him, and called upon them to work for the revival of their nation. To confuse matters still further, yet another pretender claiming to be Tsar Dmitry (referred to as the Third False Dmitry) made an appearance. He won considerable backing in the north, calling upon the population to resist Swedish occupation, and made his base at Pskov. Many Cossacks, who had previously supported various Dmitrys, were briefly enthused by this new pretender. However, he controlled Pskov by terror and during the summer of 1612 the leading citizens arrested him, and sent him to Moscow where he was executed.

Patriarch Hermogen's call-to-arms had the hoped for response. A new national movement rapidly emerged, initially based in Nizhnii-Novgorod, on the River Volga some 200 miles east of Moscow, under the leadership of Kuzma Minin, a tradesman who was given powers to raise funds for the movement, with Prince Pozharsky as its military commander. It built up a new national militia, with the clear aims of ending foreign occupation, defeating unruly Cossack groups supporting imposters, restoring social order and then electing a new tsar. By the spring of 1612 they had established a provisional government at Iaroslavl with an effective administration, and managed to negotiate a truce with Swedish forces, with the suggestion that Karl Phillip, the brother of Sweden's new king, Gustavus II Adolphus, might become tsar.

Recognising the danger, King Sigismund sent a Polish army to assist his troops who were still trapped in Moscow. But Pozharsky was able to intercept them and stop their advance. Pozharsky then negotiated with the

Cossacks still surrounding the capital. Many, led by Trubetskoi, joined his national militia, but others under Zarutsky rejected his offer and returned to the south. In October Russian forces defeated the Polish relief army and captured Moscow, with the Polish garrison in the Kremlin surrendering on 22 October 1612. Russians once again controlled their capital city.

Having defeated the Poles, the next task of the national movement was to select a new tsar. All areas of the country were invited to send representatives to the *zemskii sobor*, the 'assembly of the land', consisting of nobles, clergy and commoners (merchants and townspeople). As they arrived in Moscow during January 1613 it became clear that they would choose neither Prince Wladyslaw nor Prince Karl Filip, even though electing a foreign prince would avoid the danger of jealousies caused by the enthronement of a Russian nobleman. The remaining pretender, 'Baby Brigand' gained even less support. If it was to be a Russian there were problems. Some of the possible candidates from the leading noble families were still in prison in Poland. Others had earned the hatred of the population for their collaboration with the Poles – members of the council of seven had been ordered to leave the city during the meeting of the *zemskii sobor*. Leaders of the national movement, such as Pozharsky, were not considered to be from sufficiently distinguished families.

The Romanovs were actively campaigning, first for Ivan Romanov, the brother of Filaret (still in Poland), but he was unacceptable because he had worked with the Poles. Their efforts then concentrated on the young Mikhail Romanov, Filaret's 16-year-old son. Initially there was deadlock, giving other *boyars* such as Ivan Golitsyn, Fedor Mstislavsky, or outsiders such as Dmitry Trubetskoi, the chance to push their own names forward. But no-one could gain sufficient support. The *boyars* wished to block Trubetskoi, and the Cossacks did not wish to see one of the powerful *boyars* succeed. Romanov links with the old Rurik dynasty (Mikhail's father was the cousin of the last unquestionably legitimate tsar, Feodor I), as well as the support of many Cossacks because of Filaret's links with False Dmitry II in Tushino, were in Mikhail's favour. His youth and inexperience were also seen as a positive factor since he was not regarded as a threat to anyone. As one of the *boyars* supposedly commented: 'Let us have Misha Romanov for he is young and not yet wise; he will suit our purposes'.[6]

In February Mikhail Romanov was chosen by the *zemskii sobor* and on 21 February, after the excluded boyars had been allowed to return, the choice was confirmed. Mikhail had been living in Kostroma near his mother's convent and she had to be persuaded to allow him to travel to Moscow into what was a potentially dangerous situation. The leaders in the capital wanted him crowned as soon as possible before their consensus collapsed. He was eventually crowned as Tsar Mikhail I on 21 July 1613. Russia's problems could not be solved instantly. His government had to tread very carefully. A major effort was made to convince the population of his legitimacy as Russia's sacred ruler, the rightful successor to the Rurikid dynasty. In the early years of his reign he was dominated by the aristocratic *boyars*, at least until his father, Filaret, was released from his Polish captivity in 1519 and returned to Moscow as the Patriarch. The threat of the Cossack groups was gradually reduced. Peace with Sweden and Poland was negotiated. The remaining pretenders and their supporters were defeated. Zarutsky, along with Marina, False Dmitry's wife, and her son, 'Baby Brigand', Ivan Dmitrievich, retreated to Astrakhan where they were captured in June 1614. Sent to Moscow, Zarutsky was impaled, the three year old Ivan hanged, and Marina died soon afterwards, whether murdered or of natural causes is disputed.[7]

The fate of all the pretenders and of those responsible for the killing of the tsars, however disputed their legitimacy, was in significant contrast to that of the new tsar. Mikhail went on to reign for thirty-two years and established the Romanov dynasty. He was at heart a conservative and it has been commented that he 'put an end to the Troubles in part by crushing the very same patriotic Cossacks who had saved the country and brought him to power'[8]. His dynasty was to survive for the next three centuries until the removal of the last Russian tsar, Nicholas II, during the Russian Revolution in 1917 and his murder the following year.

UPHEAVAL IN THE OTTOMAN EMPIRE

The Killing of Osman II and Ibrahim I

'I am the khan, son of the Khans, the lord of pity and punishment, the mighty emperor Osman Khan, feeding the people in need through the assistance of the All-Bountiful God, the defender of the poor, of the faith, and of my state.'

From the introduction to a Treaty between Sultan Osman and King Sigismund III of Poland in 1519

⁕ ⁙ ⁘✦❖✦⁘ ⁙ ⁕

'Is this the precious Prince Osman who raided the coffee shops and put the sipahis *and janissaries on the galleys? Was it with mercenaries that your forefathers conquered provinces?'*

Words attributed to an eye-witness to Sultan Osman II being taken on a wagon to the Yedikule fortress before his murder, quoted by Douglas A. Howard in A History of the Ottoman Empire

⁕ ⁙ ⁘✦❖✦⁘ ⁙ ⁕

'In the end he will leave neither you nor me alive. Have him removed from the throne immediately.'

Kosem, the *Valide Sultan* – mother of the reigning sultan – agreeing to the deposition and later killing of her son, Ibrahim I, in 1648

CHAPTER 13

SUCCESSION AND THE TRADITION OF FRATRICIDE IN THE OTTOMAN EMPIRE

O sman II was the sixteenth Ottoman sultan of the dynasty founded by his namesake, Osman I, in the late-thirteenth century. In 1622 he was the first reigning sultan to be murdered in an act of regicide, although the reign of four others had been cut short, either being killed on the battlefield, dying in captivity, or being deposed. For almost three hundred years the first fourteen sultans had been succeeded by one of their sons, though not always the eldest son as primogeniture was not recognised in the Ottoman Empire. In 1617, on the death of Ahmed I, this tradition came to an end. Instead of one of Ahmed's eight surviving sons being acclaimed sultan, a small palace clique announced the enthronement of Ahmed's surviving brother, Mustafa. Although Ahmed's sons were young, Osman at 13-years-old was the eldest, and Ibrahim (3-years-old) the youngest, Mustafa at 17 was only a few years older. The outcome of this decision was not what was intended. Over the next thirty years Mustafa was to be deposed, twice, and three of Ahmed's sons became the sultan, but two of those, Osman and Ibrahim, were murdered in palace coups.

It is impossible to explain these unprecedented events without an understanding of Ottoman family structure, their traditions of succession, and the changes that were taking place within the empire during the late-sixteenth and early-seventeenth centuries. Family structure was determined by Islamic (Hanafi) law whereby the household is centred on the father, in this case the sultan. He could have up to four wives at any one time, who may or may not be Muslim, but also have sexual relations with as many female slaves (concubines) as he wished. Any son by a wife was freeborn, legitimate and able to inherit, but so were the sons of concubines, as long as they were recognised by their father.[1] In the royal household, as in others, wives and concubines were confined, creating a private female world, the harem, separate from the rest of the palace. Only the sultan was permitted to enter and by the late sixteenth century it was guarded by the black eunuchs. They were supervised by the *kizlar agha*, the chief black eunuch, whose political influence increased rapidly in the late sixteenth century because of the sultans' wish to increase the power of the palace as against outside forces and because of the close relations that the chief black eunuch was able to develop with the sultan's mother.[2]

For Ottoman sultans up to the sixteenth century marriages were entered into for political not reproductive reasons. They were used to secure a foreign alliance or extend Ottoman territory. Marrying into leading Ottoman families was avoided as it could result in jealousies and internal conflicts, as was the case in Tudor England after some of Henry VIII's marriages. Their children were born mostly to concubines, taken from across the growing empire which by this time covered much of the Middle East and Egypt, and extended into Europe across the Balkans and to the north of the Black Sea. Until the reign of Suleiman I (1520-1566) it was the tradition that after a concubine, or very occasionally a wife, gave birth to a son, her sexual relations with the sultan ceased. Each son would be brought up separately by his mother in the harem until, at the age of ten or so, he was appointed as a provincial governor. His mother would accompany him to the province, where she would become an adviser and a leading figure in the household that built up around the prince. The prince would gradually gain experience in administration and have the opportunity to develop a reputation as a leader, a protector of his subjects, a provider of justice and a patron of scholars. Daughters of a sultan before the mid-fifteenth century often married foreign princes but after that time they were increasingly married to members of the Ottoman elite. This was a useful means of linking their fortune to that of the dynasty, and keeping the sultan informed of their activities, without any danger of a rival family developing because inheritance could only be through the male line.[3]

Justice, custom and public expectation required the sultan to treat each of his sons equally. Ottoman territory was regarded as indivisible and therefore could not be divided between sons on the sultan's death. Therefore only one of a sultan's sons could become his successor. Consequently, there would be growing rivalry between them, each backed by their mother, their household, and their supporters amongst those influential in Ottoman society and the armed forces. The succession was rarely achieved peacefully. There was often a short-lived civil war between the surviving sons on the death of their father, with the victor being regarded as the rightful heir on the grounds that his 'fortune' was superior to that of his brothers[4]. He had probably demonstrated the necessary skills and abilities, both as a provincial governor and in the conflict, to gain support and become sultan.

From the time of the third sultan, Murad I, in the second half of the fourteenth century, this competition for the succession became a matter of life or death. Any surviving brothers of the new sultan, regardless of whether they had been involved in the succession struggle, would be executed, along with any sons that they had. This was usually done by strangulation with a silk cord, the honourable method of execution in the Ottoman dynasty. These fratricides meant that, once established, the only threat to the sultan was from his own sons. This brought security and stability until his own death approached. This custom was similar to that found in Turco-Mongolian dynasties that pre-dated the Ottomans, and lasted in the empire for almost three centuries until the early-seventeenth century.

The danger of a brother or nephew surviving, was that he might rebel, or even attempt to gain the support of a foreign power. In the early-fifteenth century four sons of Bayazid I fought over a period of eleven years until the only survivor, Mehmed I, became sultan. Even then a fifth brother emerged from hiding to lead a rebellion and was only captured and killed ten years later. Succeeding sultans had their brothers and nephews, however young, strangled, as soon as possible. Mehmet II, best known for the capture of Constantinople in 1453 ending a millennium of Byzantine rule, had an infant brother killed on his accession, an act that he later legalised in the so-called 'law of fratricide'. When a brother managed to avoid this fate it could certainly cause problems. In the late-fifteenth century, Jem, the brother of Beyazid II, escaped after defeat in 1482, taking refuge in Christian Europe, and remained a constant threat until his death in 1495.

Sometimes a son would take the risk of pre-empting the situation by acting before their father's death, especially if they considered that they were being treated unfairly by being given the governorship of a minor province or one further from the capital which they would have to seize if they wished to become sultan. Between 1509 and 1512 three sons of Bayezid II began manoeuvring to secure the succession. All raised armies but in April 1512 it was Selim who successfully marched on Istanbul forcing his father to abdicate. He then tracked down and killed his brothers and their sons. On Selim I's death such conflict was avoided – he had only one surviving son, Suleiman, who became Suleiman I, often known as 'the Magnificent' or 'the Lawgiver' (1520-1566). His long reign also ended in the undisputed succession of Selim II, but only because his successor's rivals had been eliminated before Suleiman's death, either by his father or with his father's support.

This was partly brought about by a major break with the tradition of each wife or concubine having only one son. Suleiman not only freed and then married his favourite concubine, Hurrem Sultan, known in Europe as Roxelana, but together they had six children. She was given the title of *Hakesi Sultan* (chief consort) and it became clear that Suleiman favoured the sons that he had with her, of whom Selim II was one, as opposed to his eldest son who many regarded as an ideal successor until Suleiman had him strangled in 1553. In the late-sixteenth century another trend became a significant factor in the succession, that of seniority. Consecutive sultans, Selim II, and his son, Murad III, left many sons, but in both cases only one of them had reached maturity on his father's death and was therefore the only realistic successor. This, however, certainly did not end fratricide. Murad III (1574-1595) had his four surviving, and much younger, brothers strangled on his accession. By 1582 he had only one surviving son with his *Haseki Sultan*, Safiye, with whom he had an essentially monogamous relationship for many years. His mother, Nurbanu Sultan, believed that he needed more sons to secure the dynasty and encouraged him to take numerous concubines. He eventually had over fifty children, including twenty-five known sons, before his death in January 1595. His eldest son, again the only one to have reached maturity, succeeded him as Sultan Mehmed III (1595-1603). He carried out a ruthless act of fratricide by having his nineteen surviving brothers, all of them under the age of ten, strangled on 28 January, as well as having seven concubines, pregnant by his father, drowned.

For 300 years, none of these killings and executions had involved the murder of a sultan, with the possible exception of Bayazid II, perhaps poisoned shortly after he abdicated in 1512. They were the result of the rulers securing their position by removing real or potential rivals – their immediate male relatives. Fratricide was justified by the claim that success in the conflict between brothers gave the victor a divine mandate to rule and that it was necessary for good order. Suleiman, Selim II and Mehmed III all claimed that they had legal backing for the killing of their brothers or sons. But traditions were changing. Sons of the sultan, except the eldest, were no longer being sent to be provincial governors to gain experience of military and civil command. They were kept in the New Palace[5] in Istanbul. There was no longer a significant struggle for power. Some authorities were beginning to question the legality of wholesale fratricide and the killings often gave rise to public unrest. In January 1595 when Mehmet III had his brothers strangled, a contemporary chronicler, Selaniki, recorded that the cortege of nineteen coffins of the princes 'dragged from their mothers' knees' leaving the Topkapi Palace was greeted by 'the crying and weeping of the people of Istanbul' which 'God Most High let the Angels around the heavenly Throne hear.'[6]

On Mehmed III's death in 1603 there was no repetition of this slaughter, although fratricide had not ended completely. The absolute power of the sultan and his immediate entourage was being challenged by the growing authority and influence of legal, religious, and military entities. Suleiman I had requested a ruling about the execution of his son Bayazid from the muftis in 1562. These were the appointed guardians and interpreters of Islamic law who were qualified to give legal opinions. Over the following decades, headed by the chief mufti of Istanbul, their influence grew, along with that of the *ulema*, 'members of the learned class, educated in Islamic law and the other Islamic sciences'[7], some of whom, known as 'the lords of the law'[8], held substantial, almost hereditary, privileges. By the early seventeenth century few sultans could have a brother or son killed without regard to their views. Even Mehmed III had requested such an adjudication before the execution of his eldest son, Mahmud, in 1603, accused of plotting against his father. All sides in political conflicts were seeking to use legal opinions in their own interests.

CHAPTER 14

DEPOSITION AND REGICIDE – THE KILLING OF SULTAN OSMAN II

Mehmed had at least eight sons (and ten daughters) but by his death in December 1603, aged 37, only two survived, Ahmed, who was thirteen, and Mustafa, only three years old. Their older brother and likely successor had been executed just six months before Mehmed's own death. The succession was decided by a powerful group within the palace who presented Ahmed as the new sultan simultaneously with the announcement of the old sultan's death at a public ceremony to which all leading public figures had been instructed to attend. The young Mustafa was not killed but instead sent with his mother, Halime Sultan, to live in the Old Palace across Istanbul. He was allowed to live probably because his death would leave Ahmed as the only surviving male member of the dynasty, and as he had yet to have a son there was a danger of the dynasty dying out. We do not know whether Ahmed subsequently considered having his brother killed, but if he had asked the chief mufti for an opinion he might well have received a negative answer. It was in the interests of the muftis to restrict the powers of any sultan. Keeping his brother(s) alive meant that the sultan could be deposed and yet the centuries old dynasty would not end. It made the sultanate less dependent on one individual because the system could continue whether or not the sultan produced a son.[1]

As it happened Ahmed, best known for the construction of the Blue Mosque in Istanbul, produced thirteen sons (and at least ten daughters) by the time of his early death fourteen years later at the age of twenty-seven, in November 1617. He had applied himself dutifully to the task of producing possible heirs, and his first son, Osman, was born just eleven months after his accession when he was fourteen years old. However, five sons had died in infancy and Osman was still only thirteen years old. Nevertheless, it was expected that he would become the sultan, but this did not happen. Instead, a small group of leading officials – Es'ad, the chief mufti, the deputy grand vizier, and Mustafa Agha, the chief black eunuch – chose Ahmed's brother, the now 17-year-old Mustafa, spared at the time of Ahmed's accession, to be the new sultan. Despite concerns about his state of mind, Mustafa Agha remarked: 'His defect in intelligence comes from his long confinement … and he might come to his senses if he has contact with people for a while'.[2]

This was a break from the tradition of over 300 years whereby a son succeeded his father. There is no official record as to why the decision was made, though it seems likely that it was an issue of age. With the early death of Ahmed, Mustafa was the oldest surviving prince of the dynasty and, according to the historian Pechevi, those in power argued that there would be public disapproval if a child was chosen when an adult was available.[3] Was Osman too young at thirteen? Ahmed had been the same age when he acceded in 1603, but the difference was that then there had been no alternative other than his three-year-old brother. It is also possible that Ahmed's *Haseki Sultan*, Kosem, had a powerful influence on the decision. Of Greek origin, she was captured and sold as a slave to the governor of the Ottoman province of Bosnia before being sent to Istanbul in 1605. Her beauty and intelligence soon caught the attention of Sultan Ahmed and over the next twelve years she bore him several children. The removal from power of Ahmed's influential grandmother, Safiye Sultan, followed by the death of his mother, Handan Sultan, left Kosem in a strong position in the harem from which, though in many ways a private world, considerable covert political influence could be exercised. It has been suggested that fearing the execution of her own sons, Murad and Ibrahim, if Ahmed's eldest son, Osman, became sultan, she first persuaded Ahmed to keep his brother Mustafa alive, then in 1617 gave her support to him becoming sultan. On his accession neither Osman nor any of Kosem's sons were killed. Instead they were secured in the *kafes*, sometimes called the 'golden cages', small private apartments within the harem, where their comfort and access to others depended on the wishes of the sultan.

Although this did not mark the end of fratricide in the Ottoman dynasty, it has been argued[4] that the law and its representatives had now entered into vital decisions about the dynasty. Whatever the reasons, the enthronement of Mustafa I marked the continuation of the shift towards seniority being the crucial factor in the succession, a principle which eventually became established and was followed for the remaining 300 years of the dynasty. Brothers and nephews of the sultan were now more likely to be confined in the *kafes* than executed on the sultan's accession. It certainly did not mean that a sultan could not be deposed, whether by peaceful or violent means. Indeed the existence of alternatives meant that such an action became more likely. In the period from 1617 to 1648, there were five reigns, four of them ended with the sultan deposed, and in two cases murdered, in palace coups. However, the new system created a clear line of succession, often from brother to brother until that generation died out, and then the eldest of the next generation.

If Osman's age had been a factor in the decision of November 1617, it was no longer an issue three months later when Mustafa was replaced. The usual explanation for this was Mustafa's mental capacity, or rather lack of it. Mustafa had survived partly because Ahmed never regarded his brother as a threat because he knew that he was not capable of ruling. Since the age of three Mustafa had been confined to the *kafes* adjacent to the harem, with little personal contact other than with servants and his mother, Halime Sultan. His education was limited, he had little knowledge of the outside world and was probably in constant fear of execution. This was not an upbringing designed to produce an able ruler. However it is possible that his mental weakness was exaggerated by those who wished to remove him. Even with an ineffective sultan the empire could have been run by a powerful grand vizier, as had happened during the reign of Selim II who seemingly had little interest in governing. However, the plotters decided to replace Mustafa and ensured that everyone knew of his odd behaviour. There were rumours, probably spread by Mustafa Agha, the chief black eunuch, of his throwing gold and silver coins to the birds and the fish in the sea, and knocking off the viziers' turbans when they were discussing government matters with him[5].

At the end of February 1618, he was deposed by almost the same court faction that had given him the throne. Mustafa Agha and the chief gardener, the title given to the head of security and chief executioner at the palace[6], played a major role, aided by the vizier Ali Pasha, who had risen quickly to become grand admiral of the navy through the support of the chief black eunuch. He was angry about being replaced by Davud Pasha, Mustafa's brother-in-law, at the beginning of Mustafa's reign. The chief mufti, Es'ad, at first opposed the plan but when the deputy grand vizier was drawn in fearing the loss of his own position, the chief mufti realised that he could do little to prevent the deposition and changed his mind. On the night of 25th February Mustafa was locked in the *kafes*, where he had already spent much of his youth, by the chief black eunuch. Osman was then released and the next morning officials were summoned to pay allegiance to their new sultan, Osman II.

Mustafa's deposition and Osman's enthronement represented a blow to the power of the new forces that had developed in Ottoman society, especially the *ulema*, and has been referred to as 'The Court strikes back'.[7] Osman's principal tutor from 1609 had been Omer Efendi, a teacher who by the early-seventeenth century had become a preacher at the prestigious *Ayasofya* (Hagia Sofia) mosque adjacent to the imperial palace where he came to the attention of Sultan Ahmed. Preachers often responded to questions about the rights and wrongs of an issue when disputes arose in daily life, providing an alternate source of advice from that of the more hierarchical and less accessible lords of the law. It is likely that Omer was influential in developing Osman's ideas about the need for social and personal discipline, shown in his preference for simple clothes, his opposition to smoking which he saw as non-Muslim decadence, and his rather restrained private life. It has been suggested that he even considered dismantling the harem.[8] Osman has been referred to as a sultan who 'enjoined good and forbade evil'[9]. He named his first son, born in October 1621, after Omer, a sure sign of respect, though the infant died in an accident, for which his mother was blamed, in February 1622.

Osman was the first sultan to have been born in Istanbul; his father had been too young to be made a provincial governor. His mother died when he was young, so he had no-one in the harem to look after his interests who could match the influence of Halime Sultan (Mustafa's mother) or Kosem Sultan. Despite being the eldest son, he had also been considered too young to be appointed to a provincial governorship, and although he was keen on hunting and the arts of war, he had not had the chance to develop close links with groups within the armed forces. His power was constrained by the influence of the grand mufti, Es'ad, who prevented him having Mustafa and his own brothers killed at the time of his accession. Kosem Sultan was sent with her sons to be confined in the 'Old Palace', but she managed to build a relationship with Osman that was strong enough to protect them. Osman must have considered himself cheated out of the throne in 1617 and, though young, he was ambitious, headstrong, and wished to assert his power. He pursued a policy of strengthening central control, which displeased many of the *ulema* and eventually managed to anger the military establishment – the cavalry divisions and the janissaries.

The Ottomans had been at war with the Safavids of Persia since 1615 but the military situation had become deadlocked. The peace of 1619 resulted in no significant gains but it had secured the eastern border. Wishing to build up his reputation and influenced by Omer and Mustafa Agha, Osman appointed Ali Pasha, who although a success as grand admiral was still a junior vizier, as his new grand vizier and announced plans for a military campaign. This was the traditional way for a sultan to strengthen his position – leading his army out of Istanbul with great ceremony in the spring or early summer on campaign against the Habsburgs, the Safavids of Persia, or rebels within the empire, and then returning having defeated his enemies, or at least claiming a victory. Suleiman, in his forty-six year reign, did so on thirteen occasions. However, of the five sultans (Selim II, Murad III, Mehmet III, Ahmed I and Mustafa I) in the fifty-five years since then (up to 1621) only Mehmet III had done so, once.[10] There had been considerable criticism of the inertia and isolation of these sultans. Many in Ottoman society believed that if the sultan was directly involved in a campaign the chances of success would be much greater. It was also thought that those who were given military command instead of the sultan were gaining too much power in other areas of government.

Osman wished to re-assert the military traditions of his ancestors. He would lead his forces north against the Polish-Lithuanian Commonwealth. In 1617 the Treaty of Busza was signed by Iskender Pasha, the Ottoman governor of the northern border areas, and Hetman Zolkiewski, the Polish commander and victor of the battle of Klushino against the Russian army in 1610. The treaty recognised Moldavia, Transylvania and Wallachia as Ottoman vassal states and the Poles promised to prevent Cossack raids into Ottoman lands along the Black Sea. In return the Ottomans gave a commitment to prevent Tatar raids across the border into the territory of the Polish-Lithuanian Commonwealth. This had done little to bring peace to the area. Raids continued on both sides and the voivode of Moldavia, Gaspar Graziani, rebelled against his Ottoman overlords, coming to an agreement with the Poles. In 1620 King Sigismund III of Poland sent forces under Zolkiewski to support Gaspar Graziani, though they got little backing from the local nobility, most of whom preferred to wait and see the likely outcome in order to be able to join the winning side. At the Battle of Cecora, in a series of engagements between 17 September and 7 October, the Polish forces were heavily defeated by the larger force commanded by Iskender Pasha. Zolkiewski refused to surrender and was killed in battle. His head was placed on a pike and sent to Sultan Osman in Istanbul.

Although hostilities paused during the winter months, Osman refused all efforts to achieve a peace and both sides expected the conflict to continue the next year. Encouraged by his advisers, especially Ali Pasha, he believed that he could take advantage of Zolkiewski's defeat. By leading a victorious campaign against the Poles, he would increase Ottoman territory at the expense of the Polish-Lithuanian Commonwealth and gain prestige and glory as a conquering sultan. There was considerable opposition to the plan from several viziers and powerful lords of the law, who argued that local commanders could deal with the situation as they had already done in 1620. The weather was unusually harsh that winter, with heavy, continuous snow in January and an extended period of sub-zero temperatures. Hunger and starvation were widespread in Istanbul and the surrounding area, but nothing dissuaded Osman to postpone the new expedition.

Before he departed he had his brother Mehmed, only three month his junior, executed in order to prevent any threat to his position during his absence, even though he failed to gain a positive legal opinion about the killing from the chief mufti Es'ad, and relied on one from the chief justice of the European provinces.[11] On the death of Ali Pasha in March 1621 he appointed Huseyin Pasha as grand vizier, a former chief gardener and still only a junior vizier, just as Ali Pasha had been, much to the annoyance of more senior ministers. He also angered the lords of the law by abolishing the tradition of giving retired judges, and those awaiting a suitable post, a sinecure of a judgeship in a small town. Instead of going to the town themselves the judges sent young protégées to carry out the work, but received most of the income. Osman's desire to weaken the power of elements in Ottoman society that could challenge the autocracy of the sultan was creating considerable hostility.

Leaving Istanbul with an army of 120,000[12] in late April 1521 Osman marched first to Edirne, the Ottoman capital before the capture of Constantinople (Istanbul) in 1453, and then over 1000 kilometres north. He confronted his enemies outside the fortress of Khotyn (Chocim), now in southern Ukraine, at the end of August. The Polish army and their Cossack allies had prepared strong field fortifications in front of Khotyn on the river Dniester. In the first week of September the besieging Ottomans forces made numerous assaults, using both infantry (janissaries) and cavalry (*sipahi*), but were repulsed, often with heavy losses. After this the Ottomans hoped to defeat their opponents by cutting off food and military supplies. A further Ottoman assault failed on 15 September and then they themselves were subjected to large scale counter-attacks in subsequent days. Despite imposing real hardship on the defenders, by 28 September Osman's army was in trouble. The poor harvest meant that food supplies were low, sickness was widespread, fodder for their horses was running out, the heavy rains had damaged tents and their heavy cannons were becoming immovable in the mud.

Given the stalemate, the lateness of the season and heavy losses of perhaps 40,000 men, they accepted the Polish request for negotiations.

In the Treaty of Khotyn, signed on 9 October, little was gained. Ottoman control of Moldavia was confirmed, but the Poles considered the halting of the much larger Ottoman army a great victory. What had been intended to be a major campaign of conquest had turned into a single, failed, siege. Osman withdrew to Edirne, planning to renew the campaign against Poland the following year. But opposition within the army, because of their lack of pay and the hardships that they experienced in 1621, forced him to give up this idea. He returned to Istanbul in early 1622.

Osman blamed the janissaries for these military failures. They were originally the elite corps of the Ottoman forces and the first modern standing army in Europe. They were made up of selected Christian children from the European provinces who were taken from their families in a form of child levy (known as *devsirme*), circumcised and raised as Muslims. These children attended the palace and military schools and went on to became administrators or members of the janissary corps, often attaining the most senior positions in the army and government, up to and including grand vizier. The janissaries were known for their strict discipline, and were expected to be absolutely loyal to the sultan. In return they received many benefits, regular payment, whether on campaign or not, and pensions on retirement.

In the late-sixteenth and early-seventeenth centuries economic and social changes meant that many of the growing middle-class looked for ways to advance their status and influence in society. One way was to join the army, in particular the janissaries. As the number of soldiers increased, recruitment methods, largely controlled by the janissary officers themselves, were loosened. Many Muslim civilians were able to buy their way in so that they could take advantage of the benefits that accrued. The janissaries became diluted and less effective as a military force, but yet another institutional threat to the power of the sultan as the members sought to defend their privileges. Together with the cavalry divisions, they had in the 1590s and 1600s used the threat of force to influence political decisions and appointments made by sultans Mehmed III and Ahmed I.

Soon after returning to Istanbul, Osman decided to go on a 'pilgrimage campaign' to Mecca, which no other Ottoman sultan had done. When this became widely known, suspicions arose. Was Osman just demonstrating devotion to his faith and seeking to gain approval as a 'righteous' sultan? Was he intending on his journey to Mecca to enforce his authority on areas of the empire where some local rulers had shown too much independence? Or was he, as many believed, using the pilgrimage as cover for a plan to recruit a new army of mercenaries from more distant parts of the empire, with which he would return to Istanbul and destroy the power of the janissaries? This did not seem as unlikely as it would have done fifty years earlier. Mercenary soldiers were widely used across Europe and various Ottoman provincial governors, as well as rebel forces within the Ottoman Empire, had made use of such troops. By the spring of 1622 there were rumours that Osman's agents were already starting to recruit in Anatolia.

Such plans were made possible by the changing nature of society. The old, essentially feudal, system based on local nobility paying tribute to the sultan, was being replaced by one in which the sultans' appointees governed the provinces. However, this pyramidal structure with the sultan at the top was now changing into a more complex web of relationships, in which the lords of the law, the viziers, the military and the more economically successful urban population, all played a part, alongside the traditional holders of power. In this structure the sultan might sit at the centre, but at various times he could be more or less active in seeking to control the web. Osman was looking to increase his control. The questions that then arose were bound to lead to friction. What authority did the sultan have to change traditional rights and privileges? Was he bound by existing laws to protect those rights or could he change them as he saw fit? What should be the influence of those who interpret divine law as against the political will of the sultan or his viziers?

It was in this context that there was considerable opposition to the pilgrimage campaign. It was asked whether the sultan should leave for such a length of time when peace with the Polish-Lithuanian Commonwealth had yet to be confirmed and while Istanbul was still suffering from food shortages, with the associated discontent. Many lords of the law expressed their concerns about the whole plan. The janissaries had already been angered by talk of payments being withheld, names being removed from the payment lists and pension rights threatened. Now, along with the cavalry divisions, they heard that Osman was going to take the imperial treasury with him on the pilgrimage, which would both endanger their pay and enable him to pay for a new army. The truth of these rumours might be questioned but, as so often, what really mattered was what people believed. Both the English and French ambassadors wrote about signs of serious unrest. In this situation Osman received much advice against going, from the grand vizier, the chief mufti and the new chief black eunuch, but he was not willing to change his plan.

On Wednesday 18th May 1622, as he prepared to leave Istanbul, janissaries and members of the cavalry divisions met at the New Barracks, and then moved to Al Meydani, the Square of the Horses, on the site of the old hippodrome. At this point they were unarmed and publicly blaming the sultan's advisers not Osman himself. They went to the homes of Omer Efendi and Dilaver Pasha, the grand vizier appointed in September 1621, with the intention of asking them to present their demands to Osman. They wanted the cancelation of the pilgrimage and the execution of Suleiman Agha, the chief black eunuch who had replaced Mustafa Agha in 1620. However, Omer fled and Dilaver Pasha's men fired arrows at them. Anger and discontent rose, though they dispersed in the early evening. There were signs that Osman might have been willing to compromise. He dismissed Dilaver Pasha that evening, and it is possible that he was reconsidering the pilgrimage.

However, the next morning the soldiers, both janissaries and cavalrymen, now armed, reassembled at the New Barracks and then moved to the mosque of Ahmed I (the Blue Mosque) adjacent to the Al Meydani. They were joined by many *ulema*, and by an increasing number of the city's population. A petition was produced for the chief mufti, Es'ad, to take to Osman. The demands were now more extensive. They wanted the execution of not just the chief black eunuch, but also Dilaver Pasha, Omer, Baki Pasha, the finance minister, and others who they held responsible for trying to cut payments to the janissaries. After some discussion between the *ulema* and the viziers, a group of them were received by Osman. Before any decision was reached the crowd of soldiers and civilians advanced to the palace. Some written accounts record that a new grand vizier read a statement from Osman to the crowd which announced an order to arrest Dilaver Pasha and the dismissal of the others, with the exception of the chief black eunuch. This compromise, if it is to be believed, is often left out by some contemporary writers who wished to demonstrate that the sultan was not willing to accede to the demands of the soldiers until much later, thus justifying the eventual outcome.

Events now developed an uncontrollable momentum. Calls started for the restoration of the former sultan, Mustafa. Sympathetic royal attendants opened the gates to the palace and many soldiers moved into the inner, third, courtyard and, having discovered where Mustafa was held, climbed up onto the roof of the harem, created a hole in it and lifted him up with ropes. Only at this point did Osman have both Dilaver Pasha and Suleiman Agha handed over to the soldiers, who killed them immediately. The aims of the lords of the law, ending the pilgrimage and weakening Osman's position, had been achieved. They now wished the crowd to disperse. But it was too late. The soldiers had come to believe that their interests could only be protected by removing Osman himself. They insisted that the *ulema* recognised Mustafa as the new sultan. Only Es'ad refused, a decision that cost him his position, though not his life.

Mustafa was taken to the Old Palace and then, on rumours that Osman might attack him there, moved on to the Orta Mosque at the janissary barracks, along with his mother, Halime Sultan. That night, under cover of darkness, Osman and his new grand vizier went to the residence of general of the janissaries, Ali Agha, and persuaded him to speak in Osman's favour to the janissaries in the hope of causing a rift between them and the cavalrymen. However, word got out and the general was murdered as he went to the Orta Mosque on the morning of Friday 20 May. Soldiers then went to his house, killed the grand vizier as he tried to escape, arrested Osman and took him to the Orta Mosque.

On the instructions of Mustafa's mother an imperial order was written, probably by a literate janissary sergeant, appointing Davud Pasha as the next grand vizier. Mustafa, who seemed to show little interest in the events unfolding around him, was taken to the New Palace to be enthroned. At the mosque Osman was treated with a complete lack of respect and unable to make himself heard when he tried to speak to the soldiers. An attempt was made to put a noose around his neck, which he resisted, and he was then unceremoniously dumped onto a wagon carrying a pile of hay and mocked by on-lookers as he was taken to the Yedikule, the Fortress of the Seven Towers. He must have known his fate. If he was to be kept alive he would have been held prisoner in the palace. Once at the fortress, his struggles subdued by having his testicles squeezed, Osman was ritually strangled on the orders of Davud Pasha in the name of the new sultan. The first regicide in Ottoman history had occurred. The former sultan's body was desecrated. His right ear was cut off and sent to Halime Sultan as proof of his death. He was buried the next day in the tomb of his father, Ahmed I.

Several accounts of the killing of Osman II hold Davud Pasha as the chief culprit. However, the soldiers could have taken any one of several opportunities to prevent the killing if they had chosen to: when Osman abandoned plans for the pilgrimage campaign; when he ordered the replacement of his advisers; when Dilaver Pasha and Suleiman Agha were executed; and even after Mustafa had been made sultan Osman could have been imprisoned. But it seems that Osman's known dissatisfaction with the janissaries and cavalry divisions after the campaign against the Polish-Lithuanian Commonwealth, threats to their pay and pensions, and his intention to take the treasury out of Istanbul so that he could raise a new army, persuaded them that he had to be killed. There seems to have been no well thought out plan to do so beforehand or any careful consideration of who should succeed him.

Although there was no immediate unrest in Istanbul after the murder, Mustafa's second reign was as unsuccessful as his first, though lasting rather longer, fifteen months instead of three months. It is possible that he issued orders for the death of his surviving nephews, Osman's half-brothers, but the princes were given protection by the chief black eunuch. Power was initially in the hands of Mustafa's mother, Halime, and Davud Pasha, but after only a month Davud was replaced as grand vizier in an effort to distance the new sultan from Osman's killing. Several grand viziers followed in quick succession, though none was able to take control of the situation. There was increasing violence in Istanbul, and a rebellion, ostensibly to revenge Osman's death, started in the provinces.

The janissaries sought to place all blame for Osman's death on Davud Pasha, and downplay their own responsibility. Davud Pasha was executed along with others in January 1623, but discontent continued until another new grand vizier, the chief mufti and other leading *ulema*, decided that Mustafa would again have to be replaced. In September 1623 his mother agreed on the condition that his life was spared. He remained confined within the palace in the *kafes* until his death in 1639, only one year before the death of his successor, his nephew Murad, Ahmed's son by Kosem Sultan.

Murad IV was only eleven years old when he became sultan, and for the early part of his reign Kosem, officially known as the *Valide Sultan* (mother of the sultan) acted as regent. After he took absolute power in 1632 he was known for his banning of alcohol, tobacco and coffee in Istanbul and his insistence on severe punishment for law-breakers. He is said to have ordered the execution of his brother-in-law for some 'act against the law of God', and to have strangled a grand vizier for beating his mother-in-law. For much of his reign the Ottomans were again at war with the Safavids, during which he personally commanded two campaigns, the second of which led to the capture of Baghdad. The resulting peace treaty in May 1639, negotiated by the grand vizier Kemankesh Kara Mustafa, established the boundary between the two sides which still remains the basis for the border between modern day Iran and Turkey/Iraq. Despite the fact that Murad had at least twenty-eight children (and possibly as many as thirty-five), all his fifteen sons died in infancy or early childhood. The execution of all but one of his surviving brothers in 1635 and 1638 meant that at his death from cirrhosis in 1640, at the age of twenty-seven, there was once again only one living member of the dynasty, his youngest brother and Kosem's youngest son, Ibrahim, born in 1615.

CHAPTER 15

THE PRICE OF FAILURE –
THE FALL OF IBRAHIM I

Ibrahim had spent his first twenty-five years in the *kafes*, as had become the norm for possible successors (and therefore threats) to the sultan. Like his uncle, Mustafa, he had effectively been under house-arrest, often with access to only a small, sunless courtyard, considered by Murad to be too unstable to rule. He had lived through the deposition of Mustafa (twice), the murder of Sultan Osman II and several of his brothers. It was even rumoured that Murad had ordered his execution from his death-bed, but the instruction was not carried out – it would have meant the end of the dynasty. It was the fact that he was the son of the influential Kosem and Ahmed I that kept him alive.

Such an early life was no preparation for ruling a large and complex empire. It is said that Kosem Sultan, and the grand vizier, Kemankesh Kara Mustafa, of Albanian origin who had risen through the ranks of the janissaries, had to persuade him to ascend the throne. He at first believed that it was a trap set by Murad in order to give his brother an excuse to execute him. He needed to inspect Murad's body before he accepted.[1] Nevertheless for the first few years he showed an interest in the affairs of state and with a competent grand vizier guiding him, the empire was efficiently run. Peace was renewed with the Habsburgs, the currency was stabilised and economic reforms achieved.[2] However, the execution in January 1644 of Kemankesh Kara Mustafa Pasha, who had lasted as grand vizier for over five years when it was common for them to be removed, and often executed, after less than a year, was followed by an on-going and venal competition for power in Istanbul. The start of war with Venice in the eastern Mediterranean over the possession of Crete also added to the problems of the empire.

At the same time there was a decline in Ibrahim's always delicate physical and mental health. He suffered frequent headaches, and spent increasing amounts of time in the harem. His duty to produce male heirs, essential for the continuation of the dynasty, seemed to become an obsession. He spent vast amounts on luxuries – fine textiles, jewellery, perfumes – and demanded more and more concubines to be provided for him, from amongst whom he created eight *Haseki Sultans* (chief consorts), thus making the title meaningless. It has been said that he was addicted to wine and sexual pleasures; the walls of his chamber were covered with mirrors, his pillows stuffed with rich furs. This was the distorted picture of the Ottoman palace and the harem in particular that developed in the imagination of Christian Europeans, a place of lascivious decadence and unbridled pleasures. Ibrahim's weaknesses were encouraged by ambitious and unscrupulous sycophants, who provided for his desires and in doing so gained power and wealth as he showered them with palaces and land.

Expenditure rose rapidly while revenues declined. After initial successes there were setbacks in the costly war, with the blockade of the Dardanelles by the Venetians not only preventing supplies being sent to the army in Crete but also causing food shortages in Istanbul. High taxes to pay for the war and for Ibrahim's extravagances became very unpopular. Poor harvests in Egypt brought famine. There were rebellions in Anatolia, with widespread looting and the destruction of villages, which although defeated were an indication of things to come. In 1647 a plague of locusts destroyed crops in Cyprus. Later in that year Ibrahim came to believe that the grand vizier, Salih Pasha and Kosem Sultan were plotting against him. Salih Pasha was executed, on the grounds that he had not enforced Ibrahim's ban on carriages in Istanbul, and Ibrahim's mother was exiled from the harem. In June 1648 Istanbul was shaken by an earthquake, killing perhaps 30,000 people and wrecking the main aqueduct. This was taken by many to be a sign of God's disapproval. Despite all the hardship suffered by the common people, they could see that the sultan's favourites still had plenty of water and that their profligate behaviour continued unchecked.

Two months later on 8 August the next grand vizier, Ahmed Pasha, who had increased taxes yet again, was seized, strangled and his body torn apart by a mob – hence his nickname *Hezarpare* (one thousand pieces). It was clear that both the janissaries and the *ulema* had turned against the sultan. The janissary commanders had already requested that the chief mufti, Abdurrahim, issue a *fatwa* (a legal ruling on a point of Islamic law) approving the removal and execution of the grand vizier, and this was then extended to the sultan. Ibrahim was taken prisoner in the Topkapi Palace and it was announced that his oldest son, six-year-old Mehmed, had replaced him as sultan. When rumours of a plot to restore Ibrahim spread, the chief mufti approved his death, as did his mother, Kosem, after a two-hour confrontation. She was later reported to have said that 'In the end he will leave neither you nor me alive. We will lose control of the government. The whole society is in ruins. Have him removed from the throne immediately.'[3] On 18 August he was strangled by the official executioner while his mother and officials watched from a window above. The second regicide had taken place just twenty-six years after the first.

The idea that Ibrahim was removed because of his degeneracy, mental incapacity and inability to govern effectively was certainly the impression that those who decided to remove him wished people to have and this explanation has been generally accepted ever since. However, despite the undoubted weaknesses and failures of his reign, it has been suggested that some of Ibrahim's actions were aimed at taking resources and power for himself and the court at the expense of the political magnates and others who wished to benefit. The motives of those who wished to remove him were therefore as much to do with limiting royal absolutism in their own interests as with ending the rule of an incompetent sultan.[4]

With his deposition and death Kosem Sultan once again became regent, this time for her grandson, Mehmed IV. The young sultan's mother, Turhan Hadice Sultan, an ambitious woman in her own right, was initially outmanoeuvred by Kosem, but three years later she had her revenge. It was believed that Kosem planned to replace Mehmed with a younger son of Ibrahim, whose mother could be more easily managed. The plot was betrayed by one of her servants. With the full backing of the chief mufti, the grand vizier drew up her death warrant and on 2 September 1651 Kosem was found hiding in a clothes chest, dragged out and killed. Her ending was in stark contrast to the influence and power that she had been able to exercise over most of the previous forty years. Turhan Sultan, now the *Valide Sultan*, became the regent, continuing this period known as the 'Sultanate of Women', when women within the harem at times exercised great power. This stretched back to Hurrem, the wife of Suleiman, through Nurbanu Sultan, the mother of Murad III, Safiye Sultan, the mother of Mehmet III, and Kosem Sultan. With Turhan's death in 1683 it came to an end.

After Ibrahim's killing in 1648 he was succeeded in turn by three of his sons, Mehmed IV (born 1642 – reigned 1648-1687 – died 1693), deposed but not executed after a reign of thirty-nine years, the second longest reign in Ottoman history, and his brothers, Suleiman II (1642 – r.1687-1691) and Ahmed II (1643 – r.1691-1695) who both reigned until their deaths. Ahmad II was followed by Mustafa II, the eldest son of Mehmed

IV. Seniority in the dynasty had now become the deciding factor in the succession. The brothers of sultans were no longer strangled *en masse* and sons had to wait out the reigns of their uncles, usually in the restricted environment of the *kafes*, until their elevation to the sultanate. They were therefore often unprepared for their responsibilities as sultan and had no opportunity to build up a group of officials and administrators around them upon whom they could rely in the early years of their rule. This limited the absolutist powers of the sultans as against those of the various factions that vied for power around them and the influence of the janissaries.[5]

This change in the nature of the succession did not result greater stability in the empire or greater security for the sultan. Until the first deposition of Mustafa I in 1617, very few sultans had been removed by internal revolt and none had been murdered while still sultan. There was no obvious successor other than a son. With changes in society and the availability of alternative princes who could become sultan, the number of depositions increased. Osman II and Ibrahim I were killed during the time when the method of determining the succession was in the process of changing. Between 1648 and the end of the dynasty in 1922, when it was the oldest male in the dynasty who succeeded, there were another eighteen sultans, of whom nine died in office, and eight were deposed, two of whom were either assassinated (Selim III, reigned 1789-1807) or executed (Mustafa IV, reigned 1807-1808) on the order of their successor, and another (Abdulaziz, reigned 1861-1876) either committed suicide or was murdered just days after his removal from office. The last sultan, Mehmed VI, born in 1861 lived for fifty-six years, first in the harem and then the *kafes*, throughout the reigns of his uncle and then three older brothers, before his accession in 1918. He went into exile in 1922 after the sultanate had been abolished by the Grand National Assembly of Turkey.

In most of the depositions the janissary corps played a significant role, just as they had in the depositions and regicides of the seventeenth century. Once a strength of the Ottoman dynasty, the influx of civilians and the loss of its uniquely military character in the late sixteenth century meant that it become a conservative, reactionary force, largely concerned with defending its own privileges. It blocked reforms in society and any efforts to reduce its own power within the empire, removing sultans who threatened to do so. It was not until 1826 that it was eventually abolished by Mahmud II in a carefully prepared campaign. He had needed to reach a compromise with them on becoming sultan in 1808. By the 1820s, their military effectiveness had long been limited, and corruption was widespread, with 135,000 men receiving salaries even though many were not active soldiers. Having strengthened his position across the empire and planned for the establishment of a more modern armed force, he announced his intention. The expected revolt took place but Mahmud was ready. In fierce conflict 4,000 janissaries died in the 'Auspicious Incident'. Many of those captured were imprisoned and eventually beheaded in the 'Tower of Blood' in Thessaloniki. Thus, the body largely responsible for the killing of both Osman II and Ibrahim I in the first half of the seventeenth century came to an end.

CHARLES I AND THE REGICIDES

PART

6

The World Turned Upside Down?

*'If we beat the King ninety-nine times yet he is King still ...
but if the King beat us once we shall all be hanged.'*

The Earl of Manchester (1602–1671), commander of the
Parliamentary army between 1643 and 1645. He later
supported efforts to come to an agreement with the
king and opposed putting Charles I on trial

———— ✦ ⊰❂⊱ ✦ ————

'I do not think one man wise enough to govern us all.'

The republican M.P. Henry Marten (1602–1680) speaking
to Edward Hyde, later the Earl of Clarendon, in 1641. As a
signatory of Charles I's death warrant he was put on trial as a
regicide in 1660 and was sentenced to life imprisonment

———— ✦ ⊰❂⊱ ✦ ————

*'I do think that the poorest man in England is not at all
bound in a strict sense to that Government that he hath not
had a voice to put Himself under.'*

Col. Thomas Rainsborough supporting the idea of universal
male suffrage at the Putney Debates in October-November
1647. He was murdered while taking part in the siege of
Pontefract Castle the following year

CHAPTER 16

THE TRIAL AND EXECUTION
OF A KING

T he English already had a reputation for executing monarchs. As the civil wars in Britain and Ireland moved towards their conclusion, King Charles was a prisoner. In April 1646 he had escaped in disguise from the besieged city of Oxford and surrendered to the Scottish army in Nottinghamshire. Nine months later they handed him over to the English Parliament and then in August 1647 officers of the New Model Army secured him at Hampton Court and later at Carisbrooke Castle on the Isle of Wight. The fate of his grandmother was recalled both in Britain and across Europe. In *'Mary Stuart or Martyred Majesty'* a play written by the Dutchman Joost van den Vondel in 1646, which had clear allusions to Charles' situation, Mary, Queen of Scots asks: 'What wonder is it then if yet another mob, increases with my corpse the count of slaughtered kings of English blood. Is't not the English custom, to hold the blood of kings of very little worth?'[1]

In the courts of France, Spain and elsewhere, horror was expressed about the events unfolding in England, though there was also a recognition that Charles had played a role in bringing about his own downfall. The French ambassador to England, Bellièvre, wrote in 1647 that Charles had failed to take much of the advice that he had been offered and that 'It is very difficult to save him against his will'[2]. Yet as late as the autumn of 1648 his death on the scaffold only three months later on a cold January day was by no means a foregone conclusion. No decision had been made to either execute Charles Stuart or to replace the monarchy with a republic. Opinion was divided on both issues, even amongst those who had fought against Charles over the previous seven years or had suffered under his rule.

One citizen who had good reason to dislike the king and his policies was William Prynne. Educated at Oxford and called to the bar in 1628 he held strong Puritan views. He was opposed to feast days, such as Christmas, for the revelry and drunkenness that he believed they encouraged. He also believed that stage plays provoked immorality and was particularly critical of female actors. Watching and even joining in plays was a favourite pastime at Charles' court and his Catholic queen, Henrietta Maria, the youngest daughter of the murdered French king, Henry IV, and her ladies, were known to take part. Prynne's views, put forward in the thousand page book, *Histriomastix*, published in 1632, were seen as a direct attack on the queen, and his criticisms of rulers who permitted such plays, using Nero and other tyrants as examples, a barely veiled condemnation of the king. He was arrested and sentenced to life imprisonment, fined £5,000, expelled from Lincoln's Inn, and deprived of his Oxford degree. In addition, as he stood in the public pillory having his ears cut off, copies of his book were burnt in front of him. They would have produced plenty of smoke.

Prynne, though, was not silenced. He became a prominent opponent of the religious policies of the king and his Archbishop of Canterbury, William Laud, appointed in 1533 and campaigned against the place of bishops in the English Church. Further punishment followed, including the branding of the letters 'S.L.' (standing for 'seditious libeller') onto his cheeks. As tensions between king and parliament rose, Prynne's conviction was overturned on the order of parliament in 1640. He was released and awarded compensation, though he was still awaiting its payment in 1648. During the civil war he wrote newspaper articles and pamphlets in support of parliament and played a leading role in gathering evidence for the prosecution of Archbishop Laud in 1644. Although the trial ended without a verdict, Parliament passed a bill of attainder, declaring Laud guilty, and the archbishop was beheaded in January 1645, at the age of seventy-one.

However, although Prynne's religious views remained unchanged, by the autumn of 1648 when he was elected as a member of parliament, he was strongly opposed to the more radical social and political views being expressed by many, especially in the army. In November the Army Council issued the Remonstrance, which expressed their anger at the generous terms that parliament seemed to be prepared to offer Charles, referring to the king as this 'man of blood' and 'the principal author ... of our late wars'. They had lost patience with Charles and wished him to be brought to justice. They also called for a new parliament to be elected as the 'Long Parliament', which had been sitting since 1640, no longer represented their views. This was ignored by parliament and on 5 December, along with the majority, Prynne voted in favour of agreeing the terms that had been negotiated with Charles' representatives as a basis for a settlement. The next morning troops commanded by Colonel Pride replaced the usual guards at Westminster. Using lists drawn up by Henry Ireton, Oliver Cromwell's son-in-law, they prevented all those who had voted for the settlement and other moderates, nearly 200 M.P.s, from entering the Commons. Forty-five M.P.s were arrested, including Prynne. Others withdrew from parliament in protest. This action, known as 'Pride's Purge', left a 'Rump' of about 150 M.P.s, mainly Independent Puritans, who were prepared to sanction further action against the king. They believed that he had rejected all reasonable peace terms and was likely to renege on any agreement that might be reached. Charles' execution and a revolution in the way that England was ruled had just become much more likely.

As usual, imprisonment did not prevent Prynne from publishing his case, which he did as early as 1 January 1649. Executing the king, he wrote, would bring parliament into disrepute. For a Protestant kingdom to remove their king would simply prove to Catholics that the Protestant religion was tainted and provide 'great encouragement to the Jesuits, papists, and all licentious persons'. Additionally, since Charles was also king of Scotland and Ireland and the execution would not have their consent, it was likely to provoke those nations to launch a 'just war against you'. Such an attack could then expect the support of all remaining English royalists and possibly several foreign countries. Finally, he pointed out that there was no law or precedent 'for what you are going about'. This was a strong defence of a king who had approved of the brutal treatment of Prynne and other religious dissenters only fifteen years earlier.

The Scottish Parliament's representatives in London agreed with Prynne that bringing Charles to trial was likely to encourage 'Popish' hostility, provoke further rebellion in Ireland and cause divisions between England and Scotland. These warnings, and threats to avenge Charles' treatment coming from France, did nothing to halt the plans for the king's trial. It was decided that a High Court of Justice would be set up and 135 commissioners were appointed to hear the case. Of those invited only fifty-three appeared at the first meeting to discuss how the trial should proceed and barely half ever sat at the trial. Many had serious doubts about the whole proceedings. Some major figures such as Thomas Fairfax, commander-in-chief of the parliamentary army, would not participate. When his name was called as the commissioners took their seats at the start of the trial and there was no response, a spectator was heard to call out that he had more wit than to be there. It turned out to be the voice of his wife, Anne Fairfax. Many more commissioners suddenly suffered from illnesses or injuries that they claimed prevented them from attending. After other, more senior, judges had refused to be named President of the Court, John Bradshaw, a respected judge from Cheshire who himself missed the first two meetings, was persuaded to accept the post after being appointed in his absence. John Cook, the Solicitor-General, was appointed as chief prosecutor, aided by his Dutch-born assistant Issac Dorislaus.

The 'Rump' House of Commons claimed that they represented the people of the country and on 1 January 1649 declared 'that it is Treason in the King of England for the time to come to levy War against the Parliament and Kingdom of England.'[3] This ignored the traditional role of the House of Lords and the king in the passing of laws, but those who were determined to see the king brought to justice believed that they were doing God's work. Even though they appreciated the extraordinary significance of their actions, their victory in the civil war and the capture of the king showed that they had God's backing. John Bradshaw, having overcome any doubts about the righteousness of their cause pointed out that 'to acquit the guilty was as much of a crime as to condemn the innocent'[4]. He knew that his job would be very difficult but he believed in the law and wished the trial to be regarded as fair and honourable. King Charles was escorted to London, the capital which he had left in early 1642 and not returned to since, in the New Year.

On Saturday 20 January 1649 Charles was brought before the commissioners in a specially prepared Westminster Hall, with paying members of the public in attendance. Bradshaw opened the proceedings by informing the king that 'the Commons of England assembled in Parliament ... have resolved to bring you to trial and judgment, and have constituted this Court of Justice before which you are now brought, where you are to hear your charge, upon which the Court will proceed according to justice.'[5] John Cook then rose to read the charges. The indictment was lengthy but essentially the charge was that 'the said Charles Stuart ... hath traitorously and maliciously levied war against the present Parliament, and the people therein represented'[6], in the interest of himself and his family, 'against the public interest, common right, liberty, justice and peace of the people of this Nation'.[7] As a result he was accused of being 'guilty of all treasons, murders, rapines, burnings, spoils, desolations, damages and mischiefs to this nation, acted and committed in the said wars'.[8]

Charles showed little respect for the court. As John Cook began to read the charges he attempted to stop the proceedings, first telling him to 'Hold' and then, when he was ignored, striking him on the shoulder two or three times with his cane. Bradshaw instructed Cook to continue with the indictment. When given the chance to reply to the charges Charles enquired that if this was a trial sanctioned by parliament, where were the Lords? When asked to answer the charge he responded by asking 'by what power I am called hither. I would know by what authority, I mean lawful authority?' He argued that he had been on the point of agreeing a treaty with both houses of parliament at Newport, on the Isle of Wight, when he had been taken away by force. He would not betray the trust committed to him by God and answer to an unlawful authority. Only when he was satisfied on that point would he answer the charges.[9] When Bradshaw responded by saying that he was answerable 'to the people of England, of which you are elected king', Charles pointed out that England was a hereditary kingdom, not an elective one. Bradshaw reiterated that the judges were satisfied that they did constitute a legal authority and adjourned the session. Charles left as soldiers shouted 'Justice, Justice', though some among the spectators called out 'God save the king'.[10]

When the court reassembled on Monday 22 January its leading members expected that Charles, having made his point, would plead not guilty. Instead, he refused to change his position, stating that he was defending the rights and liberties of the people, because 'if power without law may make laws'[11] what justice could anyone expect? He said that 'the Commons of England was never a Court of Judicature' and asked if there was any precedent for what was being done? A stalemate had been reached. When Bradshaw started to close the proceedings, Charles said that he required an answer, whereupon Bradshaw told him that it was not for a prisoner to make demands. The king responded sharply: 'Sir, I am no ordinary prisoner' and again stated that his interests were those of his subjects. Bradshaw swiftly responded: 'How great a friend you have been to the laws and liberties of the people, let all England and the world judge'. On the following day Charles still refused to answer the charges and was reminded that in an English court of law the failure to do so was taken to be a confession of guilt. After further arguments Bradshaw told Charles: 'Sir, this is the third time that you have publicly disowned this court, and put an affront on it. How far you have preserved the privileges of the People, your actions have spoke it, and truly, Sir, Men's intentions ought to be known by their actions. You have written your meaning in bloody characters throughout the whole Kingdom, but, Sir, you understand the pleasure of this court – Clerk, record the default – and Gentlemen, you that took charge of the prisoner, take him back again.'[12]

As the trial had finished, witnesses were not required to give evidence in court, but on the Wednesday and Thursday some were called to the 'Painted Chamber', the room in the Palace of Westminster that was being used by the commissioners, for a private hearing. This was not legally required but it gave time for those pushing for the death sentence to persuade any waverers to agree. On Saturday 27 January the court reassembled for its final session – the sentencing. As Bradshaw started the proceedings, Charles requested that he be heard and was told that he could make a statement so long as it was not to challenge the authority of the court. Charles said that he had an offer to make which, when put before the Lords and Commons in the Painted Chamber, would bring about satisfaction to all and peace in the kingdom. Before Bradshaw could refuse the request, one commissioner, John Downes, made the case for it to be heard. The commissioners left the court for half an hour to discuss the matter. Cromwell was furious, seeing this as yet another insincere offer by the king seeking to cause division and delay. A vote was taken and the decision made to refuse the king's proposition. Charles had made his final miscalculation; he would not be permitted to put forward his offer.

When the court reconvened Bradshaw told Charles that he had caused too much delay already and that they were unanimously determined to proceed to judgment immediately. After Charles said that a hasty sentence would 'bring on that trouble and perpetual inconveniency to the Kingdom' that even a child yet unborn would regret it[13], Bradshaw stated the prosecution's case, telling the king when he again asked to speak that 'your time is now past'.[14] Charles Stuart was judged to be a 'tyrant, murderer, and public enemy to the good people of the nation' and that he should 'be put to death by the severing of his head from his body'[15]. The sixty-seven commissioners in court stood to signify that they agreed with the judgement and sentence. When Charles, seemingly shocked, again asked to be heard he was denied and removed from the court saying: 'I am not suffered for to speak, expect what justice other people will have'[16]. On Tuesday 30 January Charles would be executed. He was secured in St. James' Palace, probably so that he did not have to hear the sound of the scaffold being erected outside Whitehall Palace.

Once Charles' death warrant had been drawn up fifty-seven commissioners immediately signed it, and two more subsequently added their names. The first to sign was the President of the Court, John Bradshaw, followed by Lord Grey of Groby, the only peer at the trial, who had commanded parliamentary armies and played a part in Pride's Purge. Oliver Cromwell was the third to sign. Many other army leaders, such as Henry Ireton, Puritan lawyers and landowners, as well as out and out republicans such as Henry Marten, mostly members of the 'Rump Parliament', also put their names to the document.

Charles used his remaining time to pray, accompanied by the Bishop of London, William Juxon, and to destroy his personal papers and letters.

On 29 January he was permitted to see his two young children who remained in the country, daughter Elizabeth (13) and Henry, Duke of Gloucester (8). His wife and other children had managed to leave England during the later stages of the civil wars. The king made Henry promise that he would never agree to become king while his older brothers, Charles and James, were still alive. He asked Elizabeth, who was in tears, to record what he said to them and pass on his love to his wife and other children. He said that she should not grieve for him for he was to die a martyr, and that he did not doubt that eventually his eldest son would become king. He divided his remaining jewels between them. After Charles' execution Elizabeth and Henry were taken to Carisbrooke Castle on the Isle of Wight. There Elizabeth died in 1650, though Henry was released to join his family in Europe in 1652. On the restoration of the monarchy in May 1660 he returned to England with his older brothers but died only four months later.

On the night before his execution Charles had little sleep, rising at 5 a.m. to begin his final preparations. The January morning was bitterly cold. The king requested two shirts because he did not wish to shiver as he awaited execution because the spectators might think that he was trembling with fear. His outer clothes were all black with the exception of his blue sash and badge of the Order of the Garter with its motto 'Honi Soit Qui Mal Y Pense', 'Shamed be whoever thinks ill of it'. After taking Holy Communion, at 10 a.m. he was accompanied by guards commanded by Colonel Hacker and the sound of drum beats, as he walked across St. James' Park back to Whitehall Palace. There he had a few hours to wait, during which he was encouraged by Bishop Juxon to eat a little bread and have a glass of claret.

The scaffold, draped in black, had been erected outside the Banqueting House on the side of Whitehall Palace facing the street. Unlike the execution of his grandmother back in 1587 which was performed in the privacy of Fotheringhay Castle, Charles' death, like his trial, was to be a public spectacle and a large crowd had started to gather early. In order to ensure that everything went according to plan and without any public display of support for the king, a large contingent of soldiers was positioned around the place of execution and more troops stationed at strategic points in Westminster and London. At the allotted time the king took the stairs up to the first floor and passed through the Great Banqueting Hall, watched by Cromwell and other parliamentary and army leaders. Twenty years earlier Charles had commissioned Peter Paul Rubens to produce the famous frescoed ceiling which adorned this same hall. Installed in 1636, it was a celebration of the reign of his father, James I. The three main panels represented the union of the crowns of England and Scotland, his peaceful reign achieved through the wisdom of the king, and the centrepiece, the apotheosis of James I as he is carried to heaven. Both Charles and Cromwell must have been aware of the symbolism. Although Charles believed in the divine right of kings and that he was therefore only answerable to the Almighty, others now regarded him as an ordinary mortal who had to answer for his actions in the here and now. Had the king shown a little more of the wisdom and judgement portrayed in the frescos, then he could probably have avoided this moment.

On Colonel Hacker's instruction Charles stepped through the window onto the scaffold where the executioner and his assistant, masked and bewigged in order to hide their identities, awaited. Charles prayed once more with Bishop Juxon, thanked him for his company and then placed a cap on his head so that he could tuck in his long hair. The ranks of soldiers surrounding the scaffold meant that few in the large crowd were able to hear his final speech, even though the hubbub had subsided as he stepped onto the scaffold. Instead he directed it towards the Bishop, who would later record and publish it. Charles said that he did not consider himself guilty of the crimes for which he was being executed, but was now suffering an unjust punishment for another unjust punishment, one that he had permitted some eight years earlier, the execution of Thomas Wentworth, the Earl of Strafford. He insisted he was no enemy of the people. Indeed he claimed to be a martyr of the people and that he was being killed for their rights 'Truly I desire their liberty and freedom as much as whosoever, but I must tell you that liberty and freedom consist in having a government by those laws, by which their lives, and their goods may be most their own. It is not for them to have a share in the government ... A subject and a sovereign are clean different things; and therefore until that be done, I mean, until the people be put into that liberty, which I speak of, certainly they will never enjoy themselves'.[17] He concluded by saying: 'I go from a corruptible to an incorruptible crown; where no disturbance can be, no disturbance in the world'. There can be little doubt that whatever his failings as a king, Charles met his death with bravery and composure.

Charles took off his cloak, gloves and garter badge and handed them to Bishop Juxon. The block was so low that Charles had to almost prostrate himself rather than kneel in order to place his neck upon it. Having done so, at shortly after 2pm he reached out his hands to signal that he was ready. In one clean blow his head was severed from his body. According to one eye-witness, Philip Henry, a royalist Oxford undergraduate, as the axe fell 'there was such a groan by the thousands then present as I never heard before or desire I may never hear again'[18], though other spectators who later wrote an account of the execution do not mention this. Certainly not

Samuel Pepys, then a 15-year-old St Paul's school boy who clearly had republican sympathies. In 1660 he recalled being called 'a great roundhead' (supporter of parliament) by a school friend[19] and saying in response that if he were to preach about the king he would take as his text, 'The memory of the wicked shall rot'.

The head of the former king was held up but the executioner did not say the traditional words: 'Behold the head of a traitor'. The crowds, some of whom approved while others were horrified by what they had witnessed, were rapidly dispersed by the soldiers. Even so quite a few of both spectators and soldiers managed to dip their handkerchiefs in Charles's blood, for some a momento of a great turning point in English history, for others a relic of a martyr. The next day Charles's head was sewn back onto his body, which was then embalmed and placed in a lead coffin. Permission to bury him at Westminster Abbey was refused and so he was taken to Windsor Castle and placed in the vault of Henry VIII and his third wife, Jane Seymour, in St George's Chapel on 9 February. Even before his burial the monarchy and the House of Lords had been abolished and shortly afterwards a Council of State was established, with John Bradshaw as its President, to act as the executive body to manage day-to-day government.

Those horrified by the execution of the king lost no time in producing propaganda against the new government. Charles' actions and words on the scaffold provided the initial focus for pamphlets that were circulated within days. These were soon followed by one of the most popular political and religious tracts ever written. *'Eikon Basilike – The Portrait of His sacred Majesty in his Solitudes and Suffering'* ran through over thirty editions in England in 1649 alone and was translated into many languages for distribution across much of Europe. First published on 9 February 1649 it started the cult of Charles the Martyr. It was written in the first-person, with short, manageable chapters, which would hold the attention of its readers. The frontispiece, originally by William Marshall and copied many times, shows Charles at an altar, with his 'Splendid and Heavy' royal crown, with its motto 'Vanitas' (Vanity), at his feet, holding a crown of thorns and looking up to the 'Blessed and Eternal' heavenly crown which contains the motto 'Gratia' (Grace). The book contains the spiritual thoughts and memoirs of Charles I (though it is now believed to be at least partly written by John Gauden, bishop of Worcester). In it Charles states that: 'I would rather choose to wear a crown of thorns with my Saviour, than to exchange that of gold, which is due to me, for one of lead' which would mean he should 'be forced to bend and comply to the various and oft contrary dictates of any factions'. He continued that 'I know of no resolutions more worthy of a Christian king than to prefer his conscience before his kingdoms'. *'Eikon Basilike'* (Icon of the King) portrayed Charles as a perhaps flawed, but essentially reasonable, generous and forgiving monarch who had done his best for the people of his lands.

The Council of State recognised the need to counter such successful propaganda. They ordered the arrest of those who produced 'scandalous pamphlets' and employed John Milton to write a response in an attempt to prevent the royalist version of the history of Charles and his reign from taking hold in the minds of the English people. In *'Eikonoklastes'* (Icon Breaker), published in October 1649, he produced a detailed rebuttal of each chapter in *'Eikon Basilike'*. Closely argued, more of an academic disputation than a popular tract and considerably longer than *'Eikon Basilike'*, it never had the same popular appeal. The new government would have to find other ways of winning hearts and minds.

Certainly no one had asked the English people whether they approved of the execution of their king. If they had been asked there would have been no universal agreement but it is likely that the majority would have been against it. Large numbers had opposed the king's policies and had even fought against his armies, but they did not all wish for his death and the establishment of a republic. As in much of Europe, monarchy was so established in the minds of the majority that it was difficult to conceive of any other sort of government. Even for those who had carried through the trial and execution this was not something that they had envisaged when the civil war in England had started in 1642 or even only a few months before the decision was made. How, then, had it come about?

CHAPTER 17

CHARLES I AND PARLIAMENT – CIVIL WAR

C harles I's relationship with many of his subjects had been difficult from the very start of his reign in 1625. The English Parliament was very critical of the failures of the Cadiz expedition against Spain in 1625 and of the attempts to assist French Huguenots in La Rochelle against the forces of Louis XIII and Cardinal Richelieu in 1627-8. Charles believed that he had not been provided with sufficient funds, and parliament, while supportive of the aims of the wars, blamed the incompetence of the king's favourite, George Villiers, the Duke of Buckingham. Having been granted subsidies worth £120,000, Charles dismissed his first parliament in 1625 after only a few weeks. He then dissolved his second parliament in June 1626 to prevent them from impeaching Buckingham. Although Charles' third parliament, which met in 1628, did not continue with this attempt in the belief that they would once more be closed down, the unpopular Buckingham was assassinated by a disgruntled army lieutenant, John Felton, later that year.

Finance was a constant source of friction between Charles and his parliaments. When he succeeded his father, James I (James VI of Scotland), parliament voted him the right to collect customs duties, known as tonnage and poundage, for only one year rather than for his whole reign as was the tradition. This immediately soured relations between them. As these customs duties amounted to about half of the ordinary revenue of the monarch, excluding additional subsidies that had to be agreed by parliament, Charles continued to have them collected in future years without parliamentary approval. In 1627, still short of money to pay for the wars against Spain and France, he raised substantial sums by a policy of forced loans. Those who refused to pay were arrested. He also cut expenditure by approving the compulsory billeting of the troops being assembled for a second expedition to La Rochelle in private homes.

Charles summoned the parliament of 1628 in order to request further subsidies. These were granted on the condition that he accepted a 'Petition of

Rights', which listed various grievances and stated that among the rights and liberties of the English people were the right not to be forced to make a loan or pay a tax without parliamentary approval, the right not to be arrested or imprisoned without due cause, and that no members of the army or navy should be billeted in private houses without the owners' consent. After much prevarication Charles accepted the petition, though later largely ignored it. In a later session of the parliament there was criticism of Charles' continued collection of tonnage and poundage, and a resolution was passed condemning those who supported its collection. Charles' reaction was to have a number of MPs arrested and to dissolve parliament once again.

The expensive wars against France and Spain were ended in 1629 and 1630 respectively and so Charles' immediate expenses were reduced considerably, so long as the country remained at peace. No parliament was called for the next eleven years. Though often referred to as the 'Eleven Years of Tyranny', such lengthy periods without a parliament were not unprecedented. Henry VIII had not summoned a parliament between 1515 and 1523, Queen Elizabeth had ruled without one for twelve years after 1572, and James I had no parliament between 1614 and 1621. Nevertheless, along with efforts to cut costs, Charles did need to find new ways of supporting his expenditure without parliamentary subsidies. Tonnage and poundage continued to be collected. Crown lands were sold. Ancient feudal dues were resurrected, such as fines imposed on those living within royal forests. The sale of monopolies to companies (as opposed to individuals, which had been banned in 1624) and the use of the crown's right to buy commodities at a reduced price, both raised significant sums. However the most profitable, as well as the most contentious, innovation was the extension of the levying of ship money. Originally raised from coastal counties in times of emergency to build a fleet, in 1634 it was extended to inland counties as well. After all, it was argued, the whole country benefitted from the defence against foreign invasion. It was also organised so that more people in the country had to pay ship money than had ever paid parliamentary subsidies. It thus raised almost £200,000 each year, but by the late 1630s there were an increasing number of people refusing to pay and numerous legal challenges, even though most people, as is usual, grumbled but still paid up.

The other major concern expressed in parliaments between 1625 and 1629, and one which grew during the following eleven years, was over religious policy. In 1625 Charles had married the French princess, Henrietta Maria, the youngest daughter of the French king, Henry IV, born just six months before his murder, and sister of his successor, Louis XIII. She was a devout Catholic and as such she did not take part in Charles' coronation ceremony. She was encouraged by the French royal family and the papacy to push for a relaxation of the anti-Catholic laws that existed in England and for the right of English Catholics to raise their children in the faith. Her early years in England were difficult. She spoke little English, took a dislike to Charles' favourite, Buckingham, and had extravagant tastes. England was at war with France and in 1626 Charles dismissed most of her French household. However, by the late 1620s Charles and Henrietta had developed a close, loving partnership. She became Charles' confidante and adviser, the more valued by Charles because of his naturally shy, reserved nature. He did not always find it easy to relax in company, perhaps a result of his stammer. Henrietta Maria's growing influence did not go unnoticed and concerned the strong Puritan element in parliament and the country as a whole.

During his father's reign there had been a careful attempt to continue the middle way in religion developed under Queen Elizabeth, one acceptable to both moderate Protestants and to those who still had some sympathy for the old religion. The monarch was the head of the church, which had a hierarchical structure with archbishops and bishops appointed by the crown.[1] Such a balance was difficult to maintain. On the one hand there were those who favoured a more ceremonial approach to worship in places of beauty, making communion the heart of church services and enhancing the authority of the clergy. Others, however, believed in the Calvinist doctrine of predestination, and wished for their places of worship to be plain and simple, in a system that had no church hierarchy. The latter became known as Puritans. There is no doubt that Charles was a committed Anglican, but it soon became clear that he favoured the former approach, with a wish for traditional ceremonies, a church hierarchy and religious uniformity. The priest at the altar was to become more important than the preacher in the pulpit.

Charles appointed men to leading positions who would move the church in that direction, such as William Laud, who became archbishop of Canterbury in 1633 and a hate figure for those against the changes. Under Charles and Laud, Puritans who openly criticised them, such as William Prynne, were dealt with harshly. Some accused the government of censorship and denying their freedom of conscience. Others claimed that this was merely the prelude to the church reverting to more a Catholic form of worship. As the influence of Henrietta Maria increased, some even talked about the royal family being sympathetic to, or even at the centre of, 'popish plots'.

However, it was in Scotland where religious problems first came to a head. Charles, though born in Dunfermline, had moved to England before his fourth birthday. England and Scotland were separate countries with the same monarch, but despite his family background he spent very little time in Scotland. He did not even go there for his coronation until 1633, over seven years after his accession to the throne. The Protestant reforms in the Scottish church had gone considerably further than in England and many people there had been concerned by some features of the coronation ceremony that Charles had insisted on. When in 1637 he ordered that a revised English Prayer Book must be used in Scottish churches there were protests in St. Giles Cathedral, Edinburgh, and across Scotland. Early in 1638 a National Covenant was drawn up and signed by many thousands of people who pledged to maintain 'the true religion of Christ' and 'abolish all false religions'. Later in the year, despite belated and half-hearted concessions offered by Charles, an assembly of Scottish church leaders approved the Covenant and passed motions to abolish episcopacy (the role of bishops) and the use of the new Prayer Book.

Charles regarded this as rebellion against his authority and ordered troops to be raised in northern England. During what became known as the First Bishops' War they advanced to the Scottish border near Berwick-on-Tweed and were faced by an army raised by the new Covenanter government in Scotland. Before the outbreak of serious hostilities an agreement was reached – the Pacification of Berwick. A Scottish parliament and a General Assembly of the Scottish Church would be called. However, when they met both confirmed the earlier decisions that had so incensed Charles. He was not prepared to accept this situation. The king recalled the able Thomas Wentworth (created Earl of Strafford in January 1640) from Ireland, where he had been an effective Lord Deputy since 1632. Wentworth, perhaps not realising the strength of opposition that had developed during his time in Ireland, recommended the summoning of a new parliament in order to raise the money needed to equip an army to defeat the Scottish rebellion.

Strafford returned briefly to Ireland and in March 1640 secured subsidies from the Irish parliament to levy an Irish army of 10,000 soldiers to be used by the king against the Presbyterian Scots. However, on his return to England, the parliament in Westminster demanded the end of ship money and refused to agree to the subsidies, worth one million pounds, that Charles was requesting. Instead parliament called upon the king to make peace with Scotland. Charles made little effort to placate the M.P.s and committed what is now recognised as a serious mistake. He dissolved the so-called 'Short Parliament' after only three weeks. Without proper funds the army sent to impose his will on the

Scots was therefore badly trained, poorly led, ill-equipped and unenthusiastic, whereas the Scots had 20,000 organised and committed troops. Scottish Covenanter forces had already crushed Scottish supporters of King Charles in the highlands. In August, commanded by Alexander Leslie, they invaded northern England, defeated the English troops at Newburn and captured Newcastle. In the Truce of Ripon that followed the Scots were allowed to occupy Northumberland and Durham and were to be paid expenses of £850 per day until the final peace terms had been agreed.

Charles had very little choice other than to call another parliament, which met in November 1640 and was not finally dissolved until 1660, thus known as the 'Long Parliament'. It was even more hostile to the king's position. The M.P.s, led by John Pym, had been emboldened by Charles' failures and the example of the Scots. They were set upon changing how both country and church had been run over the previous eleven years and removing the king's 'evil' councillors. In this way, they believed that the king's authority would be restored, though restrained, and harmony re-established. There was no thought of removing Charles. However, Strafford, Archbishop Laud and nearly all the senior judges who had backed Charles' personal rule between 1629 and 1640 were arrested and impeached.

Strafford was charged with high treason, namely of planning to send an Irish army to 'reduce this kingdom'. In the spring of 1641 this charge was rejected in the House of Lords. There was little proof and Strafford had some supporters. The House of Commons then passed a bill of attainder, which simply declared that a person was guilty of a crime without a trial. This too might also have been rejected in the Lords except for the revelation of a plot to bring soldiers loyal to the king south and, perhaps with French assistance, seize the Tower of London and release Strafford. This resulted in the Lords passing the bill of attainder. It now needed Charles' signature. The king had promised Strafford that he would save him, but the pressures on him were great. Riots in London threatened the safety of his family, and he was unable to remove parliament without provoking both the Scots and much of the country. Although it was argued by some that a king could break his word in the interests of matters of state, on 10 May 1641 he signed the bill with great reluctance. On the same day he gave his assent to another bill stating that the existing parliament could not be dissolved without its own consent. Two days later Strafford was beheaded. Charles' distress was such that eight years later at his own execution he was asking God's forgiveness for permitting this unjust punishment.

A peace was negotiated with the Scots in August 1641. Charles agreed that a substantial sum would be paid to the Scots to secure the withdrawal of Scottish troops and bishops would be abolished from the Church of Scotland. Charles announced a visit to Scotland, where he stayed for three months. By the time of his return to England the political situation in both countries had deteriorated further. Firstly, distrust of Charles had grown, especially when word got out that he had known about, and supported, a failed scheme to arrest the leading Covenanters in Scotland. Meanwhile in England some MPs wished Charles to appoint ministers who had the backing of parliament, which for others was going too far. Also, although removing some of the religious changes introduced by Laud was agreed, the plan to get rid of bishops in the Church of England being pushed by some MPs certainly did not meet with general approval. Charles perhaps had hopes of increasing his support at Westminster with judicious concessions, although that was never his strong suit.

What upset any chance of a straightforward coming to terms was rebellion in Ireland. In October 1641 Catholics in Ulster, most of whom had been displaced by Protestant settlers from Scotland and England in the 'Plantations' of the early seventeenth century turned on the newcomers. The resentment of the native Irish boiled over and spread through most the country, perhaps encouraged by the success of the Scots in resisting royal policy. Several thousand Protestants were killed and they soon retaliated. The propaganda in London was of the brutal murder of some 20,000 men, women and children, along with widespread rape and destruction of property, by Catholics. Some even believed that it had been approved by King Charles, clear evidence of a 'popish plot'. The numbers were greatly exaggerated but there is no doubt that atrocities were carried out by both sides. An army would be needed to deal with the rebellion, but parliament was very distrustful of Charles having control of such a force which might be used against them. Parliament's refusal to allow Charles to control an army was such a challenge his royal authority that he would never accept it.

As news of the Irish Rebellion reached England, in November 1641 a lengthy document, which became known as the Grand Remonstrance, was drawn up and introduced to parliament by Pym and others. It catalogued the problems faced by the country during Charles' reign and listed over two hundred individual objections to the policies that had been pursued. Without directly criticising the king, it called for ministers to be approved by parliament and for the expulsion of bishops from parliament. Many M.P.s, such as Edward Hyde, who had opposed the measures taken by the king during his 'personal rule', believed that they had no right to remove his authority in this way. After debate it was narrowly passed in the House of Commons by 159 votes to 148 votes and presented to Charles. To force the king to respond it was then published. On 23 December, after consultation with Hyde, he replied that he would not expel the bishops, nor remove any of his ministers since none had committed a crime. He declared that his views on the state of the country were very different to those of parliament. He asserted that he was opposed to Catholicism and his wish for uniformity in religion was to protect the church from schismatics, separatists and extremists. It was understandably calculated to gain the support of those in parliament who had opposed Pym.

Six days after his failed, and now infamous, entry into the Commons chamber with armed soldiers in an attempt to arrest five members – Pym, Holles, Haselrig, Strode and Hampden – on 4 January 1642, Charles decided to leave London. He was not to return until shortly before his trial seven years later. The divisions in parliament meant that with the backing of Hyde and the 'moderates' his position was strengthened, but the creation of two more evenly balanced sides brought a civil war closer. Both sides started to prepare for war. They used semi-legal means or ancient laws to claim the authority to raise troops in the counties across England. Parliament used some of the money voted for dealing with the Irish Rebellion, while Charles relied on his own funds and subscriptions from wealthy backers. Both put their case to the population. Parliament issued the Nineteen Propositions which claimed that the failure to restrain the king's power would lead to absolutism. The king argued that any such restraints would so upset the traditional balance of power that it would result in anarchy. At Nottingham on 22 August Charles raised his standard and the First Civil War began.

The events of the English civil wars, the first from 1642 to 1646 and the second in 1648, as well as the various interventions of Scottish armies, have been thoroughly described and analysed by many historians. The key fact was that King Charles was unable to defeat his opponents and eventually became their captive. The first war started reasonably well for the king but the Solemn League and Covenant signed between parliament and the Scottish Covenanters in September 1643 was a significant turning point. A Scottish army of over 20,000 men joined the fray in return for a payment of £30,000 per month and the agreement to reform religion in England and Ireland along the lines of the Scottish church. It played a major role in defeating the king's army at Marston Moor in Yorkshire in July 1644. The formation of the New Model Army by parliament in early 1645 created a well-organised force commanded by Sir Thomas Fairfax, with Oliver Cromwell as his second-in-command. All attempts at a negotiated settlement failed and when the New Model Army won a decisive victory at Naseby in June 1645, Charles' military position became almost hopeless.

London had been a parliamentary stronghold throughout the war and so the king had made his headquarters in Oxford. With the city besieged, in April 1646 Charles escaped, disguised as a servant, and surrendered to the Scottish army near Newark. He was taken north to Newcastle.

Despite their successes, divisions in and between the New Model Army, parliament, and the Scottish forces were starting to cause problems. Within the army, men like Cromwell and Ireton, wished to defeat the king's forces and then impose severe terms in any settlement. Many of these men, who became known as Independents, also wished to have liberty of conscience and toleration in religious matters (though not for Catholics). Others, such as the early parliamentary army leaders, the earls of Essex and Manchester, and the majority in parliament, wished to have a compromise with the king. As Manchester said 'if we beat the King ninety-nine times yet he is King still … but if the King beat us once we shall all be hanged'. Many were Presbyterians. They were opposed to religious toleration and wanted a national Presbyterian, church. That this had not already been established in England angered the Scots as it had been agreed in the Solemn League and Covenant.

Once the war ended these issues became more significant. Whatever settlement was reached it needed the king's involvement and eventual agreement. While he was being held by the Scots, the Newcastle Proposals were put forward. They included the abolition of bishops and the establishment of a Presbyterian Church, a parliament to be summoned at least every three years, which would control the militia for twenty years, as well as nominate some of the king's ministers. Charles requested time to consider them, though in reality he was playing for time, hoping that the divisions among his enemies would assist his cause. Parliament was not happy that the Scots were holding the king, and soldiers of the New Model Army were concerned that they would be disbanded and given little say in any final settlement negotiated by parliament. In Scotland the Covenanters were coming under increasing pressure from royalists and others who opposed them.

In January 1647 the Scots negotiated a deal with parliament. They would hand the king over and leave England in return for a £400,000 payment for their help in the war. Some in Scotland and in continental Europe accused the Covenanters of selling their king and their honour. Parliament lodged the king in Holdenby House, Northamptonshire. With the king in their power and the Scots departed, parliament now announced its plans for the army. Many soldiers were to be dismissed, others sent to fight the rebellion in Ireland and a relatively small number retained in England. Unhappy with the plans for paying the £300,000 that they were owed in wages and indemnity for actions taken during the fighting, the army refused to disband. The Independent factions in both parliament and especially the army were becoming increasingly powerful. In June Charles was taken by a force of 500 soldiers to army headquarters in Newmarket and in August moved to Hampton Court. The army also occupied London to ensure that Independent M.P.s were not prevented from attending the House of Commons.

In August the Army General Council put forward the 'Heads of the Proposals', drawn up by Henry Ireton and John Lambert with the backing of Cromwell. It was sent to the king and widely publicised. The main terms were for biennial parliaments after the dissolution of the present parliament, parliament to control the appointment of ministers and the militias for ten years, the retention of bishops but with their powers reduced, and the exclusion of royalists from running for office for five years. Charles expressed a preference for the Heads of the Proposals over the Newcastle Proposals but was still seeking to exploit the divisions between his opponents. Many of the rank and file in the army were fearful of their superiors coming to a moderate deal with the king. They had chosen representatives, referred to as 'Agitators', to put forward their views and had close links with the group known as the Levellers. In October the Levellers published the first of several manifestos, collectively known as 'An Agreement of the People'. This proposed radical reforms: freedom of religion, equality before the law, and universal male suffrage. Col. Thomas Rainsborough was one who voiced support for such ideas at the 'Putney Debates' of October/November 1647 when he argued that 'the poorest he that is in England hath a life to live ... and therefore truly, sir, I think it's clear, that every man that is to live under a Government ought first by his own consent to put himself under that Government; and I do think that the poorest man in England is not at all bound in a strict sense to that Government that he hath not had a voice to put Himself under'[2]. Such demands were discussed and ultimately rejected by the Army Council. Cromwell had to act quickly and firmly to avoid a major schism in the army.

On 11 November 1647 King Charles escaped from Hampton Court. He managed to get to the Isle of Wight believing that the governor would be sympathetic to his cause. However, this was not the case and he was secured in Carisbrooke Castle and parliament was informed. The king made further efforts to escape, attempting bribery, climbing through the roof space, starting a fire and switching clothes with a visitor, all of which failed. Charles was still able to carry out negotiations and by the end of the year he had signed a secret treaty with the Scots. They would invade England and restore him to the throne and in return he would establish Presbyterianism in England, initially for three years, appoint Scottish officials and Privy Councillors, and work for a complete union of England and Scotland. In May 1648 there were poorly co-ordinated royalist risings in Kent, Essex the south-west and south Wales all of which were easily crushed. The Scottish invasion, receiving none of the support in England that the king had hoped for, was defeated at the Battle of Preston in August.

The brief Second Civil War had left Charles in a much weaker position. He had no choice left but to negotiate with his English opponents. Although parliament had passed a motion in January 1648 barring further negotiations with him[3], with this latest defeat they believed that Charles would be more amenable. The ban was repealed and discussions reopened at Newport on the Isle of Wight, though the king was still unwilling to make the necessary compromises. The army leadership, however, had concluded that even if a deal could be done the king would be unlikely to keep his word. He had deceived them before, attempted to bring Irish and foreign troops to fight for him in England, and encouraged a Scottish invasion. He could no longer be trusted. Some people had already referred to him as 'this man of blood' and called for him to be held responsible for his actions. When the Remonstrance issued by the army high command on 20 November was ignored by parliament they purged parliament of those who still wished to negotiate and the stage was set for the trial of the king.

CHAPTER 18

THE REPUBLIC AND THE RESTORATION OF THE STUARTS: THE FATE OF THE REGICIDES

After Charles's execution it was the task of those responsible, the more radical army leaders and the members of the Rump Parliament, to run the country. They needed to establish a system of government that would be regarded as legitimate, gain the support of the majority of the population, and implement their political and religious programme. In the end this proved to be impossible, in part because there was no unanimity about how that should be achieved or indeed about their aims, and in part because their wishes did not match those of significant elements of the population. For the next eleven years England and Wales, and later Scotland and Ireland, were to see various attempts to create a workable system of governance without a monarch. The regicides, their fellow travellers, and others who sought to advance themselves in the new political circumstances, became increasingly divided, as demonstrated by the careers of the regicides John Bradshaw, Major-General Thomas Harrison and Henry Marten, as well as many others over the following eleven years.

In May 1649 an 'Act declaring England to be a Commonwealth' was agreed by the Rump Parliament. The term 'Commonwealth' was understood to mean a political community founded for the common good and general welfare. The new powers of the Rump Parliament and the Council of State, with Bradshaw as its President, were confirmed. While they initially controlled England, there was, as had been predicted, open hostility in both Scotland and Ireland. In August 1649 Cromwell was sent to Ireland, where royalists and Catholics controlled much of the country, to crush a rebellion. Many English people still remembered the horror stories, some true, many exaggerated, of Catholic massacres of Protestant men, women and children back in 1641. Cromwell himself was strongly anti-Catholic. In a nine month campaign he defeated a royalist army and stormed the fortified towns of

Drogheda and Wexford which had refused to surrender. Militarily successful, the large scale killing of both soldiers and civilians that followed has never been forgotten in Ireland. It did nothing for the reputation of either the new Commonwealth government or Cromwell himself.

Prince Charles, who the royalists recognised as King Charles II on the execution of his father, arrived in Scotland in June 1650 intent on claiming his throne. He had agreed to the demands of the Covenanter government for the establishment of the Presbyterian Church across Scotland and England. As an army was being assembled in Scotland to support him, Cromwell was recalled from Ireland. Lord Fairfax, still the commander-in-chief of the Commonwealth's army, was known to be uneasy about the establishment of the Commonwealth and when instructed to lead his troops against Prince Charles and invade Scotland, he resigned. Cromwell failed in his genuine efforts to persuade Fairfax to remain in post and was appointed in his place. Having marched north, Cromwell defeated the Scots at the Dunbar on 3 September 1650 and captured Edinburgh. This did not stop the prince's coronation as King Charles II of Scotland at Scone Abbey, near Perth, on 1 January 1651. Rather than face Cromwell's forces, Charles decided to lead his regrouped Scottish troops into England. Initially taken by surprise, Cromwell was forced to pursue him south, down the west of England. However, the mass support that Charles had hoped for in England never materialised. The foreign Scottish troops were not welcomed, even by many erstwhile royalists, and those English backers of Charles that did arm themselves were soon dealt with. On 3 September, exactly a year after his victory at Dunbar, Cromwell crushed the invading army outside Worcester. Charles, whose capture would have been richly rewarded, fled in disguise, supposedly hiding for a short time in a large oak tree. He managed to cross the Channel to Normandy the following month. He would have to wait over eight years before he returned to English shores.

Even if the Commonwealth was now militarily secure the political situation remained unstable. The members of the Rump Parliament had been in place since 1640. Now that the king had been removed they began to disagree among themselves as to the reforms that should be enacted. Also they objected to the political influence of Cromwell and other army leaders, who put pressure on them to set a date for new elections across England, Scotland and Ireland and to carry out the full set of religious reforms that they wanted. Although a much wider freedom of conscience had been introduced, many of the aspects of the old religious arrangements, such as the payment of tithes, remained in place. As early as 1651 John Bradshaw was removed as President of the Council of State for the first time in the monthly election (among its members). When the Rump Parliament eventually agreed to parliamentary elections there was consensus about the need to prevent the election of royalists and others hostile to the Commonwealth. However, it became clear that the Rump wished to control that process and Cromwell feared that they would use that power to ensure that a parliament representing their own interests would be returned. In April 1653 he took action, marching soldiers commanded by Major-General Thomas Harrison into the Commons chamber and expelling the Rump Parliament.

Cromwell and a Council of Officers selected 138 men to represent the various opinions and religious persuasions acceptable to them, some coming from the more extreme religious sects, such as the Fifth Monarchists led by Thomas Harrison, and a few from more humble origins than was usual. This group was installed as the 'Nominated Assembly', sometimes known as the 'Barebones Parliament' or 'Parliament of Saints'. Many, like John Bradshaw, were appalled by the expulsion of the Rump Parliament and were soon to fall out with Cromwell. This new experiment in government failed before the end of the year. In their meetings in the Commons chamber there were heated disagreements over issues such as legal fees, reform of the Courts and church tithes. Attendance fell, as many absented themselves, and the more moderate elements became concerned about being out-voted by the radicals. In December 1653 Cromwell was presented with a document, signed by eighty moderates who had left the chamber, requesting their own abolition. Those who remained in the parliament were ejected by troops, including Thomas Harrison.

The Instrument of Government drawn up by the leading army figure, Major-General John Lambert, approved by the Council of Officers, and issued in December 1653, stated that: 'Oliver Cromwell, Captain-General of the forces of England, Scotland and Ireland, shall be and is hereby declared to be, Lord Protector of the Commonwealth of England, Scotland and Ireland and the dominions thereto belonging, for his life'. For many who had deposed and executed the former king, the re-introduction of personal rule was against everything that they had fought for. Now it was not just Bradshaw but also the more radical elements like Thomas Harrison who opposed Cromwell. Harrison was to be imprisoned on four separate occasions during the following six years for his out-spoken opposition and religious views, while Bradshaw, though elected to the First Protectorate Parliament in 1554, refused to sign the pledge recognising the new government and so was barred from taking his seat. He was subsequently prevented from standing as a candidate in future elections.

The financial problems of the government, the uncovering of several plots and Penruddock's rising in Wiltshire in March 1655, which planned to restore the Stuart dynasty to the throne, together resulted in yet another experiment in running the country. Cromwell and the Council of State reinforced military control and combined this with an effort to regain God's approval for the regime by attempting widespread social and moral reforms. The country was divided up into regions, each run by a senior army officer, who collectively became known as the 'Major-Generals'. Their role was to identify and deal with royalist elements, sometimes by imprisonment but more often by large financial penalties. This system was to be paid for by a tax of 10% on all families of means who had ever fought against parliament – the so-called 'decimation' tax. The power of the Major-Generals was widely unpopular – even Henry Cromwell, Oliver's second son, disapproved, believing that they were dividing rather than uniting the country. In January 1657 the Second Protectorate Parliament voted down the Militia Bill, intended to continue the decimation tax, and the 'rule' of the Major-Generals ended.

In the same month a plot to assassinate the Lord Protector was uncovered. It was led by Miles Sindercombe, a former soldier in the New Model Army who had taken part in a Leveller mutiny in 1649 and then fled to the Netherlands. The plan was to kill Cromwell and restore a Puritan republic. Its leaders were executed and a banquet was held in the Whitehall Banqueting House on Friday 20 February, attended by the Lord Protector and nearly all M.P.s, to give thanks for Cromwell's safety. The following Monday a new plan was presented to parliament. It proposed to restore both the House of Lords and the monarchy, with Oliver Cromwell becoming king. The 'Humble Petition and Advice' was passed by a parliament that was increasingly influenced by moderate Presbyterians who reflected the underlying support for a more traditional form of government. After considerable soul-searching Cromwell rejected the kingship, but finally agreed to continue as Lord Protector and have the right to nominate his own successor. Even so some army leaders, such as Lambert, opposed this extension of his powers. Shortly before Cromwell died in September 1658 he made clear his wish to be succeeded by his eldest son, Richard, following the traditional custom of primogeniture. He was not the best choice. Cromwell's second son, Henry, was far more able and experienced in governmental matters, having served in Ireland for several years, and others such as Cromwell's son-in-law, Charles Fleetwood, an experienced army commander, had hopes of appointment.

As the new Lord Protector, Richard Cromwell faced increasing opposition from the army as well as serious financial problems. He also came under criticism from the supporters of a republic, who believed they were losing everything that they had achieved in 1649. Also, the divisions between the newly elected parliament and the army, whose political power it sought to restrict, came to head in April 1659 when the army, represented by his uncle, John Desborough, Charles Fleetwood and John Lambert, demanded that the Lord Protector dissolve parliament. When he refused, troops were brought in and he capitulated. The Second Protectorate Parliament was dissolved, and the Rump Parliament recalled. Richard Cromwell resigned in May and the Commonwealth was restored. The next twelve months were a time of uncertainty, intrigue and negotiation. The army and the Rump, in which an ailing John Bradshaw made his final contribution to politics, were both pleased to see the end of the Protectorate but had no common programme for running the country.

When in October 1659 the sixty-five M.P.s of the restored Rump Parliament voted to remove Lambert and Desborough from the army leadership and set up a seven-man committee under its control to replace them, Lambert and his supporters moved in troops, expelled the restored Rump Parliament and effectively seized power. Bradshaw made clear his strong objections but to no effect. He died on 31 October. However, General Monck, the army commander in Scotland, then took the army leadership by surprise. Influenced by his wife, Anne, and with the backing of the still respected Lord Fairfax, he decided that this went too far. Despite his inexperience in politics, he and Fairfax gained considerable support. When Monck marched south with the intention of restoring parliament, many soldiers in the force commanded by Lambert sent to stop him deserted. Elsewhere other army units declared for parliament. Monck arrived in London in February 1660 and reinstated those M.P.s who had been expelled from parliament by Cromwell and Colonel Pride back in 1649 with the explicit intention of them calling an election, which the Rump Parliament had persistently refused to do. William Prynne was at the head of the returning M.P.s as they entered parliament and he introduced a bill for the dissolution of the Commons to make way for new elections. He was later thanked by Charles II, had some influence in succeeding parliaments and was rewarded with public office.

Over the previous twelve months 'the Protectorate had failed, the Commonwealth had failed and the Rump had refused to fill its empty seats'.[1] Although it had not been Monck's original intention to restore the Stuarts, public opinion was increasingly made clear. The royal coat of arms was raised and those of the Commonwealth destroyed in many towns. With a new parliament likely to have a majority that favoured the end of the republic, Monck opened talks with Charles Stuart, now based in Brussels. Concessions needed to be made on both sides. The next two months were not without dangers. Monck had to move carefully to avoid the army turning against any agreement with Charles, especially after John Lambert, imprisoned in the Tower of London since March, escaped in April and attempted to stir up armed resistance. On 4 April Charles issued the Declaration of Breda indicating his acceptance of the major terms that Monck had outlined. These included a free and general pardon for actions taken during the civil war and since, with exceptions to be decided upon by the new parliament; a degree of religious toleration where it did not disturb the peace of the kingdom; a full settlement of any back-pay owed to the soldiers; and his agreement to parliament's decisions about property taken from royalists and sold after 1649.

The newly elected parliament met in late April. It contained more country gentlemen and far fewer republicans and soldiers than any since 1640.[2] They approved Charles' proposal that the King, Lords and people should be restored 'to their just, ancient and fundamental rights' and the terms of the Declaration of Breda. In early May their recognition of Charles as King Charles II was presented to him by their representatives, led by Lord Fairfax. Charles landed at Dover on 26 May and entered London three days later, on his thirtieth birthday. His coronation took place at Westminster Abbey on 23 April 1661. By the end of August 1660, a Bill of Free and General Pardon, Indemnity, and Oblivion had passed all stages in both houses of parliament and received royal assent. The inter-regnum period between the execution of Charles I and the restoration of Charles II was to be treated as though it never happened. In 1649 Charles had declared that he wished to be a 'severe avenger' of his father's 'innocent blood'. Since then his stance had been moderated by political considerations. He needed to compromise with many who had participated in the ruling of the Commonwealth and the Protectorate, such as General Monck, if he was to avoid widespread opposition. It was now parliament's task to decide who should be excluded from the pardon, but it was clear that retribution would be concentrated on members of the court which condemned Charles I rather than on those who ruled England after him.

The inability to establish an agreed alternative form of government had resulted in the restoration of the monarchy. Not all the regicides had supported Cromwell in the dismissal of the Rump Parliament or his becoming Lord Protector. Many had opposed these moves, but it was certain that none of them wished to see Charles I's son on the throne. The pardon and indemnity which Charles had agreed to was never going to include them. But what was the precise meaning of the term 'regicide' and who could be regarded as one? There was, and still is, uncertainty about who should be included in the definition. The responsibility of those commissioners at the trial who had signed the death warrant and of course the executioners was clear. They would certainly be exempted from the pardon. But what of commissioners who had not signed the warrant and the soldiers who had guarded the king in his final days and escorted him to his death? Their fate depended on a number of factors – what they had actually said and done, how willing they were to implicate others, who they knew that could plead their case in parliament, and the amount of money that they had available to pay their way to safety. There was also the complication that a degree of leniency had been promised to those who willingly handed themselves in to the authorities by 20 June 1660.

Although what follows appears to be a list of severe penalties against those involved in Charles' death, the Act of General Pardon, Indemnity and Oblivion meant that the numbers involved were relatively small. Many M.P.s, including Prynne, wished to see far more people exempted from the general pardon. One example was Richard Cromwell, Oliver's son and successor as Lord Protector. He might have been expected to be a major target, but he was not exempted. He moved to France in 1660 and for the next twenty years travelled around Europe. There is the story that he was once invited to dinner by a French nobleman who did not know his true identity. When he was asked about Richard Cromwell, who his host described as 'the basest fellow alive', he replied that the Lord Protector had been 'betrayed by those he most trusted, and who had been most obliged by his father'[3]. In about 1680 he returned to England and led a quiet life in the country until his death in 1712 at the age of eighty-four. There would have been far more retribution and bloodshed if the royalists who had fled abroad, as well as those who had remained in England and had been heavily fined or had property taken from them during the eleven years of the Commonwealth and Protectorate, had been given a free rein.

Twenty of the fifty-nine commissioners at Charles I's trial who had signed the death warrant in January 1649 had already died by May 1660. Of the seventeen commissioners who had sat for at least one day at the trial but had not signed the warrant, four were dead. There were also some lawyers and soldiers who were exempted from pardon because of their role in the trial and execution of the king. Only one of these, Issac Dorislaus, who had helped draw up the charges against Charles I, was dead. He had been murdered by a group of royalist refugees, led by Walter Whitford, in May 1649 while negotiating on behalf of the Commonwealth in The Hague. Most of the dead were exempted from the Act of Immunity, which made it possible for the state to confiscate property that had formerly belonged to them. The bodies of some, such as Richard Deane and Sir William Constable, were disinterred and reburied in a common pit. However, for those deceased considered to be most responsible for the former king's execution – Oliver Cromwell, John Bradshaw, and Henry Ireton – a more gruesome spectacle was arranged. A similar sentence was passed on the body of Colonel Thomas Pride but it was never carried out.

The three bodies were disinterred on 28 January 1661 and taken to the Red Lion Inn at Holborn. On the twelfth anniversary of Charles' execution, 30 January 1661, which many wished to be a day of remembrance for 'Charles the Martyr', their bodies were subjected to the same treatment as traitors. Their open coffins were dragged through the streets on hurdles to the public gallows at Tyburn. It was possible to buy a close look at Cromwell's corpse in his coffin.[4] The bodies were then pulled out and hanged from the Tyburn 'tree', a horizontal wooden triangle supported by three uprights erected in 1571. As had been intended, many thousands turned out to watch the display. Samuel Pepys avoided the scene but recorded that his wife, Elizabeth, then aged twenty, went to Tyburn with a friend. Ireton had died ten years earlier and his embalmed body was described as being 'like a dried rat'[5]. Bradshaw's body, buried just over a year before, was still in the process of decay with liquid oozing through the winding sheets. Cromwell's corpse had also been embalmed after his death, just over two years before, and was reported to have looked remarkable fresh. As dusk approached they were cut down, beheaded, and their bodies dismembered before being thrown into a pit. Their heads were taken to the south front of Westminster Hall where Charles' trial had taken place, and placed on twenty-foot-long poles facing Whitehall, the site of his execution. This was one of the busiest parts of the capital and the heads remained there for the whole of Charles II's reign, a warning to republicans and any would-be rebels. Cromwell in particular was the subject of a sustained campaign to vilify him.

Few heads have had such a varied history or been subjected to as much examination as Cromwell's. After over twenty years at Westminster it is believed that a great storm broke the pole and his head fell to the ground where a sentry picked it up and took it home. On hearing that it was being looked for and believing that he might be punished, he hid it up his chimney. In the early eighteenth century, it was sold to a private museum and became a curiosity and a potentially popular attraction. Towards the end of the century it was in the ownership of a Samuel Russell, who then gave it to a goldsmith, James Cox, in lieu of debts of £100. Cox regarded it as an investment and sold it in 1799 to the Hughes brothers for £233. They hoped to hold a profitable exhibition with Cromwell's head as its centrepiece. However, interest in the head had waned. The high entry price of two shillings and sixpence and the widespread rumours that it was a fake, doomed their efforts. In 1815 the head was purchased by Josiah Wilkinson in whose family it remained until 1960. During the nineteenth and early twentieth centuries it was scientifically examined on a number of occasions, along with another head stored in the Ashmolean Museum, Oxford, which was also claimed to be that of Oliver Cromwell. Each report supported the Wilkinson head as being the genuine article and dismissed that in the Ashmolean as a fake. In 1960 the family offered it to Sidney Sussex College, Cambridge, where Cromwell had studied. It was buried in March 1960 in a secret location near the antechapel, in the oak box in which it had been kept for the previous one hundred and fifty years.

Those regarded as regicides who remained alive in 1660 came from a variety of walks of life. There were various relations of Cromwell, cousins and in-laws, along with others who had served as officers in the parliamentary armies. In addition, there were numerous lawyers, landowners and wealthy merchants, as well as religious radicals like the Fifth Monarchists. Whatever their background they had good reason to believe that their exemption from the Act of Indemnity and Oblivion would result in a trial followed by execution. As some of the exemptions needed to be agreed by parliament there was often disagreement as to who should be included, with William Prynne leading the demands for more trials and executions. Such debates continued for almost two years, leaving many of the individuals under consideration fearing for their lives.

Some regicides who were initially exempted had handed themselves in by the deadline of 20 June 1660. Of the others who remained in the country a few, such as Thomas Harrison, stayed at home to await arrest, while the rest, some of whom went into hiding, were quickly rounded up. Others fled abroad, most to the Netherlands, Germany or Switzerland, but three made it as far as New England in North America. Two who had managed to escape abroad, Sir Hardress Waller and Thomas Scott, returned to England voluntarily. Starting on 11 October 1660 the twenty-eight regicides who were then in custody were brought to trial at the Old Bailey over the following week. Another, William Hewlett (Hulet), a Captain of the Guard, was added to the list of the accused during the trials.

Charged with responsibility for the death, or as it was now referred to, the murder, of King Charles, only two pleaded guilty, including Waller. The verdicts were a forgone conclusion. All were found guilty, and most were sentenced to death with the words: 'That you … be drawn upon a hurdle to the place of execution, and then you shall be hanged by the neck and, being alive, shall be cut down, and your privy members to be cut off, and your entrails be taken out of your body and, you living, the same to be burnt before your eyes, and your head to be cut off, your body to be divided into four-quarters, and head and quarters to be disposed of at the pleasure of the King's majesty. And the Lord have mercy on your soul.'

The first execution, on Saturday 13 October at Charing Cross, was that of Thomas Harrison. A well-known republican and religious zealot, he had become the chief hate figure of the new regime as Cromwell, Ireton and Bradshaw were already dead. A clerk at the Inns of Court in the 1630s, Harrison had enlisted in the parliamentary army at the start of the civil war and risen through the ranks to become a Major-General. His regiment was known for its Leveller sympathies. He had commanded the escort that brought Charles to London for his trial and had signed the death warrant. He became a spokesperson for the Fifth Monarchists, had opposed the creation of the Protectorate, but was clearly still regarded as a threat to the Restoration. At his trial he had pointed out that he had given himself up and despite many opportunities had not attempted to escape because 'I had been engaged in the service of so glorious and great a God'[6]. According to Edmund Ludlow, a fellow regicide who escaped to Switzerland, in his posthumously published '*Memoirs*', Harrison argued that he had acted on the authority of parliament and then only on the principles of conscience and justice. He was prevented from finishing his speech, found guilty and sentenced. As he was taken from the court he shouted that he had no reason to be ashamed of the cause in which he had acted. Pepys was in the large crowd that turned out to see the execution. He was impressed with the courage and dignity demonstrated by Harrison, and didn't join in with the shouting and cheering as Harrison's head and heart were held up for the crowd to see.[7]

This execution was followed two days later by that of John Carew, a fellow commissioner and Fifth Monarchist. He was hanged, but unlike Harrison and most of those whose deaths were to follow, he was spared being dismembered and having his 'quarters' displayed on various city gates. On the following day Hugh Peters, a radical preacher, condemned for inciting regicide, and John Cook, the chief prosecutor at the trial, were executed. Peters' head was placed on London Bridge and that of Cook above the entrance to Westminster Hall. Then on Wednesday 17 October four commissioners who had signed the death warrant, Thomas Scott, Gregory Clement, John Jones and Adrian Scrope were hanged, drawn and quartered, the latter being the only person who had handed himself in before the 20 June deadline to be executed. On Friday 19 October officers of the guard who had participated in Charles' death, Francis Hacker and Daniel Axtell, met their fate. These final two executions of the week were moved from Charing Cross further out to the traditional place of execution, Tyburn. It seems that many people had seen enough bloodshed and the crowds turning up were much smaller. Perhaps some felt like Pepys, who recorded that walking home one evening he passed the limbs of some of those executed which had been placed on Aldersgate, which he thought 'was a sad sight to see; and a bloody week this and the last have been'.[8]

These executions seemed to have satisfied much of the public's desire for retribution. The carrying out of other death sentences was delayed, partly because of the need for another act of parliament to confirm the sentences on most of those who had freely surrendered by 20 June. This proved to be a slow process partly because of the failure to agree to the list – some wished to add more names – and partly because both the Commons and the Lords wished to be seen to be diligent in their work. In early 1662 several prisoners were still awaiting a final decision as to whether the death penalty would be carried out. One, Owen Rowe, had already died in the Tower of London in December 1661. The general expectation was that more executions would take place, ideally on 30 January 1662. Three of the commissioners who had not signed the death warrant and had already been sentenced to life imprisonment, Sir Henry Mildmay, William Mountson (First Viscount Monson) and Robert Wallop, suffered the horrendous experience of being dragged through the streets to Tyburn on hurdles in a dress rehearsal.

However, the much-delayed bill, having been passed by the Commons and under consideration by the Lords, was quietly dropped by May 1662. It seems possible that by then King Charles II had indicated that while he did not wish to be seen to be pardoning the regicides, he did not wish to confirm any more death penalties. As a result, several of those who signed the death warrant of Charles I as well as other commissioners who had not signed it had their death sentences commuted to life imprisonment. All eventually died while still in prison. They were held in a number of different prisons and their conditions varied considerably. Some were closely confined while others had far more relaxed gaolers. Sir Hardress Waller, Henry Smith, and Gilbert Millington all died while in prison in Jersey during the 1660s. Peter Temple died in the Tower in 1663 while Sir Robert Tichborne died after over 20 years there in 1682. The last survivors was Thomas Waite who died in 1688.

Henry Marten seems to have been particularly fortunate in both the sentence and his eventual imprisonment. An avowed republican, he had called for an end to the monarchy as early as 1641, stating that 'I do not think one man wise enough to govern us all'.[9] Two years later he had declared in the House of Commons that he knew of 'no cause why the destruction of any one family should be put in the balance with the destruction of the whole kingdom' and made clear that he was referring to 'the king and his children'.[10] Not many parliamentarians agreed with him so early in the civil war. He was expelled from parliament for three years and spent some time in the Tower. Later he had supported Cromwell's purge of parliament in 1648, though had vehemently opposed the creation of the Protectorate. At his trial he effectively defended himself but said that he would be a loyal subject of King Charles II because this king had been 'called in by the representative body of England'.[11] Imprisoned at first in the north of England and then Windsor Castle, he was moved in 1668 to Chepstow Castle. There his confinement did not appear to have been unduly arduous, living with his common law wife until his death in 1680.[12]

Only two of those who signed Charles' death warrant were pardoned. Sir Richard Ingoldsby, an army officer and cousin of Oliver Cromwell, had supported General Monck in 1660 and had been in command of the troops who recaptured John Lambert after his final effort to prevent the Restoration. Ingoldsby also claimed that he had refused to sign the death warrant but had been forced to do so by Cromwell 'who with a loud laugh, taking his hand in his, and putting the pen between his fingers, with his own hand wrote Richard Ingoldsby'.[13] It has been commented that the signature on the death warrant looked no different from his usual signature and so his claim must be doubted. John Hutchinson also supported General Monck against Lambert. He made the dubious claim that he was fully convinced of his own errors of the past and that he was inspired by the wish to see the monarchy restored. Backed by an influential kinsman, the royalist Richard Byron, it was decided that he should be pardoned. However, in 1663 he was implicated in a plot against the new king and imprisoned, dying the following year.

Of the non-signing commissioners and soldiers involved, a few were also pardoned. John Dove had taken no part in the trial though had been present when Charles's sentence had been decided. He made a grovelling apology to parliament and went unpunished. Sir Gilbert Pickering had attended two sessions of the trial. He was the brother-in-law of Edward Montagu, who although a parliamentary military commander and a member of the Council of State in the Commonwealth had played a prominent part in the restoration of Charles II. He was created the earl of Sandwich in 1660, and we know from Samuel Pepys, a friend, that Montagu's influence was able to secure a pardon for Pickering. Matthew Tomlinson had been in charge of Charles's guard in the last month of his life but had refused to become a commissioner at the king's trial, an act that saved his life. He was pardoned for the respect that he had shown to the king and for testifying against other guards, Hacker and Axtell. Another senior guard who testified against them was Hercules Huncks. He was also pardoned though he died shortly afterwards in October 1660.

Two other men, John Lambert and Sir Henry Vane the Younger, who were not at the trial of King Charles or directly involved in his execution, were exempted from the Act of Indemnity after much debate in parliament. Lambert, although named as a commissioner for the trial, never attended, as he was involved in the siege of Pontefract at the time. As the leader of the army faction that wished to prevent the Restoration he had been arrested in 1660, before Charles II's return to England. He remained in prison in Guernsey until 1662 when parliament charged him with high treason. He threw himself on the mercy of the court and it was decided that he should be retained in custody until further orders were issued. He was never released, though he was later permitted some limited freedom of movement 'consistent with the security of his person', first in Guernsey and then from 1667 on Drake's Island near Plymouth, until his death in 1684. Sir Henry Vane the Younger was a leading parliamentary figure during the civil war and during the early years of the Commonwealth. A convinced republican, even though he had not supported King Charles's execution, he too was opposed to the return of the Stuarts. Initially granted clemency by Charles II, he remained in prison until, at the instigation of parliament, he was charged with high treason in 1662 for previously 'imagining the death of Charles II' in 1659. His political beliefs were still regarded as a danger to the new regime and he made no attempt to disguise them. He argued that it was impossible to commit treason against a king who had not been crowned and that if a king violated the agreement between him and the people then his powers should be withdrawn. Found guilty, he was sentenced to death. The king retracted his clemency but granted Vane the dignity of being beheaded at Tower Hill. Pepys recorded that he died 'justifying himself and the cause that he stood for' confident that he was going to Christ's right hand.

Nearly twenty of the commissioners and others exempted from the pardon fled from England in 1660 and took refuge in Europe. Most went to the Netherlands, Germany or Switzerland. They were joined in 1664 by Thomas Wogan. He must have had influential friends who helped him to avoid the trials of October 1660 and then to escape from York Castle and flee to Europe. All were regarded as fugitives by the English government under Charles II. In 1662 the English ambassador in the Netherlands,

Sir George Downing, was responsible for the tracking down and capture of three regicides. Downing had held important administrative and diplomatic positions during the time of the republic, ending as ambassador in The Hague, where he organised spies to watch the activities of royalist exiles. As the restoration of the Stuarts became increasingly likely he used his position to keep Charles, who was based in Brussels, informed about English affairs, acknowledged the error of his past allegiances and declared his loyalty to the monarchy. At the Restoration he was knighted, retained his position as ambassador, and used his contacts to find his former associates. John Barkstead and John Okey had fled to Germany and Miles Corbet to the Netherlands. Downing's agents tracked down Corbet and then managed to lure Okey and Barkstead to the Netherlands in the belief that they would be meeting their colleague and some relations. Once they had arrived, Downing's men moved in and arrested them. They were extradited to England. As fugitives they had already been declared outlaws and had no right to a trial, other than to confirm their identity. All three were to be hanged, drawn and quartered, though it is believed that when the sentence was carried out in April 1662 they were hanging for long enough for them to be dead before they were cut down. It was perhaps their executions that saved those who were still in prison in England awaiting the outcome of parliament's deliberations by persuading the king that more deaths were unnecessary.

Another fugitive, Sir John Lisle, was murdered in Lausanne in 1664 by James FitzEdmond Cotter, an Irish royalist who had set about hunting escaped regicides. His murder and the arrest of the three regicides in the Netherlands meant that the remaining exiles always lived in fear of capture or murder, with one eye looking over their shoulder, finding it hard to trust any of their countrymen who might try to befriend them. Some did not live for long. Valentine Walton (in Germany) and Thomas Chaloner (in the Netherlands) both died of natural causes in 1661. However, some lived for many years. Edmund Ludlow was the last to die, living in Bern, Switzerland, where he died in 1692. Even their relations who remained in England could not afford to be seen to be hostile to the Stuarts. John Lisle's second wife, Alice, was arrested in 1685 for giving overnight shelter to a non-conformist preacher and an associate after the defeat of Monmouth's rebellion against King James II, who had succeeded his brother, Charles II. Found guilty, she was condemned to be burned at the stake by Judge Jeffreys at the 'Bloody Assizes' in Winchester. The new king refused to commute the death sentence but allowed her to be beheaded as befitted her social status.

Two regicides, Edward Whalley, and his son-in-law William Goffe, managed to board a ship bound for North America the day before warrants for their arrest were issued. They hoped that because of the non-conformist religious persuasion of many of the people who had left England for the new colonies during the 1620s, 1630s and 1640s there would be more sympathy for their cause. Landing in Boston, Massachusetts, in July 1660, they were at first welcomed by the governor and lived openly in Cambridge. As news of their status as fugitives became known and agents were sent from England to track them down, it became necessary for them to go into hiding. They moved to Connecticut, where they sheltered in New Haven and then Milford. For some time they lived in a cave when those hunting for them came close. In 1664 they moved one hundred miles north to Hadley, Massachusetts, where they remained for the rest of their lives, Whalley dying in about 1675 and Goffe probably in 1679.[14] A third regicide, John Dixwell, also reached the New England colonies. It is believed that he first went to Germany and then Switzerland before crossing the Atlantic. He briefly stayed with Whalley and Goffe before finally settling in New Haven, Connecticut, under the name James Davids. He had the advantage that the English authorities, having lost track of his movements, believed that he had died in Europe. Unlike Whalley and Goffe, whose families in England were only able to have minimal correspondence with them because of the dangers of detection, Dixwell seems to have had no family in England. He married twice in America and had three children by his second wife before his death in 1689.

In Scotland a separate Act of Indemnity and Oblivion was passed in September 1662, naming specific individuals who were excluded from any pardon. Another Act of the Scottish parliament named 700 supporters of the Covenant who had to pay substantial fines in order to benefit from the pardon. Earlier some Scots had been arrested and charged with high treason. A number of them were executed. Archibald Campbell, the Earl of Argyll, was found not guilty of complicity in the execution of Charles I but condemned for his leading role in the defeat of royalist uprisings during the 1650s. He was beheaded on 27 May 1661. A few days later James Guthrie, a leading churchman and opponent of royal ecclesiastical authority was hanged, along with Captain William Govan, who was found guilty of desertion and of assisting Cromwell's invasion of Scotland in 1650. The other Scot to be executed was the judge and statesman, Archibald Johnston, Lord Warriston. He had played a leading role in drawing up the National Covenant in 1638. He later opposed any concessions to King Charles I during the negotiations of 1648 and then had positions under the Lord Protector. He fled abroad at the restoration of Charles II and was sentenced to death *in absentia*. In 1663 he made the mistake of travelling to Rouen, in France, where he was identified, arrested and sent to England. He was taken to Edinburgh to be hanged in July 1663.

There were two other individuals that the authorities after the Restoration would have liked to have detained and almost certainly executed. They were described in the list of names exempt from indemnity as 'those two persons ... who being disguised by frocks and vizors, did appear upon the scaffold erected before Whitehall'. In other words, the executioner, or headsman, and his assistant. They had taken care to be unrecognisable, the executioner had never even spoken the traditional words when holding up the head, and their identities were never revealed. There has been much speculation as to who the executioner was. Back in January 1649 there had been some difficulty in finding someone to perform the task. A considerable sum was offered to soldiers of the guard but none immediately volunteered. Later it was suggested that one of them, William Hewlett (Hulet), offered his services. The fact that he received a promotion after the execution tends to back up this idea. He was charged in 1660, found guilty and sentenced to death. However, the punishment was never carried out and he was pardoned strongly suggesting that those in power did not believe that he was their man. The most likely executioner was the common hangman, Richard Brandon, who had certainly beheaded people before, such as Archbishop William Laud in 1645. The fact that Charles's head was severed from his body with one blow, which was by no means always the case, would suggest someone with experience. It is known that Brandon also beheaded other royalists, James Hamilton, Duke of Hamilton, Henry Rich, Earl of Holland and Lord Capel, on 9 March 1649, but died only a few months later.

Although the restoration of Charles II was achieved without too much bloodshed, religion remained a potentially divisive issue. Dissenters still had a strong support base and were concerned about the apparent Catholic sympathies of the Stuarts. Such concerns grew during the 1670s, culminating in the Exclusion Crisis after it became known that Charles's heir, his brother James, was a Catholic. There were rumours of a 'popish plot' to restore Catholicism and several failed efforts were made to exclude James from the succession because of his religion. On Charles II's death in 1685 without a legitimate heir, James did indeed become king, accepted by many as the price of stability and because his heir was his eldest daughter, Mary, a Protestant. Within less than four years his policies had lost him support. When in June 1688 his second wife gave birth to a son, James, creating the likelihood of a permanent Catholic dynasty, events came to a head and he was deposed in the 'Glorious Revolution'. William, Prince of Orange, the wife of James' daughter, Mary, was invited to lead an army to England in order to force James to make Mary his heir. When William did so in November 1688 he received widespread support. James fled. He was at first captured but then allowed to escape to France, where he was received by his cousin and ally, Louis XIV. A Stuart king had been removed again, but this time he had not lost his life. Mary and William became joint monarchs of England, Scotland and Ireland. James II died in exile in 1701 though both his son, Edward, the 'Old Pretender', and his grandson, Charles, the 'Young Pretender', both attempted and failed to regain the crown.

Had the world been turned upside down by the civil wars and then the trial and execution of Charles I? At the time it might have seemed so, with the removal of the king and the introduction of a republic. This was revolutionary in a world in which monarchy was the accepted form of government. The radical ideas of the Levellers had been rejected by those who came to power, but the various experiments in government between 1649 and 1660 had all failed to gain legitimacy in the eyes of the majority of the population. In 1660 people turned to the security of what they knew and King Charles II was restored to the throne. Even after the deposition of his successor, James II, monarchy was not abandoned. However there had been a permanent shift in the balance of power between crown and parliament, even if only a small proportion of the population were represented at Westminster and power was still held by a relatively small group of people. It was to take several centuries of gradual change to see many of the demands of the Levellers – a wider franchise, regular elections, more equal constituencies, equality before the law – to be accepted as the basis for a modern democracy.

CONCLUSIONS

The fact that regicide has been a central element in many dramatic productions from classical times onwards suggests that it has always been seen an act of the greatest significance, usually regarded with horror. Thus, in Sophocles' *'Oedipus Rex'* the central theme is Oedipus' quest to find the killer of his father, Laius, King of Thebes, in order to end a plague in the city. His search eventually reveals that he had unwittingly killed his father and then married his mother, Jocasta. She hangs herself and Oedipus gouges out his own eyes in remorse. The psychological and physical punishment of those who have killed a monarch is at the centre of Shakespeare's *'Macbeth'*, for his murder of King Duncan, and *'Hamlet'*, in which the prince seeks revenge on his uncle, Claudius, for murdering his father and seizing the throne. In recent times the backstory to *'A Game of Thrones'*, based on the fantasy novels *'Songs of Ice and Fire'* by George R. R. Martin was the end of the Targaryen dynasty fourteen years earlier. As Aerys II, King of the Seven Kingdoms of Westeros, became ever more unpredictable and brutal, he was killed by a member of the kings-guard, Jamie Lannister. As one of the main characters in the series, Lannister is often insultingly referred to as 'king-killer', despite the fact that almost everyone in Westeros was relieved that Aerys was removed.

In Europe at the beginning of the sixteenth century monarchy was widely accepted as the natural form of government. Monarchs derived their authority from God and represented the head of the body politic beneath which every individual had their place in the hierarchical social structure. Yet in the years between 1550 and 1650 many monarchs were killed by their own subjects. Some of these monarchs were generally regarded at the time as being incompetent, corrupt or tyrannical. Others, however, such as Henry IV of France, were thought of as effective rulers, a belief upheld in the court of history. The underlying political, social and religious circumstances differed, as did the motives of those responsible and the consequences of the killing, for both those directly involved and the country as a whole.

Nevertheless there are some common features that can be identified in these acts of regicide in England, France, Russia and the Ottoman Empire.

Invariably a disputed succession resulted in significant problems. If there is any doubt as to who the legitimate monarch should be, whether the result of dubious genealogical claims, family intrigues or religious convictions, violence was often seen by the rival claimants as the only way to secure the throne or impose a change of monarch. The succession issue was at its most straightforward in England. All monarchs wished to control who their successor should be – essentially their own eldest son or, failing that, in some jurisdictions, daughter. But what happened when a monarch was childless? Laws and customs that defined the line of succession existed, but Henry VIII had altered these laws until, after the birth of his son, he eventually reinstated his daughters to the succession without repealing the laws that declared them to be illegitimate. However, that son, Edward VI, wished to prevent the accession of his sister Mary, the rightful heir, because of her religion. He could only do this by excluding both his sisters as illegitimate. In his 'Devise for the Succession' he therefore named the young Lady Jane Grey to be his successor. Although civil war was avoided by Mary's unexpectedly determined response and the unwillingness of the establishment to go through with the plan, Jane Grey remained a focus of rebellions. She was eventually executed several months after the beheading of John Dudley, Duke of Northumberland, regarded as the instigator of the plot.

The case of Mary, Queen of Scots was slightly different. She was the legitimate heir to the throne as long as Queen Elizabeth remained unmarried and childless. Mary never renounced her right to the English throne. As a Catholic, with the potential support of her co-religionists in England and that of foreign powers who wished to bring England back into the Catholic Church, she was always going to be central to any plots to remove Elizabeth. She had a greater responsibility for bring about her own execution than Jane Grey because of her willingness, despite her denials, to show an interest in plans for foreign invasion and her accession. The executions of both Jane Grey and Mary, Queen of Scots were carried out, after a legal process, in order to remove a threat to the reigning monarch.

In Russia, France, the Ottoman Empire and England in the late 1640s it was the reigning monarchs themselves who were killed. In Russia, with the end of the Rurikid dynasty on the death of the childless Feodor I, civil war could not be avoided for long. Although delayed by the firm hand of Boris Godunov, the opposition to his family becoming the established dynasty which had built up during his reign, erupted on his death. His son Feodor II was murdered within months of his accession. There followed a succession of 'pretenders' claiming to be the deceased Prince Dmitry of Uglich, and the *boyar* Vasily Shuisky establishing himself as Tsar Vasily IV. His failure to defeat an invasion by the Polish king, Sigismund III, led to his overthrow. The 'Time of Troubles' only came to an end with the recognition, by most of the elite as well as the population as a whole, that they would have to accept one of their own as a legitimate monarch. The Romanov dynasty which emerged survived for the next three hundred years.

The succession, linked with religious conflict, was also a major factor in the French Wars of Religion and the murders of both Henry III and Henry IV. Henry III accepted the traditional Salic Laws that excluded both the accession of a woman and the inheritance of a claim to the throne through the female line. It meant that after 1584, for as long as he remained childless, his heir was the Protestant, Henry of Navarre. This was completely unacceptable to many Catholics who therefore argued that the coronation oath, which required the French monarch to defend the Catholic religion, was more important than the Salic Laws. Henry III's murder of the leaders of the Catholic League and his alliance with Henry of Navarre was followed by his own assassination in 1589. The Huguenot leader then became King Henry IV as a result of military success, but he recognised that he needed to convert to the Catholic faith if he was ever to be accepted by the majority of the French people. This, however, did not win over everyone. Some believed that his conversion was insincere and deceitful. The more extreme claimed that he was planning to overthrow Catholic rulers across Europe, hence his assassination.

It does not seem coincidental that the killing of monarchs in France, Russia and the Ottoman Empire took place over a relatively short space of time. The monarch had been given almost sacred status and such acts would have seemed almost inconceivable fifty years earlier. However, in France the belief developed that Henry III had broken his contracts with both God and the French people, thereby he had become a tyrant and lost his right to rule. It became acceptable to talk about his removal and even murder. In this atmosphere of heightened tensions and vitriolic rhetoric in a divided society some individuals came to believe that it was their duty to act. After one king had been murdered it became easier to contemplate the killing of another. There were numerous attempts to kill Henry IV before the success of Ravaillac in 1610.

Similarly in Russia, after almost 300 years of the Rurikid dynasty, the killing of Tsar Feodor II in 1605 set off a chain of events which resulted in civil war, the murder of Tsar (False) Dmitry I and other pretenders, as well as the removal of Tsar Vasily IV, all within five years. In the Ottoman

Empire any of the previous sultan's sons could rightfully succeed him. War between brothers, followed by fratricide, usually resolved the issue by removing rivals. However, the end of wholesale fratricide meant that alternative candidates remained alive and so sultans could not only be deposed, like Mustafa I (twice), but murdered as in the cases of Osman II and Ibrahim I. Once such an action was accepted by certain groups in society and started to become normalised then the chances of it reoccurring were dramatically increased. Violence gave rise to more violence in many countries.

Another factor that had an influence in the Ottoman Empire was the changing balance of power between the sultan with his immediate circle and other groups who wished to have greater power and influence over policy. These included administrators and the janissaries, as well as rival court factions. The palace coups that removed Mustafa I (twice) and had Osman II and Ibrahim I strangled required the backing of some of these groups who then believed that they could dominate the new sultan. None were the result of conspiracies involving their successors. They were too young to have been involved – Osman II's successor (after the second removal of Mustafa) was Murad IV who became sultan aged 11, while Ibrahim's successor was his six-year-old son, Mehmed IV. In 1622 Osman II lost the support of the janissaries who believed he was planning to create a new army so he could disband, or severely undermine their influence. In 1648 after the killing of Ibrahim I considerable effort was put into persuading the population of his increasing mental instability to justify his death.

The issue of over-mighty subjects and powerful factions with personal rivalries, even blood feuds, was also an important factor in creating the conditions for regicide in France and Russia. The impact of the Guise family throughout the French Wars of Religion, combining personal ambition with their backing of the Catholic Church, together with the actions of Conde, Coligny and Henry of Navarre, the Huguenot leaders, contributed greatly to the development of the conditions in which the assassination of a king could be contemplated. In Russia the opportunities opened up in the minds of some of the *boyars* by the end of the Rurikid dynasty can be seen most clearly in the actions of Vasily Shuisky He successively supported and then turned against Boris Godunov, Feodor II and False Dmitry I when it suited his own ambitions, culminating in him becoming tsar.

What was never disputed after these regicides was that the dead monarch would be replaced by a new one. Very few of the killers doubted that they were restoring the natural order of things, by removing a monarch who had lost the backing of God, who was failing to fulfil his duties to the country and its people, or who was simply unable to fulfil the role. The murderers of the French kings and the Russian tsars were not planning to establish a new form of government. Instead, they wished either to have a monarch who satisfied their demands, both political and personal, or place themselves on the throne. In the Ottoman Empire a new sultan was always enthroned, but after 1648 their absolute authority was restrained by other power brokers.

A similar result eventually emerged in seventeenth-century England, but only after the execution of a king at first resulted in the creation of a republic. The death of Charles I was not something that many of those who had fought against him in the civil wars had originally intended. Very few questioned his legitimate right to be king. However, by the time of his trial, the men who eventually signed his death warrant had no intention of replacing him with another monarch, even though most of them had only come to that conclusion a matter of months or even weeks earlier. Their problem was that without a monarch a new form of government had to be established and gain the backing, or at least the acquiescence, of the population as a whole. Over the next ten years there were various efforts to create a new system – the Commonwealth, the rule of the Major-Generals, the Protectorate – but none took root in the minds of the people of England and Scotland. No solution was found that would satisfy the various political and religious groups that had been unified only in their opposition to the personal rule of King Charles I. This failure opened the way for the restoration of the Stuarts in the form of Charles II, though with certain restrictions on his absolute power and with the influence of parliament significantly enhanced.

There were many motives for the regicides of the sixteenth and seventeenth centuries but most can be grouped into a limited number of categories – personal or family ambition, religious fervour, the desire to have a more effective ruler, personal revenge, and the wish to introduce a new system of government. The killings were never random acts of violence. Even those perpetrated by lone individuals, as in France, were closely connected to the political and religious situation of the time. What all had in common was the wish of those responsible to provide a legal or moral justification for their actions. This could be achieved in a formal trial for treason, by claiming that the monarch had lost the right to rule by becoming a tyrant, by demonstrating that (s)he had no legitimate, hereditary right to rule, or by affirming that the monarch was grossly incompetent and a danger to the country.

Despite these efforts, the outcome for those directly involved was rarely what they had planned. The executions of Lady Jane Grey and Mary, Queen of Scots effectively removed threats to the Tudor monarchy. However, Queen Mary I's death in 1558 meant that her attempt to undo the changes brought about by the Reformation came to nothing and Mary Stuart's execution left her son, James VI of Scotland, to inherit the English crown in 1603. As a Protestant he was acceptable to the English establishment, but still experienced probably the best known and certainly the most remembered attempt to assassinate an English monarch – the Gunpowder Plot. Those regicides in England responsible for the execution of Charles I failed in their attempt to establish a republic. With their different ideas and beliefs they fell out amongst themselves and were helpless to prevent Charles II's restoration eleven years later. Those still living, with only few exceptions, were then either executed or spent the rest of their lives in prison or in exile.

In France the assassins of Henry III and Henry IV were both killed, the former immediately at the scene of the murder, the latter in a painful public execution. But Henry III's murder did not achieve the wish of the Catholic League to prevent the Huguenot, Henry of Navarre, taking the throne as Henry IV. His subsequent murder deprived France of an able ruler, who had already converted to Catholicism, gone a long way to restoring royal authority and founded the dynasty that ruled for the next 180 years. Similarly in Russia the perpetrators of regicide gained little in the end. False Dmitry, having had Feodor II killed, seemingly with the population of Moscow fully behind him, ruled for only one year before his own killing by a group led by Vasily Shuisky, who achieved his aim to become tsar. But during his four-year reign, as Vasily IV, Russia experienced almost perpetual civil war and a Polish invasion. Vasily was removed from power by fellow Russian nobles, and died, most likely murdered, in a Polish prison. After the palace coups in Ottoman Empire few of the participants benefitted for long. Almost all of those who had Osman II killed were themselves executed with months, in an attempt by the new regime to disassociate itself from the murder. Likewise, after 1648 and the killing of Ibrahim I, Kosem Sultan and her supporters held sway for a couple of years before being removed and themselves executed.

Once in power it can prove to be very difficult to retain it, especially if it is achieved by dubious or outright illegal means. In a democracy there is a means of removing an unpopular, incompetent incumbent. Public opinion can sometimes shift rapidly. Support for politicians or a political party can erode quickly, especially if it has been gained in the first place by trickery and false promises. In dictatorships and autocratic states not only is it more difficult to remove leaders by peaceful means, but it is perhaps easier to control public opinion. The censorship of information and the constant repetition of propaganda are powerful tools, especially when backed-up by the use of fear to discourage opposition. None of the states in sixteenth and seventeenth century Europe can be regarded as democracies but it was still important for their rulers to have the support of a substantial proportion of the political elite and the economically powerful, as well as the ability to call upon the majority of the people, especially in the capital cities, to back them. As Machiavelli pointed out 'Principality [monarchy] easily becomes tyranny'. Once a 'prince came to be hated, and since he was hated, came to be afraid, and from fear soon passed to offensive action', this 'quickly brought about a tyranny'[1]. Once regarded as a tyrant any monarch could only expect there to be scheming and plotting against them.

The populace, often referred to as the 'mob', can be fickle in their sentiments. In a crowd there is a loss of the sense of individual responsibility, and people follow the predominant emotions of the crowd having gained the impression that their behaviour is the norm. In such situations peoples' behaviour tends to become more extreme than that of any single individual in that crowd. Key members of a crowd can create the prevailing mood and thus to some extent control the outcome. At times the 'mob' can be a powerful independent force but it has sometimes been carefully manipulated to help achieve the particular aims of the powerful elite or a charismatic speaker. An angry crowd can be fired up to identify a hate figure to blame for their perceived problems and when this became the monarch, rather than foreigners, ministers or court favourites as was often the case, the very survival of the ruler was threatened.

The 'mob' played a part in events leading to the death of several monarchs, though were only directly responsible for the death Tsar Feodor II when in 1605 the fear of False Dmitry I's army motivated the crowds to turn on the young tsar. A year later Vasily Shuisky skilfully managed to have the Moscow mob believe that it was the Poles who were attacking the Kremlin, inciting anti–Polish riots, while he and his men killed False Dmitry I. In Paris those that planned the murder of fifty or so Huguenot leaders in August 1572 lost control of the situation, resulting in thousands of deaths in the St Bartholomew's Day Massacre. In 1588 King Henry III had to flee his capital when large numbers turned out to support the demands of the Catholic League in the 'Day of the Barricades'. In 1622 the initial protests by the Janissaries were given greater impetus by the large numbers of the Istanbul population who aided them in the removal of Osman II. When Charles I left London in 1642, fearing for his safety and that of his family, it was a clear sign that a large section of the city's population had turned against him. He only returned, as a prisoner, weeks before his execution.

Since the seventeenth century most of the monarchies in Europe and around the world have come to an end, some peacefully, some violently. The monarchies that still exist in Europe are constitutional monarchies where the king or queen has a significant though usually ceremonial role, and their position is clearly circumscribed by law, custom and tradition. In modern political structures, whether regarded as democratic or autocratic, the succession might not be such a significant concern, but some leaders show a tendency to make use of family members, some extend the length of time that they are permitted to hold office, and most have a wish to see their policies continued by their successors, sometimes hand-picked. Just as in the royal families of the past, in present-day political parties the critic and rival from within is often more dangerous than an external threat and almost certainly more difficult to deal with. The removal of the leader of a political party, particularly one in power at the time, is regarded as a major step. However, in a time of national difficulty and disharmony it can become a habit in a desperate effort to find the 'right' person who can win the next election. This will often have unforeseen consequences and rarely benefit those responsible. In a democracy winning the support of the population is now more important than it has ever been, but governments still grapple with many of the same issues and problems faced by the monarchs of the sixteenth and seventeenth centuries.

LIST OF PRINCIPAL CHARACTERS

PART 1: LADY JANE GREY

Edward VI (1537-1553), son of Henry VIII and Jane Seymour. King of England from 1547 until he died at the age of 15 in 1553.

Elizabeth I (1533-1603), daughter of Henry VIII and Anne Boleyn. Queen of England from 1558 until 1603.

Henry VIII (1491-1547), second son of Henry VII and Elizabeth of York. King of England from 1509 until his death.

Mary I (1516-1558), daughter of Henry VIII and Catherine of Aragon. Queen of England between 1553 and 1558.

Lady Jane Grey (1537-1554), daughter of Henry Grey, Earl of Suffolk, and Frances Brandon (the daughter of Charles Brandon and Henry VIII's youngest sister, Mary). She was named in Edward VI's will as his successor.

Henry Grey, Duke of Suffolk (1517-1554), the great-grandson of Elizabeth Woodville, the wife of Edward IV, by her first marriage. He married Frances Brandon, thereby becoming Duke of Suffolk. He was the father of Lady Jane Grey and executed early in the reign of Queen Mary.

Frances Brandon, Duchess of Suffolk (1517-1559), daughter of Mary Tudor (the younger sister of Henry VIII) and Charles Brandon, and mother of Lady Jane Grey.

Lady Katherine Grey (1540-1568), the younger sister of Lady Jane Grey.

John Dudley (1504-1553), Lord Lisle, Earl of Warwick, Duke of Northumberland. A successful general and admiral, he became Lord

President of the Council in 1549. He was beheaded in 1553 after his failed attempt to establish Lady Jane Grey, his daughter-in-law, as queen of England instead of Mary.

Guildford Dudley (1535-1554), a younger son of John Dudley, Duke of Northumberland, who was married to Lady Jane Grey in 1553 and was executed on the same day as his wife.

Robert Dudley (1532-1588), a son of John Dudley, Duke of Northumberland, he was condemned to death along with his father and brother but reprieved in 1554. He later became a favourite of Queen Elizabeth and was created Earl of Leicester in 1564.

Edward Seymour (1500-1552), Earl of Hertford, Duke of Somerset. The brother of Henry VIII's third wife, Jane Seymour and uncle of Edward VI, he became Lord Protector during the minority of Edward VI until he was overthrown in 1549. He was executed in 1552.

Thomas Seymour (1508-1549), the younger brother of Edward Seymour. He married Katherine Parr, Henry VIII's last wife in 1547 and both Princess Elizabeth and Lady Jane Grey spent some time in their household. He was executed for treason in 1549.

Thomas Wyatt (1521-1554), the son of Thomas Wyatt, the courtier, diplomat and poet. He was executed in 1554 after rebelling against Queen Mary.

PART 2: MARY, QUEEN OF SCOTS

Mary, Queen of Scots (1542-1587), Queen of Scotland from 1542 until her forced abdication in 1567. She was married to Francis II, king of France, until his death in 1560 after which she returned to Scotland. In 1565 she married Henry Stuart, Lord Darnley and in 1567 James Hepburn, Earl of Bothwell, suspected to be one of those responsible for Darnley's murder. In 1568 she fled to England where she was closely guarded until her execution in 1587.

Mary of Guise (1515-1560), member of a powerful French family who married King James V in 1538. Mother of Mary, Queen of Scots, she played an important role in supporting the interests of Mary, France and the Catholic Church in Scottish affairs, while Mary spent her youth in France.

James V (1512-1542), king of Scotland from 1513 until his death, just six days after the birth of his daughter Mary.

Henry Stuart (Stewart), Lord Darnley (1546-1567), the son of the earl of Lennox and second wife of Mary, Queen of Scots. Murdered in Edinburgh in February 1567.

Matthew Stewart, Earl of Lennox (1516-1571), the father of Henry Stuart, Lord Darnley. He spent some of his early life in France and from 1544 until 1564 he lived mainly in England. He was a significant participant in Scottish internal conflicts of the period. In 1570 he became regent for his grandson, King James VI, but was killed in a skirmish near Stirling the following year.

Margaret Douglas, Countess of Lennox (1515-1578), the wife of Matthew Stewart. She was the daughter of Margaret Tudor, the sister of Henry VIII, and dowager queen of Scotland (widow of King James IV), by her second marriage.

David Rizzio (1533-1566), an Italian courtier who became private secretary to Mary, Queen of Scots. He was murdered in March 1566 in the Palace of Holyroodhouse while dining with Mary.

James Stewart, Earl of Moray (1531-1570), the illegitimate son of King James V and a leading figure in Scottish affairs during the 1550s and 1560s. He was a supporter of the Reformation in Scotland and became regent for James VI in 1567. He was assassinated in January 1570.

John Knox (1514-1572), a leader of the Reformation in Scotland. His outspoken views often brought him into conflict with secular powers, resulting in periods of imprisonment and exile. He was very critical of Mary, Queen of Scots when she returned to Scotland.

William Cecil (1520-1598), created Lord Burghley in 1571. He was Elizabeth I's chief adviser for most of her reign. He wished to ensure that Scotland was controlled by pro-English factions and played a significant role in the trial and execution of Mary, Queen of Scots.

Francis Walsingham (1532-1590) Elizabeth I's principal secretary from 1572. He is best remembered as her 'spymaster', controlling an efficient intelligence network which uncovered plots against the queen, including those involving Mary, Queen of Scots.

PART 3: FRANCE – HENRY III AND HENRY IV

Henry II (1519-1559), the king of France from 1547. Married to Catherine de' Medici in 1533, three of their sons became kings of France after his death from injuries sustained while jousting.

Catherine de' Medici (1519-1589). After the death of her husband, King Henry II, she played a major role in French political life during the Wars of Religion when three of her sons (Francis II, Charles IX and Henry III) came to the throne while still young.

Francis II (1544-1560), the eldest son of Henry II and Catherine de' Medici and king of France for just seventeen months, dying shortly before his seventeenth birthday. He was the first husband of Mary, Queen of Scots.

Charles IX (1550-1574), king of France from the age of 10 in 1560. It was during his reign that the Wars of Religion intensified and the St. Bartholomew's Day massacre took place in 1572.

Henry III (1551-1589), king of France from 1574 until his murder in 1589. In 1573 he was elected as king of the Polish- Lithuanian Commonwealth but he returned to France on the death of his brother Charles IX and was deprived of the title. He struggled to impose royal authority in France and became the first French monarch to be assassinated. He had no children and was the last of the Valois dynasty.

Hercule / Francis (1555-1584), Duke of Alencon, created Duke of Anjou in 1576, often referred to as *'Monsieur'* a title used for the eldest surviving brother of the French king. Christened Hercule, he changed his name to Francis in honour of his late brother, Francis II. His death in 1584 created a major crisis in France because it meant that the heir to the childless Henry III was Henry of Navarre, a Protestant.

Henry IV (Henry of Navarre) (1553-1610), the first Bourbon king of France. Raised as a Protestant by his mother, Jeanne d'Albret, queen of Navarre, he became the leader of the Huguenots in the Wars of Religion. When he became the heir to the French throne in 1584, Catholics were determined to prevent his accession. He converted to Catholicism in 1593, though he was assassinated in 1610 by a Catholic extremist.

Jeanne d'Albret (1528-1572), queen of Navarre and mother of Henry IV. She was the daughter of Henry II of Navarre and Margaret of Angoulême, the sister of King Francis I. She converted to Calvinism in 1560. Well educated, with a strong personality, she was an able ruler of her territories.

Marie de' Medici (1575-1642), the second wife of Henry IV. She was the mother of King Louis XIII and head of the *Conseil de Roi* during his youth, and of Henrietta Maria, the wife of Charles I of England. A keen patron of the arts, her political intrigues resulted in her being exiled from France in 1631.

Francis, Duke of Guise (1519-1563), leader of the Catholic forces in the First War of Religion, he was killed by a Protestant assassin. His murder led to a feud between the Guise family and the Huguenot leader, Coligny. He was the brother of Mary of Guise and father of Henry, Duke of Guise and Louis II, Cardinal of Guise.

Henry, Duke of Guise (1550-1588), a leading Catholic figure in the religious wars from the late 1560s. He was the main instigator of the murder of Admiral Coligny and the St. Bartholomew's Day Massacre. A founder of the Catholic League, he was assassinated on the order of King Henry III in December 1588.

Louis II, Cardinal of Guise (1555-1588), brother of Henry, Duke of Guise, also murdered in December 1588.

Mary of Guise – see above in Part 2.

Admiral Coligny (1519-1574), became the military leader of the Huguenots after the death of the Prince of Condé. He was murdered in Paris in 1572 at the start of the St. Bartholomew's Day Massacre.

Antoine de Bourbon (1518-1562), the father of King Henry IV, descended from King Louis IX (1214-1270). He became king of Navarre on the death of his father-in-law. He died from wounds in the early stages of the Wars of Religion.

Louis I, Prince of Condé (1530-1569), younger brother of both Antoine de Bourbon (see above) and the Cardinal of Bourbon (see below). He commanded the Huguenot forces in the early Wars of Religion and was executed after defeat at Jarnac in 1569 on the orders of Henry of Anjou, later King Henry III.

Charles, Cardinal of Bourbon (1523-1590), a leading French nobleman and prelate. He became the candidate of the Catholic League, supported by Philip II of Spain, to be king in the event of the death of Henry III instead of the Huguenot, Henry of Navarre (Henry IV). He died less than a year after Henry III's murder while still being held prisoner by Henry IV.

PART 4: RUSSIA'S TIME OF TROUBLES

Ivan IV (1530-1584), known as 'the Terrible', he became Grand Prince of Moscow at the age of 3 and Tsar of All Russia in 1547. In 1581 he killed his eldest son, Ivan Ivanovich, in a fight, leaving Feodor as his successor.

Anastasia Romanovna (1530-1560), the first wife of Ivan IV and mother of both Ivan Ivanovich and Feodor I. She was the link between the Rurikids and the Romanovs, being the aunt of Feodor Romanov and great-aunt of Tsar Mikhail I.

Feodor I (1557-1598) the younger son of Ivan IV. Good natured, pious, rather simple minded and with little interest in politics, he married Irena, the sister of Boris Godunov, his chief minister. He and Irina had one daughter who died as a young child. He was the last of the Rurikid dynasty.

Maria Nagaya (1553-1608), the seventh and last wife of Ivan IV and the mother of Dmitry of Uglich. She later accepted False Dmitry I as her son in order to further her family's interests.

Dmitry of Uglich (1582-1591), the youngest son of Ivan IV, born to his last wife, Maria Nagaya. He almost certainly died, whether by accident or design, at the age of eight. His death was first used to blacken the name of Boris Godunov but then various pretenders to the throne claimed to be Dmitry, who had escaped Godunov's assassins.

Boris Godunov (1552-1605) became Tsar in 1598 on the death of his brother-in-law, Feodor I. An able ruler, Russia suffered various natural disasters during his reign. Many people did not accept him as the legitimate Tsar and supported other claimants to the throne.

Feodor II (1589-1605), the son of Boris Godunov, who succeeded his father. He was overthrown and murdered in an uprising in support of False Dmitry I after only two months as Tsar.

False Dmitry I (1582?-1606) claimed to be Dmitry of Uglich but was in all probably Grigory Otrepev, a former monk. He successfully raised an army and led it into Russia gaining much support there. He was crowned Tsar after the murder of Feodor II in 1605. Within a year he was in turn deposed and murdered.

False Dmitry II (1582?-1610). In 1607 he claimed to be Dmitry and gained considerable support amongst the Cossacks and others discontented with Tsar Vasily. He besieged Moscow in 1508-1509, making his base at Tushino, until defeated by the Tsar Vasily's forces and later, Polish troops. He retreated to Kaluga, where he was murdered by members of his bodyguard.

Vasily Shuisky (1552-1612), a member of a *boyar* family related to the Rurikid dynasty. He opposed both Boris Godunov and his son Feodor, and then turned against False Dmitry I playing a leading role in his murder. He became Tsar in 1606, but like his predecessors was never widely recognised as the legitimate ruler. Overthrow by leading nobles in 1610 with the support of Polish troops, he died in prison in Poland.

Marina Mniszech (1588-1614), the daughter of a Polish landowner, she married False Dmitry I. Her arrival and coronation in Moscow in May 1606 provoked anti-Polish protests, giving Vasily Shuisky the opportunity to have False Dmitry I murdered. Sent back to Poland, Marina then returned to Russia and married False Dmitry II. After his defeat and death she was eventually captured and died in prison in 1614.

Feodor Romanov (1553-1633), a leading Russian nobleman, involved in numerous plots, who was exiled and forced to take holy orders (and then known as Filaret). He was the cousin of Feodor I and father of Mikhail I.

Mikhail Romanov (1596-1645), became Tsar Mikhail I in 1613, chosen by delegates of the *Zemsky Sobor* (Estates of the Realm) after the expulsion of occupying Polish troops. A compromise candidate, gaining much support through respect for his father, he founded the dynasty that ruled Russia for the next 300 years.

Sigismund III Vasa (1566-1632). The son of the king of Sweden, he was a devout Catholic and was elected King of Poland in 1587, which he ruled until his death. King of Sweden, which was largely Protestant, between 1592 and 1599, he was deposed there by his uncle. He had ambitions to become Tsar of Russia but this was prevented by renewed Russian unity under Mikhail I.

Stanislaw Zolkiewski (1547-1620), a Polish nobleman and general who defeated Russian and Swedish troops at Klushino in 1610, opening the way for the occupation of Moscow. He was killed at the Battle of Cecora against Ottoman troops.

PART 5: THE OTTOMAN EMPIRE

Murad III (1546-1595) was sultan from 1574 until his death.

Mehmed III (1566-1603) became sultan in 1595 and immediately had nineteen brothers strangled and seven concubines pregnant by his father drowned.

Ahmed I (1590-1617) was sultan from the death of his father, Mehmed III, in 1603. Three of his children eventually became sultans, though two were removed from office and murdered.

Mustafa I (1600-1639), was the brother of Ahmed I. He was proclaimed sultan twice, first in 1617 and then in 1622. He was generally regarded as being incapable of ruling and on both occasions he was deposed after a brief reign.

Osman II (1604-1622). The eldest son of Ahmed I who was initially passed over on the death of his father in favour of Mustafa. He became sultan in 1618, when still only 14, but his attempts to strengthen royal power against vested interests, especially the janissaries, resulted in his deposition and murder four years later.

Murad IV (1612-1640). Another son of Ahmed I who became sultan in 1623 after the second deposition of Mustafa I. His mother Kosem Sultan acted as regent during his minority. Although he had at least fifteen sons, none survived childhood.

Ibrahim I (1615-1648), the youngest son of Ahmed I and Kosem Sultan. He had spent most of his life in the *kafes* until he became sultan in 1640 as the only remaining male member of the dynasty. Regarded by most as increasingly mentally unstable, in the face of increasing problems in the empire, he was first deposed and then murdered in 1648.

Mehmed IV (1642-1693), became sultan at the age of 6 on the deposition of his father, Ibrahim I. Kosem Sultan, his grandmother, at first acted as regent until displaced by his mother, Turhan Sultan. He was deposed in 1687, but not killed, and replace by his brother.

Kosem Sultan (1589-1651), of Greek origin, became the *Haseki Sultan* (chief consort) of Ahmed I. She had a good grasp of Ottoman politics, and as *Valide Sultan* (mother of the sultan) acted as regent for her son, Murad IV, during his youth. She agreed to the execution of another son, Ibrahim, in 1648 and was initially the regent for her grandson, Mehmed IV. She was overthrown and executed in 1651, having played an influential role in the Ottoman Empire for forty years.

Davud Pasha (1570-1623) An Ottoman statesman who held various posts under Ahmed I and Mustafa I, who was his brother-in-law. He has been held responsible for the murder of Sultan Osman II in May 1622, after which he was briefly Grand Vizier, effectively head of the government, under Mustafa I. However, within a month all those who were involved in Osman's murder, including Davud Pasha, were arrested and eventually executed in January 1623.

PART 6: CHARLES I, THE REPUBLIC
AND THE REGICIDES

James VI and I (1566-1625), son of Mary, Queen of Scots and Henry Darnley. King of Scotland (as James VI) from the deposition of his mother in 1567, and king of England (as James I) from 1603.

Charles I (1600-1649), second son of James I and Anne of Denmark, who became heir to the throne on the death of his older brother, Henry, in 1612. He married Henrietta Maria, the daughter of King Henry IV of France in 1625 shortly after becoming king. Defeated in the English civil wars and executed on 30 January 1649.

Charles II (1630-1685), eldest son of Charles I. He went into exile in 1646, spending time in The Hague and France. His attempt to gain the throne in 1650-51 was defeated and it was another nine years until the 'Restoration'. He had numerous illegitimate children but no legitimate one so he was succeeded by his brother James.

James II (1633-1701), king of England, Scotland and Ireland between 1685 and 1688. He was deposed in the 'Glorious Revolution' of 1688, was defeated in Ireland when attempting to recover the throne, and thereafter lived in exile in France.

John Bradshaw (1602-1659) acted as President of the High Court of Justice at the trial of King Charles. Between March 1649 and December 1651 he was President of the Council of State, the executive arm of government in the Commonwealth. He opposed the establishment of the Protectorate under Cromwell. Along with those of Cromwell and Ireton, his body was exhumed and posthumously executed in 1661.

Oliver Cromwell (1599-1658), a Member of Parliament who became a successful commander in the New Model Army during the civil war against Charles I and later campaigned in Ireland and Scotland. A religious independent and believing that he was doing God's work, in 1648 he opposed compromising with the king and supported his execution. He was later created Lord Protector, though he turned down the offer of the crown.

Sir Thomas Fairfax (1612-1671), was appointed Lord General of parliament's New Model Army, with Cromwell as his Lieutenant-General. He refused to be associated with the trial and execution of King Charles and resigned his commission rather than lead the army against the Scots in 1650. His support for General Monck in 1659-60 helped to bring about the restoration of Charles II.

Henry Ireton (1611-1651), a general in the New Model Army, who became Cromwell's son-in-law. He originally wished to come to terms with the king but eventually accepted that this was impossible. He became the commander of forces in Ireland, when Cromwell was recalled to lead the campaign against Scotland. He became ill and died there in November 1561.

John Lilburne (1614-1657), was whipped, placed in the pillory and imprisoned during the late 1630s for writing, printing and distributing unlicensed books and pamphlets. He fought in the early stages of the civil war but then campaigned for freedom of religion and the 'freeborn rights' of all Englishmen, and was closely involved in producing 'An Agreement of the People'.

Henry Marten (1602-1680) was a republican M.P. whose outspoken views resulted in his expulsion from parliament between 1643 and 1646. He was associated with the Levellers and was a commissioner at the king's trial, signing his death warrant. A member of the Council of State he opposed the setting up of the Protectorate. After surrendering himself at the time of the Restoration he was sentenced to death, though this was commuted to life imprisonment.

William Prynne (1600-1669), a puritan opponent of Charles I's religious policies. He was imprisoned for his beliefs and had his ears cut off. He became a member of parliament though later he opposed the trial of the king and was purged. He was once again imprisoned for refusing to declare his loyalty to the Commonwealth. He supported the restoration of Charles II in 1660.

Acknowledgements

I would like to thank all those who encouraged and nurtured my love of history from an early age – my parents, my teachers and the authors whose books I enjoyed and learnt so much from. The resources at Cambridge University library have been invaluable, and I appreciate the Metropolitan Museum of Art in New York and the National Gallery of Art in Washington D.C. for making many of their works of art readily available. I am indebted to Laura Hirst, Susan Last and Lucy May at Pen and Sword for their guidance and support. Most of all I am again grateful to Deborah for giving her time so generously and for her valuable comments on all aspects of this book.

Cambridge
30th July 2024

LIST OF PLATES

Plate 1 Lady Jane Grey. Engraving by Willem and Magdalena de Passe, published in 1620. National Gallery of Art, Washington D.C. – Rosenwald Collection. (CC0)

Plate 2 The future Edward VI. From the workshop of Hans Holbein, 1547. Metropolitan Museum of Art, N.Y. – The Jules Bache Collection, 1949. (OA – Public Domain)

Plate 3 An Extract from Edward VI's 'Devise for the Succession'. (Public Domain)

Plate 4 Queen Mary I of England. The obverse of a bronze medal by Nizzola da Trezzo, Milan. Metropolitan Museum of Art, N.Y. – Robert Lehman Collection, 1975. (OA – Public Domain)

Plate 5 Mary, Queen of Scots 1558–1559. Frans Huys (1522–1566) National Gallery of Art, Washington D.C. – Rosenwald Collection. (CC0)

Plate 6 Henry Stuart, Lord Darnley. Engraving by Renold Elstrack(1571–1625). National Gallery of Art, Washington D.C. – Rosenwald Collection. (CC0)

Plate 7 Queen Elizabeth I. 1592. Engraving by Crispijn de Passe I (1564–1637). Metropolitan Museum of Art, N.Y. – Harris Brisbane Dick Fund, 1928. (OA – Public Domain)

Plate 8 William Cecil, Lord Burghley. Engraving by Willem and Magdalena de Passe, published in 1620. National Gallery of Art, Washington D.C. – Rosenwald Collection. (CC0)

Plate 9 Sir Francis Walsingham. Engraving by Willem and Magdalena de Passe, published in 1620. National Gallery of Art, Washington D.C. – Rosenwald Collection. (CC0)

Plate 10 The Death of Mary, Queen of Scots (from *European Magazine and London Review volume 1,* London, 1782). William Walker (1729–1793) after Bernard Picart (1673–1733). Metropolitan Museum of Art, N.Y. – Gift of Susan Dwight Bliss, 1958. (OA – Public Domain)

Plate 11 Catherine de' Medici, Wife of Henry II of France. Engraving by Johan Wierix (1549–1618). National Gallery of Art, Washington D.C. – Rosenwald Collection. (CC0)

Plate 12 Francis II, King of France. Engraving by Thomas de Leu (c.1560–c.1620) after Francois Clouet (1520–1572). National Gallery of Art, Washington D.C. – Rosenwald Collection. (CC0)

Plate 13 Henry III of France. Engraving by Thomas de Leu (c.1560-c.1620). National Gallery of Art, Washington D.C. – Rosenwald Collection. (CC0)

Plate 14 Jeanne d'Albret, Queen of Navarre and Mother of Henry IV of France. Engraving by Marc Duval (1530–1581). National Gallery of Art, Washington D.C. – Rosenwald Collection. (CC0)

Plate 15 Henry IV, King of France, 1590. Engraving by Crispijn de Passe (1564–1637). National Gallery of Art, Washington D.C. – Rosenwald Collection. (CC0)

Plate 16 Marie de' Medici, Wife of Henry IV of France. Engraving by Thomas de Leu (c.1560-c.1620). National Gallery of Art, Washington D.C. – Rosenwald Collection. (CC0)

Plate 17 Tsar Ivan IV 'the Terrible'. Great State Book of 1672. St Petersburg. (Public Domain)

Plate 18 Feodor II. Unknown artist, Eighteenth century.

Plate 19 False Dmitry I. c.1606. Simon Boguszowicz (1575–1648). State Historical Museum, Moscow. (Public Domain)

Plate 20 Tsar Vasily IV. Unknown artist, Eighteenth century. (Public Domain)

Plate 21 Sultan Ahmed I, with the Blue Mosque below. Unknown painter. (Public Domain)

Plate 22 Kosem Sultan. Oil on canvas. Unknown painter of the Venetian School. Seventeenth century. (Public Domain)

Plate 23 Sultan Mustafa I. Unknown painter. (CC BY – SA4.0)

Plate 24 Sultan Osman II. Unknown painter. (Public Domain)

Plate 25 Sultan Ibrahim I. Unknown painter. (CC BY – SA4.0)

Plate 26 King Charles I (1600–1649). Oil on canvas, Daniel Mijtens, 1629 Metropolitan Museum of Art, N.Y. – Gift of George A. Hearn, 1906. (OA – Public Domain)

Plate 27 Queen Henrietta Maria with Sir Jeffrey Hudson and Pug the monkey. Anthony van Dyke, 1633. National Gallery of Art, Washington D.C. – Samuel H. Kress Collection. (CC0)

Plate 28 Oliver Cromwell. Stipple engraving by Francesco Bartolozzi (1802) after Robert Walker (1607–1660). National Gallery of Art, Washington D.C. – Gift of Hermann Wunderlich. (CC0)

Plate 29 The Execution of King Charles I (Title page: *'Engelandts Memotiael'*) Etching published by Joost Hartgerts, 1649. Metropolitan Museum of Art, N.Y. – Gift of Joseph Verner Reed, 1950. (OA – Public Domain)

Plate 30 Charles I: The Juxon Medal (obverse). Gold, cast and chased, Nicholas Briot, 1639. National Gallery of Art, Washington D.C. – Gift of Drs. Yvonne and A. Peter Weiss. (CC0)

Plate 31 Frontispiece to *Eikon Basilike – The Portrait of His Sacred Majesty in his Solitudes and Suffering* (a version of William Marshall's design) by Wenceslaus Hollar, 1649. Metropolitan Museum of Art, N.Y. – Gift of Carl J. Ulmann, 1924. (OA – Public Domain)

Plate 32 The Second Great Seal of England, Under the Commonwealth. Lead, produced by Thomas Simon c.1656. National Gallery of Art, Washington D.C. – Gift of Mark Wilchusky in honour of Douglas Lewis. (CC0)

Plate 33 Oliver Cromwell – A Genealogy of Anti-Christ. George Bickham Sr. (1684–1769). National Gallery of Art, Washington D.C. – Rosenwald Collection. (CC0)

Plate 34 King Charles II in Coronation Robes (obverse) and King Charles II Enthroned, being crowned by Peace (reverse) 1661. Medal in silver washed with gold by Thomas Simon (1618–1665) National Gallery of Art, Washington D.C. – Gift of Lisa and Leonard Baskin. (CC0)

References and Notes

Introduction

1. Regicide, from the Latin '*regis*', meaning king, and '*cidium*', meaning kill or murder,
2. Eisner, Manuel, *Killing Kings: Patterns of Regicide in Europe AD 600-1800 (Abstract)*
3. Ibid.
4. Joost van der Vondel (1646), quoted in Jackson, Clare, *Devil–Land: England Under Siege: 1588-1688,* 288
5. Greengrass, Mark, Ch.2 *Politics and Warfare* in Cameron, Euan (ed.) *The Sixteenth Century,* 60
6. *Kanterorowitz, H, 219-220*
7. Greengrass, in Cameron, 66

PART 1: RELIGION AND THE TUDOR SUCCESSION: THE TRAGEDY OF LADY JANE GREY

Chapter 1: 'My soul will find mercy in God' – Execution

1. Ives, 252
2. Floria, *Historia*, 61, in Ives, 252
3. Vertot, *Ambassades*, ii. 211, in Ives, 187
4. Fox *Acts and Monuments* (1570), 1568, in Ives, 192
5. MS Harley 2342 ff. 78-80, in Tallis, 266-7
6. Plowden, Alison, *Lady Jane Grey*, 144-5
7. Commendone, *The Accession, Coronation and Marriage of Queen Mary,* 45
8. Foxe, *Acts and Monuments*, X, 1621-2, in Tallis, 264-5
9. Ibid.
10. Ibid.

11. Florio, *Historia*, 73, in Tallis, 265
12. Commendone, 48-9, in Tallis, 267
13. Ibid. Tallis. 268
14. Commendone, *The Accession, Coronation and Marriage of Queen Mary,* ed. C.V.Malfatti, in Ives, 273-4
15. Florio, Historia, 76, in Ives, 275
16. Details of Lady Jane Grey's execution are taken mainly from Nichols, (ed) *The Chronicle of Queen Jane* 39-42 and Commendone 45-50, in Ives, 275-7, Tallis, 272-7 and Plowden, 146-7
17. Davey, Richard, *The Nine Days' Queen: Jane Grey and her Times,* 345-6 and Vertot, *Ambassades* iii 126

Chapter 2: Edward VI's 'Devise for the Succession'

1. Tallis, Nicola, *Crown of Blood – The Deadly Inheritance of Lady Jane Grey*
2. Ives, Eric and Beer, B.L.
3. The Act was passed in the calendar year of 1534, but at the time the legal year began on 25 March and so the Act is considered as being in 1533.
4. Heath, Richard, *Henry VIII and Charles V: Rival Monarchs, Uneasy Allies,* 168-70, provides a useful summary.
5. The verdict of guilty of plotting to kill Northumberland and others was obtained mainly through the false evidence provided by Sit Thomas Palmer.
6. Hoak, Dale, *The King's Council in the Reign of Edward VI,* 66-9
7. Calendar of State Papers Spain 12 June Mary to Charles V, in Ives, 87, ref.305(5)
8. Plowden, Alison, 85
9. Ives, Eric, 94
10. Ibid, 8
11. Loach, Jennifer, 159-169
12. In this plan, if Edward were to die before an heir reached the age of 18 then the heir's mother should be his governess until he was 18, but do nothing without the approval of a minimum of six members of a Council (of 20 members) that Edward would appoint in his will. If the mother died before her son reached the age of 18 then the council would govern, provided that after the king became 14 'great matters of importance be opened to him'. If there was no male heir at the time of his death, then Lady Frances should be regent, and if she died, Lady Jane would take that role, and so on through the daughters, until such

time as a boy was born and then the boy's mother, whoever she might be, would become his governess and effectively regent.

13. Stedall, Robert, 52
14. Ives, Eric, 62
15. Ibid., 51
16. Plowden, Alison, 86
17. Paul, Joanne, 223
18. Commendone, in Paul, 222

Chapter 3: The Rightful Queen Restored

1. Stedall, Robert, Elizabeth I's Secret Lover; Robert Dudley, Earl of Leicester, 55
2. Paul, Joanne, 222
3. Sir John Gates was a close associate of Northumberland. He had been Chief Gentleman of the Privy Chamber from 1549, and late Captain of the Guard, responsible for the security of the Monarch.
4. A soldier and courtier, Sir Thomas Palmer had disturbed the proceedings at the trial by shouting at his judges that they were as guilty as he was.
5. Queen Matilda, while Henry I's heir, was never formally declared queen of England.

PART 2: MARY STUART, MARY QUEEN OF SCOTS: THE UNWANTED MONARCH

Chapter 4: Queen without Power

1. Wormald, Jenny, *Mary, Queen of Scots: A Study in Failure*, 102
2. Guy, John, *Mary Queens of Scots*, 110

Chapter 5: Return to Scotland – Marriages and Murders

1. Ibid. 132
2. Doran, Susan, *Mary, Queen of Scots: An Illustrated Life*, 78 and Guy, 150
3. Wormald, Jenny, 105

4. Ibid. 117
5. Ibid. 105
6. Doran,Susan, 91-4
7. Mina, Denise, *Rizzio*, 20-35
8. Doran, Suan, 106
9. Ibid. 112
10. PRO SP 52/13, 17 in Williams, Kate, *Rival Queens, The Betrayal of Mary, Queen of Scots*, 180-1

Chapter 6: Fellow Queen or Dangerous Conspirator?

1. Doran, Susan, 131-35. For a detailed consideration of the Casket Letters see Guy, John, 396-436
2. Quoted in Jackson, Clare, 26 – *from HMC Salisbury Part 1 400-1 26 Feb. 1569*
3. Williams, Kate, 289
4. Ibid. 290
5. Guy, John, 457
6. Doran, Susan, 166
7. Williams, Kate, 303
8. Maxwell-Scott, Mary, *The Tragedy of Fotheringay*
9. Jackson, Clare, 26 – from *CSP Foreign, Vol XXI, Part 1; June 1586-June 1588* (London 1927, p119 (November 1586)
10. Fraser, Antonia, *Mary, Queen of Scots*, 524
11. T.E. Hartley (ed), *Proceedings in the Parliaments of Elixabeth I Vol II 1584-89* (London 1995) 229 used in Jackson, Clare, 28
12. John Morris (ed), *The Letter-Books of Sir Amyas Paulet: Keeper of Mary, Queen of* Scots (London 1874) 362 used in Jackson, Clare, 34
13. Jackson, Clare, 30 from *CSP Scotland, Vol IX: 1586-88, p163 (24 NOV 1586)*
14. Freebairn, James, *The Death of Mary, Queen of Scots*, 2
15. Williams, Kate, 329-30 and Guy, John, 501
16. Freebairn, James, 10
17. Freebairn, James, 6-7; Williams, Kate, 332
18. Freebairn, James, 12
19. Jackson, Clare, 38

PART 3: VALOIS AND BOURBON: REGICIDE AND CHANGING DYNASTIES IN FRANCE

Chapter 7: The French Wars of Religion

1. Holt, Mack P. *The French Wars of Religion 1562-1629*, 2
2. See Knecht, R.J., *The French Wars of Religion, 1559-1598,* Holt, Mack P. *The French Wars of Religion 1562-1629*, and Knecht, R.J., *The Rise and Fall of Renaissance France 1483-1610.*
3. Carroll, Stuart, *Martyrs and Murderers: The Guise Family and the Making of Europe,* 19
4. Briggs, Robin, *Early Modern France 1560-1715*, 24

Chapter 8: The Death of a Tyrant? The End of the Valois Monarchy

1. Knecht, R.J., *Hero or Tyrant? Henry III, King of France 1574-89*, 230
2. Ibid. 133 Ch.8 119-144
3. Potter, David, *The French Wars of Religion: Selected Documents*, 190-2
4. Ibid. 192-4
5. Knecht, R.J., *Hero or Tyrant? Henry III, King of France 1574-89*, 243
6. Ibid. 246
7. Potter, David, *The French Wars of Religion: Selected Documents*, 206-7
8. Holt, Mack P. *The French Wars of Religion 1562-1629*, 130
9. Filippo Cavriana, Catherine de' Medici's physician, in Knecht, R.J., *Hero or Tyrant? Henry III, King of France 1574-89,* 269
10. L'Estoile, Journal 581-2 in Holt, Mack P., *The French Wars of Religion 1562-1629*, 130
11. Pitts, Vincent J., *Henri IV of France: His Reign and Age*, 140
12. Potter, David, *The French Wars of Religion: Selected Documents*, 215-6
13. Holt, Mack P. *The French Wars of Religion 1562-1629*, 131-2
14. Knecht, R.J., *Hero or Tyrant? Henry III, King of France 1574-89,* 303

Chapter 9: Henry IV and the New Dynasty

1. Pitts, Vincent J., *Henri IV of France: His Reign and Age*, 162
2. Ibid. 169
3. Ibid. 226

4. Ibid. 322
5. Mousnier, Roland, *The Assassination of Henry IV,* 25
6. Pierre de Lestoile (1878) in Mousnier, Roland, *The Assassination of Henry IV,* 24
7. Pitts, Vincent J., *Henri IV of France: His Reign and Age,* 329
8. Mousnier, Roland, *The Assassination of Henry IV,* 50

PART 4: RUSSIA'S 'TIME OF TROUBLES': FROM RURIKIDS TO ROMANOVS

Chapter 10: Descent into Chaos and Regicide

1. See Platonov's division of the 'Time of Troubles' into the dynastic, social and national phases. Sergey Platonov (1860-1933) was a Russian historian, who specialised in 'The Time of Troubles'. He spent most of his career at St. Petersburg University. He did not change his views and interpretations after the Russian Revolution and was eventually exiled to Samara in 1930, although much of his writing was never banned. His work was formally rehabilitated in 1967.
2. Crummey, Robert, *The Formation of Muscovy 1304-1613,* 163
3. Perrie, Maureen, *Pretenders and Popular Monarchism in Early Modern Russia: The False Tsars of the Time of Troubles,* 9. It is possible that Ivan had eight wives, with another wife immediately before his final wife, Maria Nagaya.
4. Ibid. 12
5. Dunning, Chester S.L., *Russia's First Civil War,* 23
6. Crummey, Robert, 212
7. Ibid. 211
8. Besides the more politically inspired character assassinations, Boris Godunov has been the subject of an opera by Mussorgsky and a play by Pushkin, and recent television and radio series in both Russia and the United Kingdom.
9. Perrie, Maureen, 35-6
10. Massa, Issac, *A Short History of the Muscovite Wars down to the Year 1610,* 51-2. Massa (1586-1643) was a Dutch trader who was in Russia between 1601 and 1609. He then returned to Russia on various trading and diplomatic missions during the 1610s, 1620s, and 1630s.
11. Bussow, Conrad, *The Disturbed State of the Russian Realm,* 32. Bussow (1552-1617) was a German mercenary soldier who fought first for

Poland, then Sweden and finally Russia, when he was recruited by agents of Boris Godunov. He also served under False Dmitry and Tsar Vasily.

12. Ibid. 33
13. Perrie, Maureen, 37. Brahin is a small urban settlement in modern day Belarus, close to the Ukrainian border and the nuclear plant at Chernobyl.
14. Platonov, S.F., *The Time of Troubles*, 66-7
15. Dunning, Chester, 127
16. Perrie, Maureen, 41
17. E.g. Skrynnikov, Ruslan, *The Time of Troubles: Russia in Crisis, 1604-1618.*
18. Dunning, Chester, 131-2
19. Ibid. 131
20. Massa, Issac 77
21. Ibid. 109
22. Perrie, Maureen, 74
23. Massa, Issac, 105
24. Dunning, Chester, 195-6
25. Perrie, Maureen, 76
26. Bussow, Conrad, 49
27. Ibid. 48

Chapter 11: Pretender and Usurper – Tsar Dmitry and Tsar Vasily

1. The square was created by clearing properties in the early sixteenth century outside the Kremlin. St Basil's Cathedral was built in the south-east corner of the square in the 1550s. Originally known as *Torg* (Trade) Square and then *Troitskaya* (Trinity) Square, after the small church, which was destroyed in the Tatar invasion of 1571. It was first called Red Square in the seventeenth century, when the word *krasnaya* was used, as it was for many main squares in Russian cities. It could be translated as either 'red' or 'beautiful', but more recently, especially after the Bolshevik Revolution of 1917, it has come to mean 'red'.
2. Ibid. 52
3. Perrie, Maureen, 86-8
4. Bussow, Conrad, 55
5. Perrie, Maureen, 98
6. Massa, Issac, 136

7. Ibid. 139
8. Ibid. 138
9. Dunning, Chester, 237
10. Ibid. 245
11. Skrynnikov, Ruslan, 47
12. Massa, Issac, 163
13. Dunning, Chester, 320
14. Ibid. 398

Chapter 12: Foreign Occupation and the Rise of the Romanov Dynasty

1. Zolkiewski, Stanislas, *Expedition to Moscow: a Memoir by Hetman Stanislas Zolkiewski,* 117. Zolkiewski (1547-1620) was Polish nobleman and a senior general (Hetman) in the army of the Polish-Lithuanian Commonwealth. At one time he was governor of Kiev Province and by the end of his career he was Great Chancellor of the Crown.He commanded Polish forces in their major victory against Russia at Klushino in 1610 and the occupation of Moscow. He died in battle against the Ottomans in 1620.
2. Skrynnikov, Ruslan, 99
3. Zolkiewski, Stanislas, 104
4. Skrynnikov, Ruslan, 259
5. In what Platonov referred to as the 'national' phase of Russia's Time of Troubles', following the 'dynastic' and 'social' phases.
6. Dunning, Chester, 442
7. Perrie, Maureen, 227
8. Dunning, Chester, 442

PART 5: UPHEAVAL IN THE OTTOMAN EMPIRE: THE KILLING OF OSMAN II AND IBRAHIM I

Chapter 13: Succession and the Tradition of Fratricide in the Ottoman Empire

1. Imber, Colin, *The Ottoman Empire 1300-1650,* 87-8
2. The tradition of having eunuchs to guard and control access to the royal palace and in particular the harem, was long established. Originally all

guards in the palace were under the *Kapi Agha* (the chief white eunuch), but in the late sixteenth century control of those slaves guarding the harem passed to the *Kizlar Agha* (the chief black eunuch). During the reign of Murad III the holder of this position became the most senior official in the palace.

3. Imber, Colin, 95-6
4. Tezcan, Baki, *The Second Ottoman Empire. Political and Social Transformation in the Early Modern World*, 60
5. The New Palace was built during the reign of Mehmet II after his capture of Istanbul, and is now known as the Topkapi Palace (Museum).
6. Imber, Colin, 109
7. Ibid. 354
8. Tezcan, Baki, 36

Chapter 14: Depositions and Regicide – the Killing of Osman II

1. Tezcan, Baki, 61
2. The words of the Chief Black Eunuch, Mustafa Agha, arguing for the enthronement of Mustafa I in 1617, as reported by the historian Pechevi (1572-1650).
3. Imber, Colin, 110
4. Tezcan, Baki, 72-6
5. Imber, Colin, 110
6. The *Bostansi-Bashi*, which has the literal translation of 'Chief Gardener' was the head of the body of men that protected the sultan and the grounds of the palace. He was also the chief executioner, who 'pruned' those who became considered to be undesirable at court. Some Chief Gardeners went on to become Grand Vizier.
7. Tezcan, Baki, 'Chapter 3 *The court strikes back: The making of Ottoman absolutism*', in *The Second Ottoman Empire*, 79-114
8. Tezcan, Baki, 120-8
9. Ibid. 128
10. Karateke, Hakan T., Chapter 8 ('*On the Tranquillity and Repose of the Sultan*') in Woodhead, Christine (ed.) *The Ottoman World*, 116-121
11. Tezcan, Baki, 62
12. Estimates of the size of armies at the time vary considerably and can only give an approximate idea of their size.

Chapter 15: The Price of Failure – The Fall of Ibrahim I

1. Imber, Colin, 82-3
2. Imber, Colin, 83
3. Quoted in Lucienne Thys-Senocak. *Ottoman Women Builders: The Architectural Patronage of Hadice Turhan Sultan.*
4. Tezcan, Baki, 214
5. Tezcan, Baki, 13

PART 6: CHARLES I AND THE REGICIDES: THE WORLD TURNED UPSIDE DOWN?

Chapter 16: The Trial and Execution of a King

1. Quoted in Jackson, Clare, *Devil-Land: England Under Siege 1588-1688,* 289
2. Jackson, Clare, 289
3. Rushworth, John, *Account of the Trial of Charles I* in *The Trial of Charles I* Roger Lockyer (ed.) 72
4. Keay, Anna, *The Restless Republic,* 25
5. Rushworth, John 82
6. Ibid 83
7. Ibid 85
8. Ibid 86
9. Scolar Press Trial 5-6
10. Tomalin, C Samuel Pepys, 34
11. Scolar Press, *The Trial and Execution of Charles I,* 11
12. Rushworth, John in Wedgwood, C.V. *The Trial of Charles I,* 95
13. Ibid 29-30
14. Ibid 44
15. Ibid 47
16. Ibid 46
17. Part of Charles I's speech on the scaffold, as recorded by Bishop Juxon and reproduced by Edward Chamberlayne.
18. Tomalin, Claire, *Samuel Pepys: The Unequalled Self,* 34
19. Ibid. 35

Chapter 17: Charles I and Parliament – Civil War

1. Seel, Graham, *Regicide and Republic: England 1603-1660*, 19
2. Carlton, Charles: *This Seat of Mars: War and the British Isles 1485 – 1746,* 155
3. Jackson, Clare, 292

Chapter 18: The Republic and the Stuart Restoration – The Fate of the Regicides

1. Keay, Anna, 340
2. Keay, Anna, 343
3. Kimber, Issac, *The Life of Oliver Cromwell, Lord Protector of the Commonwealth of England, Scotland and Ireland (5th edition)* (1743, J. Brotherton and T. Cox, London, 406
4. Tomalin, Claire, 117
5. Keay, Anna, 349
6. Noble, m. The Lives of the English Revolution (1798) 332 quoted in Tomalin 115
7. Tomalin, Claire, 115
8. Ibid. 116
9. Worthen, John, *Regicide: The Trials of Henry Marten*, 10
10. Ibid 12
11. Ibid 95
12. Ibid. 177
13. Edward Hyde, Earl of Clarendon, *The History of the Rebellion and Civil Wars in England* in David L.Smith; *Oliver Cromwell 1640–1658*.
14. Harris, Robert

Conclusions

1. Machiavelli, Nicolo, The Discourses, Book 1.2, p106-7

BIBLIOGRAPHY

Askan, Virginia and Goffman, Samuel (eds.), *The Early Modern Ottomans: Remapping the Empire* (CUP, Cambridge, 2007)

Beer, Barrett L., *Northumberland: The Political Career of John Dudley, Earl of Warwick and Duke of Northumberland* (Kent State University Press, 1973)

Bergin, Joseph (ed.), *The Seventeenth Century: Europe 1598-1715* (O.U.P., Oxford, 2001)

Briggs, Robin, *Early Modern France 1560-1715* (O.U.P., Oxford, 1977)

Bussow, Conrad, *The Disturbed State of the Russian Realm.* Translated by G Edward Orchard (McGill-Queens University Press, 1994)

Cameron, Euan (ed.) *The Sixteenth Century* in the *Short Oxford History of Europe* (O.U.P., Oxford, 2006)

Carroll, Stuart, *Martyrs and Murderers: The Guise Family and the Making of Europe* (O.U.P., Oxford, 2011)

Commendone, Giovanni, *The Accession, Coronation and Marriage of Mary Tudor,* ed. C.V. Malfatti (Barcelona, 1956)

Crummey, Robert, *The Formation of Muscovy 1304-1613* (Longman, London and New York, 1987)

Davey, Richard, *The Nine Days'Queen: Lady Jane Grey and her Times* (ed. M. Hume 1909)

Doran, Susan, *Mary, Queen of Scots, An Illustrated Life* (The British library, London, 2007)

Dunning, Chester S.L., *Russia's First Civil War: The time of Troubles and the Founding of the Romanov Dynasty* (Pennsylvania State University Press, 2001)

Eisner, Manuel, *Killing King: Patterns of Regicide in Europe AD 600-1800.* (British Journal of Criminology, Vol. 51, Issue 3, May 2011)

Florio, Michelangelo, *Historia de la vita e de la morte de l'illustriss. Signora Giovanna Graia* (Middleburg, 1607)

Foxe, John, *Acts and Monuments (1563-83)*

Fraser, Antonia, *Mary, Queen of Scots* (Weidenfeld & Nicolson, London, 1994) First published in 1969

Freebairn, James, *The Death of Mary, Queen of Scots* (Signet Press, Greenock, 1960) (From: *'The life of Mary Stewart, Queen of Scotland and France'* written originally in French based on an eye-witness account printed in Paris in 1588, and now done into English by James Freebairn, first printed in Edinburgh in 1725)

Friedeburg, Robert von, (Ed.) *Murder and Monarchy: Regicide in Europe 1300-1800* (Palgrave MacMillan, Basingstoke, 2004)

Greengrass, Mark, *Politics and Warfare* in Cameron, Euan (ed.) *The Sixteenth Century* (O.U.P., Oxford, 2006)

Gundulic, Ivan, *Osman*, Transl. E.D. Goy (Yugoslav Academy of Sciences and Arts, Zagreb, 1991)

Guy, John, *Mary, Queen of Scots* (4th Estate, London, 2018) First published as *My Heart is My Own* (2004)

Grey, Lady Jane, *Here in this Booke ye have a godly Epistle* (1554)

Harris, Robert, *Act of Oblivion* (Hutchinson Heinemann, London, 2022)

Heath, Richard, *Henry VIII and Charles V: Rival Monarchs, Uneasy Allies* (Pen and Sword, Barnsley, 2023)

Hoak, Dale, *The King's Council in the Reign of Edward VI* (PhD thesis, University of Cambridge, Dept. of History, 1971)

Holt, Mack P., *The French Wars of Religion 1562-1629* (C.U.P., Cambridge, 1995)

Howard, Douglas A., *A History of the Ottoman Empire* (C.U.P., Cambridge, 2017)

Hurstfield, Joel, *Elizabeth I and the Unity of England* (English Universities Press, London, 1964) First published in 1960

Imber, Colin, *The Ottoman Empire, 1300-1650* (Palgrave-MacMillan, Basingstoke, 2002)

Ives, Eric, *Lady Jane Grey: A Tudor Mystery* (Wiley-Blackwell, Chichester, 2008)

Jackson, Clare, *Devil-Land: England Under Siege 1588-1688* (Allen Lane, 2021)

Keay, Anna, *The Restless Republic: Britain without a Crown,* (William Collins, London, 2023)

Knecht, R.J., *The French Wars of Religion, 1550-1598* (Longman, London, 1989)

Knecht, R.J., *The Rise and Fall of Renaissance France 1483-1610* (Blackwell, Oxford, 2nd edition, 2001)

Knecht, R.J., *Hero or Tyrant? Henry III, King of France, 1574-89* (Ashgate, Farnham, 2014)

Kolodziejczyk, Dariusz, *Ottoman-Polish Diplomatic Relations (15th – 18th century), Vol. 1* (Brill, Leiden/Boston/Koln, 2000)

Loach, Jennifer, Edward VI (Yale University Press, New Haven and London, 1999)

Loades, David, *John Dudley, Duke of Northumberland 1504-1554* (Clarendon Press, Oxford, 1996)

Lockyer, Roger (ed.), *The Trial of Charles I* (The Folio Society, London, 1959)

Machiavelli, Niccolo, *The Discourses*, (ed. Bernard Crick, Penguin Classics, London, 1970)

Mackay, James, *In My End is My Beginning* (Mainstream Publishing, Edinburgh and London, 1999)

Massa, Isaac, *A Short History of the Muscovite Wars down to the Year 1610*. Translated by G Edward Orchard (Univ. of Toronto Press, Toronto, Buffalo and London, 1982)

Maxwell-Scott, Mary, *The Tragedy of Fotheringhay: Founded on the Journal of D. Bourgoing, Physician to Mary, Queen of Scots* (Adam a& Charles Black, London, 1895)

Mousnier, Roland, *The Assassination of Henry IV* (Originally published by Editions Gallimard, Paris, 1964. English edition, translated by Joan Spencer, Faber and Faber, London, 1973)

Muddiman, J.G., *The Trial of King Charles the First* (William Hodge and Co., Edinburgh and London, 1928)

Paul, Joanne, *The House of Dudley* (Penguin Random House UK, 2023)

Perrie, Maureen, *Pretenders and Popular Monarchism in Early Modern Russia: The False Tsars of the Time of Troubles* (Cambridge University Press, 1995)

Pitts, Vincent J., *Henry IV of France, His Reign and Age* (John Hopkins University Press Baltimore, 2009)

Platonov, S.F., *The Time of Troubles* Translated by John T. Alexander (University Press of Kansas, 1970)

Plowden, Alison, *Lady Jane Grey: Nine Days Queen* (Sutton Publishing, Stroud, 2003)

Potter, David, *The French Wars of Religion – Selected Documents* (Macmillan Press, Basingstoke, 1997)

Scolar Press, *The Trial and Execution of Charles I* (The Scolar Press, Leeds, 1966)

Seel, Graham, *Regicide and Republic: England 1603-1660* (C.U.P., Cambridge, 2001)

Skrynnikov, Ruslan, *The Time of Troubles: Russia in Crisis, 1604-1618* Ed. And translated Hugh F. Graham (Academic International Press, 1988

Stedall, Robert, *Elizabeth I's Secret Lover* (Pen and Sword, Barnsley, 2020)

Tallis, Nicola, *Crown of Blood: The Deadly Inheritance of Lady Jane Grey* (Michal O'Mara Books, London, 2016)

Tezcan, Baki, *The Second Ottoman Empire. Political and Social Transformation in the Early Modern World* (C.U.P., Cambridge, 2010)

Tomalin, Claire, *Samuel Pepys: The Unequalled Self* (Penguin, London, 2003)

Thys-Senocak, Lucienne, *Ottoman Women Builders: The Architectural Patronage of Hadice Turhan Sultan.* (Ashgate, Aldershot, 2006)

Upton, Anthony, *'Politics'* in Bergin, Joseph (ed.), *The Seventeenth Century: Europe 1598-1715* (O.U.P., Oxford, 2001)

Wegdwood, C.V., *The Trial of Charles I* (Penguin, London, 1983) (First published 1964)

Williams, Kate, *Rival Queens, The Betrayal of Mary, Queen of Scots* (Hutchinson, London, 2018)

Wilson, Derek, *The Uncrowned Kings of England: The Black Legend of the Dudleys* (Robinson, London, 2005)

Woodhead, Christine (ed.) *The Ottoman World* (Routledge, Abingdon, 2012)

Wormald, Jenny, *Mary, Queen of Scots: A Study in Failure* (George Philip, London, 1988)

Worthen, John, Regicide: *The Trials of Henry Marten* (Haus Publishing, London, 2022)

Zolkiewski, Stanislas, *Expedition to Moscow: a Memoir by Hetman Stanislas Zolkiewski.* Translated by M.W. Stephen, Intro. by Jedrzej Giertych (Polonica Publications, London, 1959)

INDEX